The United States
and Cuba under
Reagan and Shultz

The United States and Cuba under Reagan and Shultz

A Foreign Service Officer Reports

KENNETH N. SKOUG, JR.

Westport, Connecticut
London

Library of Congress Cataloging-in-Publication Data

Skoug, Kenneth N.
     The United States and Cuba under Reagan and Shultz : a foreign
service officer reports / Kenneth N. Skoug, Jr.
          p.   cm.
     Includes bibliographical references and index.
     ISBN 0–275–95467–6 (alk. paper)
     1. United States—Foreign relations—Cuba. 2. Cuba—Foreign
relations—United States. 3. United States—Foreign
relations—1981–1989. I. Title.
E183.8.C9S544   1996
327.7307291—dc20   95–42964

British Library Cataloguing in Publication Data is available

Library of Congress Catalog Card Number: 95–42964
ISBN: 0–275–95467–6

First published in 1996

Praeger Publishers, 88 Post Road West, Westport, CT 06881
An imprint of Greenwood Publishing Group, Inc.

Printed in the United States of America

The paper used in this book complies with the
Permanent Paper Standard issued by the National
Information Standards Organization (Z39.48–1984).

10 9 8 7 6 5 4 3 2 1

For Martha
Wife and Life's Companion

Contents

Introduction

This is an account of U.S.–Cuban relations during 1982–1988, while I was Coordinator of Cuban Affairs in the Department of State. The period covered coincides with the incumbency of George P. Shultz as Secretary of State.[1] It deals with diplomacy—more than many expected—and confrontation, and with the interaction between them.

✗ Shultz set the tone for a policy less "ideological" than critics supposed. In 1983 he authorized migration negotiations with Cuba, and four years later it was his decision that helped restore the bilateral agreement of 1984 that Cuba had suspended less than six months after its signature. President Reagan laid great store by his popularity among anti-Castro Cuban-Americans. If his public involvement with Cuban matters frequently was to tell the émigrés what they wanted to hear, Reagan came down pragmatically on most issues. He kept rhetoric apart from action.

The period was rich in anomaly:

—Despite an overall hardline approach to Cuba, a foremost Reagan administration objective became negotiation, and later restoration, of an agreement establishing normal migration.

—A high-profile opponent of administration foreign policy helped willy-nilly to launch the migration negotiations that Cuba had hitherto resisted.

—A staunch critic of Radio Marti in the U.S. Senate became the catalyst for its enactment by Congress as a surrogate radio.

—The Cubans delayed Radio Marti's start by threatening retaliation they never carried out; their surprise sanction damaged Havana's interests as much as ours and ruled out a modest improvement in relations.

—The only military combat ever to occur between U.S. and Cuban forces took place on Grenada, in part owing to faulty communications, although both sides hoped to avoid bloodshed.

I write as a United States foreign service officer, retired 1990. I was prepared by training and experience to coordinate U.S. policy toward Cuba. My career began in Washington in 1957 working on security in the Eastern Caribbean at the time Fidel Castro, his objectives well concealed, was winning power by a twenty-five-month Fabian war of attrition. I served in the Soviet Union, Czechoslovakia, and Germany, as well as in Latin America. By 1982 I knew Latin America and the East-West conflict reasonably well. Cuba was part of each.

Under the overall responsibility of George Shultz, I served with Under Secretaries of State for Political Affairs Lawrence Eagleburger (1982–84) and Michael Armacost (1983–88) and Assistant Secretaries of State for Inter-American Affairs Thomas Enders (1982–83), Langhorne A. ("Tony") Motley (1983–85), and Elliott Abrams (1985–88). The Principal Deputy Assistant Secretary of State for Inter-American Affairs (1983–1987) was James H. Michel, attorney, career civil servant, and subsequently ambassador to Guatemala, on whose integrity and judgment the Inter-American Affairs Bureau (ARA) relied in turbulent times. While others received more headlines, Michel bore an immense load.

Ronald Reagan left office in 1989 in the aura of dawning Russo–American understanding that his policies facilitated. Regarded by many in 1981 as a dangerous dilettante, he left office viewed as a peacemaker. But when Reagan assumed office, he was confronted in every continent except Australia and Antarctica by Cold War conflict. Cuba was involved in many of these quarrels. In the Caribbean, Central America, southern Africa, and the Horn of Africa, Cuban military forces or advisors were on the cutting edge, in syncopation with a Soviet Union which gave little hint of the vast changes the Reagan years would later see and facilitate.

In the beginning, Reagan faced struggle. The U.S.–Cuba relationship, endemically hostile after Fidel Castro gained power in 1959, was more inimical than ever. Policy focused on obliging Cuba to repatriate persons from the Mariel Boatlift of 1980 who had committed serious, non-political crimes in Cuba or in the United States or who were mentally ill (the Mariel Excludables, as they were called because they had never been legally admitted to the country and were to be "excluded" therefrom).

Although the administration would gladly have had it otherwise, the detritus from Mariel required negotiations to undo a gratuitous act of aggression by Cuba during the Carter administration. While it conducted as tough a policy toward Cuba as any administration in Washington since 1959, the Reagan administration faced restraints on its options because of this burden.

Dawning awareness that rapid, dramatic achievements could not be made with Cuba left policy management more to foreign affairs professionals than might otherwise have been the case. Specific guidance from higher authority was relatively rare, but this was not required because the aspirations of the administration concerning Cuba were clear enough. The Department of State largely shaped policy, but its implementation required the cooperation of other agencies with different agendas.

As Coordinator for Cuba, I sometimes felt that "internal" struggles were as great a challenge—and often less exhilarating—as matching wits (and endurance) with the formidable representatives of the Cuban government. This account follows a chronological order so as to best capture the crosscurrents.

NOTE

1. Shultz was Secretary of State from July 16, 1982 until January 20, 1989. I was Coordinator for Cuban Affairs from August 30, 1982 until August 8, 1988.

1

The Trouble with Cuba

The air traveler from Miami to Havana perceives the white sandy beaches of Varadero minutes after the last sight of Florida. The island is on the tip of the continent, its western extremity due south of Detroit and its easternmost part due south of New York City. As technology progressively reduces geographical distances, U.S.–Cuban relations are condemned to become even closer.

Until January 1, 1959, most Americans viewed Cuba with sympathy if not always understanding. They welcomed its fight for independence as the last Spanish colony in the Western Hemisphere. After U.S. intervention in 1898 secured Cuban independence, Washington helped steer the island republic's course for a third of a century.

For the next quarter-century Cuba coped largely for itself, dominated by the authoritarian hand of Fulgencio Batista, who, with an eye to Washington, permitted three reasonably free elections (1940, 1944, and 1948). American business and tourism contributed to Cuban prosperity. Whatever the legacy of four hundred years of Spanish rule and American proximity, intervention, and influence, Cubans enjoyed considerable personal freedom and ranked among the most affluent denizens of Latin America.

But Cuban democracy was not spared the vices common to contemporary Latin America: widespread corruption, discrepancies between rich and poor, and the proclivity of military men to overthrow civilian governments. Representative government broke down definitively in 1952 when Batista overthrew the elected but scarcely popular government of Carlos Prio Socarras. After 1952 Cuba would not see democracy again.

In January 1959, when Fidel Castro took power, our close neighbor was abruptly transformed into a hostile, personalized dictatorship which soon closely aligned itself with Soviet power. In 1958, Castro had vowed to a confidante, privately but not in jest, that when his civil war with Batista ended, his *destiny* would be to conduct a longer, larger struggle against the United States. For Washington the trouble with Cuba had begun, and when it would end no man could foretell.

Assured of Soviet political and military support, sustained increasingly by Soviet economic assistance, Castro was free to create in Cuba a militant, Spartan society. Eventually he turned a small island into a regional power. It was the misfortune of the United States that the zeal of this man and the small nation he led was directed primarily against what he viewed as his enemy to the north. His objective was to be a model for a new Latin America.

From the beginning Castro's revolution alienated a substantial portion of Cuba's own population, and his system ineluctably produced *new* alienation. For the alienated, there was no relief or redress in Cuba. They suffered on the island, both in and out of prison, for having opposed Castro. Many of the disaffected, however, sought refuge in the United States, where their bitter memories of Castro's revolution fueled existing animosity toward Cuba. This result did not deter him. He relished it. He thrived on defying the United States.[1]

For Castro, emigration of the enemies or victims of his revolution was a tacit safety valve. It was also a weapon he learned to exploit against the U.S. government. By a stroke of irony, however, the hundreds of thousands of Cubans who fled the island became a powerful interest group in their new home. United by their antipathy to Fidel Castro, the Cuban–American "community" came to present a formidable obstacle to any change in U.S. policy toward Cuba, at least as long as Castro held power.

THE SOVIET–CUBAN SYMBIOSIS

When Castro invited the Soviet Union to his defense so that he could mold Cuba in a new image and challenge the international order in Latin America and the Caribbean, the Russians exploited this windfall to draw Cuba progressively into their "camp." The intimate relationship established, which exacerbated U.S.–Cuban tensions, would end only when the Soviet Union did. A senior Soviet diplomat later said that the Soviet–Cuban alliance remained "a constant, major factor hampering the progress of mutual efforts by Moscow and Washington to narrow their differences in periods of detente and exacerbating their contradictions in times of heightened tension."[2]

The military alliance was not one-sided. In the 1970s Castro demonstrated in Africa the efficacy of Cuban military intervention under favorable circumstances. In Angola and in the Horn of Africa, Cuban soldiers showed their mettle. Meanwhile, Moscow's reticence to become involved in Third World struggles far from the USSR was weakened as opportunities proliferated and risks diminished in the wake of President Nixon's resignation.

In 1979, events in Central America showed a new "revolutionary" tide that both Havana and Moscow welcomed and abetted. The Kremlin, which had earlier restrained Castro's restless activism in Latin America, would resist it no longer. With substantial Cuban help, a pro-Communist regime took power in Nicaragua.[3] On Grenada, close to South America and on Havana's supply route to southern Africa, a band of conspirators seized control. A struggle was on in El Salvador, where the revolution had a "Jacobin cast" and where the insurgents admired and sought to emulate Fidel Castro.[4]

Economic trends, however, were less favorable to Cuba as a member of the "socialist camp." Cuba's growing distress was due mainly to economic dependency on its Soviet benefactor. After 1962, the Russians, as the major consumer of Cuban sugar, stimulated monoculture. In 1972, Cuba joined the Council for Mutual Economic Assistance (CMEA) as a full member. The USSR wanted Cuba as a full member in order to exert more control on its economic policy and to share the burden of sustaining it with Eastern Europe.[5]

As the terms of trade between overabundant sugar and scarce oil altered, this barter-trade inevitably became a growing soft currency subsidy from Moscow to Havana, a genuine Soviet economic sacrifice. The bargain began to damage the Cuban economy. Cuba did not seek alternative markets or untraditional exports while there was a guaranteed market for sugar in the Soviet Bloc.[6]

Cuba could no longer earn convertible currency from exports of its own production. Instead the major "export" for dollars became so-called "surplus" oil which the Soviets provided to Cuba in excess of Cuban consumption. Thus arose the paradox of Fidel Castro defending high world oil prices. He imported oil with soft currency—a debt Cuba could not, hence need not, repay—and resold part for real money.

While hard currency credits from Europe and Japan in the late 1970s gave Cuba temporary respite from total envelopment in CMEA, this did not touch the basic problem. Moreover, it created a new headache. By 1982 Cuba could no longer service its Western debt. Thus, although by 1981 the

Soviet–Cuban politico-military relationship seemed stronger than ever, with prospects for mutually beneficial strategic gains in Latin America and the Caribbean, Havana's socioeconomic problems were of increasing concern to itself and Moscow.

THE CARTER ADMINISTRATION AND CUBA

In 1977, after nearly two decades of hostility and minimal intergovernmental contact—mainly over migration and hijacking—Jimmy Carter's administration undertook to negotiate normalization of diplomatic relations between Havana and Washington. Secret talks continued throughout his presidency. Their enduring result was establishment in 1977 of "interests sections" in the respective capitals. The U.S. Interests Section in Havana was formally under the Swiss Embassy, its Cuban counterpart in Washington under Czechoslovakia. But the "sections" were substantial—twenty accredited expatriates, including U.S. Marines in Havana and Cuban security personnel in Washington—and they were quartered in the old U.S. and Cuban embassies. This was not formal diplomatic relations, but it permitted direct discourse whenever desired.

The U.S. embargo on Cuba, established in 1962, was relaxed by President Carter. Cuba, moved by need for dollars, permitted expatriates to return for visits, which had an unforeseen impact on the Cuban population. The contrast between the visitors' relative affluence and the poverty of the average Cuban aggravated the latter's despair.

If Castro miscalculated the destabilizing effect of the émigrés, however, Carter was misled in assuming that the prospect of better ties to the United States would restrain Castro from pursuing his "destiny." Despite negotiations and relaxation of U.S. pressure, Cuban military engagement in Africa expanded. Cuban support for the Sandinistas helped the latter achieve power in Nicaragua. The belated discovery of a Soviet brigade in Cuba, which President Carter infelicitously called "unacceptable" but which he was unable to counteract, further undermined the relationship. Despite Carter's attempted show of goodwill, the trouble with Cuba did not abate. Indeed, things were about to get much worse.

THE MARIEL BOATLIFT OF 1980

The event which destroyed any prospect of improved bilateral relations under President Carter, and which helped establish the framework for the

next eight years, was unrelated to the outreach of the Soviet
into Central America and the Caribbean.

Fidel Castro had long manipulated his internal opposition by
valve of emigration. Although he permitted departures only on his terms,
he built no Berlin Wall around Cuba. Castro probably recognized that East
Germany could withstand a higher degree of domestic discontent, given the
massive Soviet military presence, than could Cuba. He may have suspected
that an uprising in Cuba similar to that of June 17, 1953 in East Berlin could
bring Americans to its support rather than Soviet tanks to its demise.

By November 1965 nearly 290,000 Cubans had arrived in the United
States. A subsequent U.S.–financed airlift brought almost 350,000 more
Cubans by 1973. Cuba ended the airlift in April 1973 after deciding that the
"brain drain" and other costs exceeded the benefits.[7]

By 1977, Castro's removal of the historic safety valve created renewed
internal pressure which the "dialogue" with Cuban-American visitors exacerbated. On March 8, 1980, Castro warned that he might open a port to
permit emigration, as he had done fifteen years earlier at Camarioca. The
following month, thousands of desperate Cubans sought asylum on the
grounds of the Peruvian Embassy in Havana.

Efforts by the Carter administration and several Latin American and West
European governments to bring these persons to Spain or Latin America in
an orderly fashion failed, largely because Castro did not want evidence of
internal unhappiness to impair Cuban influence in the Hispanic world. That
was precisely where he wished post–1959 Cuba to appear attractive. Castro
directed the exodus instead to the United States, sacrificing any prospect of
reconciliation with Washington. For him, domestic security and Cuba's
image in Latin America took precedence.

Closing an airlift to Costa Rica, Castro opened the Port of Mariel on April
20 and invited Cuban-Americans to come for their relatives. Professor Jorge
Dominguez of Harvard University comments, "As in 1965 (at Camarioca)
they would cooperate with their enemy."[8] The Mariel Boatlift brought over
125,000 persons to the United States, mainly to southern Florida, in a few
tumultuous weeks. In their ranks were thousands of persons who had
committed common (non-political) crimes in Cuba, including some released directly from prisons. State and local governments in the United
States were overwhelmed. The migration-accepting consensus toward
Cuba broke down.[9] Violent demonstrations outside the U.S. Interests Section in Havana caused the Carter administration to suspend consular activities, including a program for ex-political prisoners. The boatlift ended only
when the Cuban government concluded that it was undermining the pros-

pects of President Carter for reelection.[10] Castro had no wish to help Ronald Reagan gain office.

The lame duck Carter administration made a final but unsuccessful effort to negotiate with Cuba on the boatlift. A U.S. delegation met with Cuban officials for the return of persons who were ineligible to remain in the United States because of their common crimes. The Cubans, however, were prepared to accept only persons willing to return, and those on a case-by-case basis. These conditions were not acceptable to the United States for reasons of principle and because very few persons whom the U.S. government wished to repatriate would have gone voluntarily.

Fidel Castro presumably saw little reason to reach an agreement with an expiring administration in Washington, even one that had shown him unprecedented goodwill. Facing a less friendly new administration, Cuba decided to hold the Mariel issue as a bargaining chip against Ronald Reagan.

HAIG: TALKING TO THE SOURCE

The transition in Washington came with the United States under challenge from the Soviet Union in Europe and elsewhere. The adversarial relationship with Castro was accentuated by conflict in the Caribbean Basin and burdened by the residue of the Mariel Boatlift.

During his relatively short period as Secretary of State, General Alexander Haig epitomized the U.S. approach to the conflict by his oft-cited statement that we should "go to the source." By "source" Haig clearly had Cuba in mind, but the sense of "go" was less definite. Cuban outreach could be combatted, but it was hard to come to grips with the island itself.

Viewing Cuban interference in Nicaragua and especially in El Salvador as the key to the struggle for Central America, Haig believed an overwhelming show of military force could make Cuba back off—without need for the United States to invade the island. A military man, Haig felt U.S. economic and military superiority could be used peacefully to tame Cuba. He wrote: "But it was obvious that Cuba, an island nation of 11 million people lying 100 miles off the coast of a United States with a population of 230 million, simply could not stand up to the geostrategic assets available to the larger country."[11] But even though the preponderant assets of the United States supplied leverage, this had not reined in Castro during the previous twenty years.

Although personally skeptical that a dialogue with Cuban leaders would be productive, Haig had to take into account President Reagan's notion that such contact might produce a desirable result. He made Cuba's willingness to take back criminals from Mariel a test of Havana's willingness to engage in fruitful dialogue.

After Fidel Castro indicated a willingness to discuss this or other issues, Haig went to Mexico City in November 1981 to meet Cuban Vice President Carlos Rafael Rodríguez, whom he tried to persuade that the United States was deadly serious about Cuban activity in Central America and that time was running out. Rodríguez, after reciting Cuba's inalienable sovereignty and unbreakable friendship with the USSR, offered no give on Cuban conduct. From this meeting and other evidence, however, Haig concluded that the Cubans were "very anxious."[12]

At Reagan's request, Lieutenant General Vernon ("Dick") Walters was sent secretly to Havana in March 1982 to remind Fidel Castro and Rodríguez that Cuba must cease supporting the El Salvador insurgents, end military assistance to Nicaragua, and "accept the return of the criminals." Castro told Walters that the question of the criminals was solvable but that El Salvador and Nicaragua were "more difficult."[13]

Meanwhile the Mariel Cubans in the United States were causing growing concern. Justice Department reports about the situation agitated the president. Haig recommended that Castro be warned to take the criminals back or face unspecified U.S. action. "If he failed to respond, we would simply load them aboard an expendable ship, sail it into a Cuban anchorage under escort of the U.S. Navy, and inform Castro that we had returned his citizens to him."[14] Haig's recommendation was not accepted. In light of subsequent events, it seems inconceivable that U.S. courts would have permitted these persons to board the expendable ship. So far, "going to the source" had merely underscored the United States' unhappiness with the situation.

Frank McNeil, who argues without much supporting evidence for the utility of "serious talks" with Cuba, nevertheless comments sagaciously on the Haig–Rodríguez and Walter–Castro conversations: "Perhaps we didn't have much of substance to say to each other."[15] Beyond mere willingness to engage in talks, successful diplomacy requires readiness by at least one party to make concessions on and adjustments to the issues at stake. This was missing. The residue of Mariel remained the chief bilateral Cuba problem. In June 1982, Associate Attorney General Rudolph Giuliani testified before the Senate Judiciary Subcommittee on Immigration and Refugee Policy that there were some fifteen to twenty thousand Cuban criminals at large in the United States.[16] A plan was slowly emerging in the Department of State. It involved formally asking Havana to take back the Mariel criminals. At face value, the plan was little more realistic than Haig's expendable ship, but it would start the process. By July 1982, the administration had a new Secretary of State, George Shultz, a prudent man not averse to negotiating when necessary.[17]

NOTES

1. Edward Gonzalez and David Ronfeldt, *Castro, Cuba and the World* (Santa Monica, CA: The Rand Corporation, 1986), p. vii.

2. Yuri I. Pavlov, *Soviet-Cuban Alliance, 1959–1991* (New Brunswick, NJ: Transaction Publishers, North-South Center, University of Miami, 1994), p. 199.

3. Frank McNeil, *War and Peace in Central America* (New York: Charles Scribner's Sons, 1988), p. 113. McNeil writes, "Only after the revolution had triumphed in July 1979 did the United States learn the full scope of the Cuban effort."

4. Ibid., p. 105.

5. Pavlov, *Soviet-Cuban Alliance*, p. 94.

6. Ibid., pp. 189–190.

7. Jorge L. Dominguez, "Cooperating with the Enemy? U.S. Immigration Policies Toward Cuba," in *Western Hemisphere Immigration and United States Foreign Policy* (University Park: Pa.,: The Pennsylvania State University Press, 1991), pp. 33–34, 41.

8. Ibid., pp. 55–56.

9. Ibid., p. 57.

10. McNeil, *War and Peace in Central America*, p. 143. McNeil contends that Castro shut the Mariel faucet when he saw pressures building for U.S. military intervention. This is doubtful. It seems unlikely that Castro feared the use of military force by the Carter administration.

11. Alexander M. Haig, Jr., *Caveat: Realism, Reagan, and Foreign Policy* (New York: Macmillan Publishing Co., 1984), pp. 129–130.

12. Ibid., pp. 132–136.

13. Ibid., p. 136.

14. Ibid., p. 137.

15. McNeil, *War and Peace in Central America*, p. 142.

16. Dominguez, "Cooperating with the Enemy?," p. 78.

17. In his confirmation hearings Shultz told the Senate Foreign Relations Committee, "I think on the basis of realism and on the basis of strength, part of that strength itself is the self-confidence to undertake negotiations when they are called for." George Shultz, *Turmoil and Triumph: My Years as Secretary of State* (New York: Charles Scribner's Sons, 1993), p. 20.

2

1982–1983—Bilateral Conflict

When I became Coordinator for Cuban Affairs in the Inter-American Affairs Bureau (ARA/CCA) of the Department of State on August 31, 1982, the Reagan administration was presenting a different face to Cuba than had its predecessor, or even previous Republican administrations. It was deeply concerned about Cuba's regional role and the close Soviet–Cuban alliance. It sought to inhibit Cuban overseas activities, strengthen the embargo, and take the ideological offensive by broadcasting directly to the Cuban people.

The most pressing bilateral problem with Cuba remained, however, the still rising cost of the Mariel Boatlift. While this had indisputably resulted from hostile Cuban action, it could be solved only with some Cuban cooperation. That was the rub. How was such cooperation to be obtained from a government as unfriendly and combative as Cuba's, particularly when the administration wanted to be tough?

THE FRONTIER WAR—THE AFTERMATH OF MARIEL

During the Mariel Boatlift, newspaper columnist James Reston asserted that the influx of refugees was only the most dramatic evidence that the United States was unable to protect its borders or enforce its laws against illegal aliens.[1] This was a severe charge.

If there was a Cuba-related objective which united all factions in the United States at the outset of the Reagan administration, it was to expel criminals included in the Mariel influx. The majority of persons from Mariel was absorbed into U.S. society, but many released from Immigration and Naturalization Service (INS) detention were committing serious crimes.[2] Others still in U.S. detention centers were rioting. This conduct was eroding traditional American receptivity to victims of political oppression abroad, already strained by Vietnam boat people.

One pressure point against Cuba was to withhold processing of preference immigrants and former political prisoners in the U.S. Interests Section in Havana. Processing had been curtailed after a Cuban government-inspired mob attack on such persons occurred outside the interests section on May 2, 1980. The Reagan Administration did not resume processing in 1981 on grounds that Cuba had made it impossible. It also hoped that resumption of processing would be a U.S. bargaining chip because Havana had so much interest in the departure of these persons.

Havana viewed the former prisoners and their families as *reclusos* (recluses, although "outcasts" would have been a more accurate description). Another stimulus for Havana was the dollars that could be extracted in the process of their departure from Cuba. Their relatives in the United States would pay for their freedom.

Under normal immigration procedures, the United States would process visa applications from preference immigrants in Cuba as in other countries. Since many outcasts would not qualify as preference immigrants, however, a special program would be required to bring them to the United States as "refugees," even though they were in their own country and not in a third state.

The pressure of withholding processing had not been enough to sway Cuba in the talks at the twilight of the Carter administration. Moreover, Cuban representatives left Reagan administration officials with the impression that Cuba's stand was unchanged—hence unacceptable to the United States.

This policy was not cost-free to the U.S. government. It presented a severe hardship for persons involved. Family reunification was delayed. Crimes committed by Cubans from Mariel, together with Cuba's unwillingness to take them back, harmed persons still in Cuba whose suffering was due to their opposition to Castro. The irony of this for an avowedly anti-Communist administration was clear.

Influential members of Congress critical of the administration and those with large Cuban-American constituencies, such as Representative Peter W. Rodino, Jr., of New Jersey—where the second largest number of Cuban exiles lived—and Senator Edward Kennedy, began to demand that processing be resumed in Havana. They inquired about the legal grounds for withholding processing of preference immigrants.

In the Department of State, a memorandum proposing that the issue be raised formally with Cuba was under consideration when I arrived at the end of August 1982. It proved no simple task to coordinate a consensus on what to propose and then to win the endorsement of all concerned in the U.S. government. The proposal was lucid enough: (a) ask Cuba to take back all of the persons whose names the U.S. government would present, and (b) pledge that once this had been accomplished, that the United States would resume processing of immigrants and former political prisoners in its interests section in Havana. The bureaucracy expected that this would involve negotiations since Cuba was unlikely to respond favorably to the offer as formulated. Secretary Shultz sent back the proposal on January 12 with a request for a "scenario" of all steps involved. He did not want the U.S. to be a supplicant. As I wrote the scenario, I felt that the Secretary of State would much prefer to avoid formal negotiations with Cuba—if that were possible—but was prepared to accept them if inevitable.

A key element in the approach to Cuba was to ask the Attorney General to invoke Section 243 (g) of the Immigration and Nationality Act. This section of the law provided that when a foreign country refused upon request of the United States to take back one or more of its citizens, immigrant processing would be suspended in that country. Since Cuba was refusing to take back several thousand of its citizens, the applicability of the law seemed appropriate.

Attorneys for the Bureau of Consular Affairs, which was taking congressional heat for not processing preference visas in Havana, believed invocation of Section 243 (g) would make the Department of State less vulnerable to litigation to force resumption of visa processing. Invoking this section was also intended to increase pressure on Cuba to negotiate by giving current sanctions a more stable basis.

On January 10, 1983, key elements of this plan were revealed by Guillermo Martínez in the *Miami Herald*. Quoting only "high ranking officials," Martínez announced that the State Department had developed a plan to solve the Mariel problem, adding that a decision by Secretary Shultz was expected shortly. The article spelled out the intended invocation of Section 243 (g) of the Immigration and Nationality Act, which the source had explained quite accurately as "no more than a legalization of what the government has been doing since May 1980."[3]

According to Martínez, his sources said that for the first time since the last days of the Carter administration "high-level officials in the State

Department" were willing to talk to the Cubans about returning the Mariel criminals. They reported that George Shultz did not have the same objections to negotiations with Cuba as did his predecessor. Thus, halting visa issuance in Cuba by invoking Section 243 (g) "would be accompanied by a strong signal to the Cuban government that the Reagan administration is now willing to talk." Opinion in Washington was that Cuba would welcome the move.

Martínez concluded that a serious question remained. Cuba had invited a new round of talks with the United States but not on immigration matters alone, whereas U.S. officials "would feel more comfortable" if the negotiations were limited to immigration problems—simply an exchange of criminals for legal immigrants.

On January 14 Secretary Shultz signed a letter to Attorney General William French Smith to set the plan in motion. But Smith's February 18 reply rejected the request. He asked that it first be shown that Cuba had refused to take back persons the United States wished to expel.

On February 23 the same view was expressed by Senator Edward Kennedy, who—apparently basing his judgment on comments provided by a retired U.S. diplomat unsympathetic to Washington's policy—asserted that the administration had *not* asked Cuba to take back the Mariel criminals. This was nit-picking. Although there was no formal diplomatic record on this point, Cuba had refused upon request to accept these persons in the negotiations during the last days of the Carter presidency, and subsequent discourse with responsible Cuban officials had revealed no change in Havana's stand.

Assistant Secretary of State for Inter-American Affairs Thomas Enders, the main principal in the Mariel issue, insisted that negotiations must await invocation of Section 243 (g) of the Immigration and Nationalty Act. State would not proceed if Justice held back an action that State deemed crucial to its negotiating posture. After Justice received additional data, the Attorney General dropped his objection. On April 21, more than three months after the Miami newspaper account, he invoked Section 243 (g). It read:

Upon the notification by the Attorney General that any country upon request denies or unduly delays acceptance of the return of any alien who is a national, citizen, subject or resident thereof, the Secretary of State shall instruct consular officers performing their duties in the territory of such country to discontinue the issuance of immigrant visas to nationals, citizens, subjects, or residents of such country until such time as the Attorney General shall inform the Secretary of State that such country has accepted such alien.

The stage finally seemed set for the Department of State to call in the chief of the Cuban Interests Section in Washington, Ramón Sánchez-Parodi y Montoto, to receive the United States proposal. Sánchez-Parodi, who had opened the Cuban Interests Section in 1977 and who enjoyed ambassadorial access in the Carter administration, was invariably received at the Coordinator for Cuba level in the Reagan administration. For this meeting, however—to underscore the importance which the U.S. government attributed to the issue—Sánchez-Parodi was to be permitted to deal directly with Assistant Secretary Enders. This incurred a new delay. The delicacy of receiving the chief Cuban diplomat in Washington at the assistant secretary of state level meant that the meeting had to be postponed. The administration wished no action which might conflict with an important speech by President Reagan to a joint session of Congress on April 27, appealing for aid to El Salvador in its struggle against the FMLN (Farabundo Marti National Liberation Front). Another possible meeting was aborted because the president was addressing Cuban-Americans in Miami.[4] News of a confabulation between Enders and Sánchez-Parodi might have spoiled the euphoric atmosphere, since the émigrés were deeply suspicious of any formal negotiations with Cuban authorities.

The approach would now have to take place during a spate of aircraft hijackings to Cuba and after four ranking Cuban officials were indicted by a U.S. grand jury for assisting a Colombian drug trafficker in bringing narcotic drugs to the United States. There would never be a trouble-free time in dealing with Cuba.

On May 25, 1983, three years after the boatlift began, Enders received Sánchez-Parodi in his sixth floor office. The session between the tall, coldly austere Enders and the short, uncharacteristically subdued Sánchez-Parodi lasted only fifteen minutes. Unsmilingly, Enders handed the Cuban representative a diplomatic note together with a list of 789 Cuban nationals who had come with the boatlift and whom we wanted the Cubans to take back at once.[5] When this had been done, Enders explained, a new list would be provided, and we would expect those persons also to be taken back. Once all of the Excludables whom we identified were repatriated, normal migration processing would resume in the U.S. Interests Section in Havana.

Sánchez-Parodi listened with attention, then inquired if that was the only subject for discussion. He wished to know if it would be "like the last time" (i.e., when formal discussions had taken place in New York). Enders responded, "No, sir." After the meeting, in which I was a silent notetaker, Enders approved my memorandum of conversation verbatim except for striking out the word "sir." He presumably did not want the official record to show him saying "sir" to a Cuban official.

This was the only time during the Reagan administration when Sánchez-Parodi would be received by Enders or by his two successors, Tony Motley and Elliott Abrams. Considering the terse exchange and the chilly atmosphere, which Enders told me to record as "businesslike," it is doubtful that Sánchez-Parodi enjoyed the experience. Enders had seemed to rule out negotiations. Nevertheless, such was Cuba's satisfaction at the level of the meeting that in subsequent negotiations the Cubans referred almost with nostalgia to that shining quarter-hour when their Washington representative sat down with Enders.

If the Cubans applied their brand of "Kremlinology" to U.S. government behavior, however, they must have been taxed to their intellectual limits by news on May 27, two days after this meeting, that Enders was being relieved as Assistant Secretary for Inter-American Affairs. (He was reassigned as ambassador to Spain.) In his memoirs, Secretary Shultz states that Enders was removed because his free-wheeling style and the exclusion of so many people from his confidence had cost him the indispensable support of his boss (i.e. Shultz).[6] (It was particularly fortunate for the U.S. government that in February 1983 James Michel had been appointed the principal—and for a while the only—Deputy Assistant Secretary of State in the Bureau of Inter-American Affairs. Without the order brought about by the hard-working, unflappable Michel, the management of the bureau would have suffered even more in the first half of 1983.) The Cubans never inquired why Enders was transferred. It had nothing to do with Washington's proposal on migration matters. Nor did it seem to affect Cuba's response.

On June 3, Bernie Gwertzman of *The New York Times* called to ask me about former political prisoners whom we were not processing in Havana and who were in limbo. While I did not, of course, tell Gwertzman, there was no piece of received doctrine which I, personally, at that time found so hard to explain as failure to process these humble, anti-Communist persons whom the Cuban regime had severely punished and then condemned to the outermost margin of a society that provided amenities only to privileged insiders. It seemed questionable on ethical grounds.

Only later, during the lengthy negotiating process in 1984, did I realize that (a) the intense Cuban desire to expel these persons from Cuba was indeed essential leverage in inducing Havana to take back the criminals whom it had included in the Mariel Boatlift, and (b) many Americans, including some in positions of high influence, would not have accepted a Cuban refugee program without a Mariel settlement.

Before Cuba responded, an incident occurred that illustrated continuing bureaucratic indecision in dealing with illegal migration from Cuba. On June 10, news that a U.S. cabin cruiser was in Varadero, Cuba, possibly preparing to conduct Cubans to Florida, aroused anxiety that Cuba might be hinting at a "Second Mariel."

At a June 13 meeting involving State, Justice, and Coast Guard, the Justice representative urged State to ask Cuba not to repeat its 1980 actions, contending that if the boat reached the United States, hundreds of such cruisers would head south to take on human cargo. This had occurred in 1980 when Washington failed to stop Cuban-Americans from violating U.S. law to rescue relatives—and to transport common criminals at the insistence of Cuban authorities.

I was appalled. If our defense against a "Second Mariel" was to ask Cuban forbearance, we were in bad shape. Diplomacy requires bargaining chips—either inducements or credible warnings. Otherwise a request to Cuba under duress would only acknowledge weakness.

Fortunately, the cabin cruiser brought back no illegal immigrants. In 1983, as in 1980 and thereafter, the most effective defense against massive, organized violation of U.S. borders would have been swift action against shipowners, ship captains, and other persons abetting illegal immigration by fines, confiscation, and imprisonment—and, if necessary, by temporarily closing U.S. ports.[7]

The administration took the position that if there were another Cuban effort to infringe U.S. sovereignty, it would know how to react. This was in part bluff, but the legal and technical means to deter a "Second Mariel" were available. The administration was not put to a test. In view of strong Cuban–American influence, it would have been a wrenching decision for President Reagan, who would have had to risk alienating their affection or permit another disorderly boatlift.

On June 17 the Cubans presented a response in Havana to the U.S. Mariel initiative. Although argumentative in tone, it did not close the door. Apparently the Cubans made the text of the note available to the press. As printed in part in *The New York Times*, the response stated: "Cuba does not refuse to discuss establishment of conditions which would permit normalization of migration between both countries, including norms to follow concerning persons who, having committed illegal acts in one country, travel illegally to the other." Havana said it was willing to discuss return of some citizens who went to the United States illegally, but only as part of negotiations on normalization of migration between the two countries. The note complained that the United States had been unresponsive to Cuban requests to return "criminals" from the Batista period who had fled to the United States. Havana wished to discuss "standards" for returning persons who committed illegal actions and then illegally left the country.[8]

Since the illegality we were concerned about was illegal entry into the United States, and not illegal departure from Cuba, there was apprehension that we were being asked to sign onto a quasi-fugitive slave law. Cuba wanted the U.S. government to accept an obligation to return persons who had violated Cuban law. In the Reagan administration this was not negotiable.

On July 7, I provided Sánchez-Parodi the second U.S. diplomatic note on Mariel. The conduit for messages between the United States and Cuba on migration matters was thereafter either my office or the U.S. Interests Section in Havana. Such sessions never invited press scrutiny or public attention. Sánchez-Parodi spoke of legal difficulties in getting people to return involuntarily to Cuba. Despite evidence to the contrary, he maintained that Cuba did not need emigration as a safety valve.

On July 19 Sánchez-Parodi assured me that Cuba would respond "constructively" to our July 7 note. But Havana was in no hurry. Only on September 22 did it deliver an ambiguous answer that neither opened nor closed the door to talks. Whatever the Cubans had in mind, however, was postponed indefinitely by events in late October 1983, which saw the first deadly clash of arms between American and Cubans.

 ## THE ETHER WAR—THE FIGHT FOR RADIO MARTI

As the two sides sparred about Mariel, they engaged in a contest over radio broadcasting, another old battleground with new weapons at play. The proximity of the United States and Cuba made it inevitable that stations broadcasting in the one country could be heard in the other. To regulate broadcasting and limit harmful interference, the United States, Cuba and other countries in the region affirmed the North American Radio Broadcasting Agreement, signed in 1950. Despite this accord, Cuban interference on the AM band began to grow in the 1960s after Castro came to power. By the 1970s it was a serious problem.

Late in 1979, moreover, Cuba submitted an inventory of requirements to the International Telecommunications Union (ITU) which, if implemented, would have greatly increased the level of radio interference in the United States and other countries. The inventory indicated that Cuba planned to double the number of AM stations broadcasting from 90 to 180 and develop two stations transmitting with 500,000 watts of power (500 kw), a volume ten times the limit permitted to any U.S. radio station.

In November 1980, Cuba formally abrogated its commitment to the broadcast agreement. It nevertheless participated in the regional AM radio conference in November and December 1981 in Rio de Janeiro to propose a so-called "block shift," which would have lessened current and anticipated interference problems with third-party countries but transferred them to the United States. When their proposal was rejected, the Cubans walked out of Rio.

In 1981, the United States and Cuba conducted three rounds of technical-level talks to try to reduce mutual interference. At the last of these, in August 1981, Cuba maintained its intent to implement the two 500,000-watt stations. It advised that it would shift the frequencies of these stations to 1040 and 1160 kHz, respectively.

Although notification of plans for augmented Cuban radio broadcasting had preceded the election of Ronald Reagan by more than one year, Havana's decision to alter the frequencies of its super stations was plainly addressed to plans by the new administration in Washington to put a radio station on 1040 kHz that would provide surrogate broadcasting to Cuba. Strongly urged by Cuban-Americans in southern Florida and especially by the Cuban–American National Foundation (established in January 1981), the Reagan administration planned to broadcast to Cuba in a form analogous to Radio Free Europe and Radio Liberty, which had been communicating for over a quarter-century as "home-service" radios for Eastern Europe and the USSR, respectively.

In contradistinction to the Voice of America, whose mission was to tell foreign audiences (including Cuba) about the United States, Radio Martí, as the intended station was to be called, would tell Cuba about itself.[9] (The prospective station was named after José Martí, a Cuban patriot killed fighting against Spain, who was ambivalent about the many years of exile he spent in the United States. Cuban exiles honored Martí for his democratic sentiments while their foes in Cuba revered Martí for his pungent criticism of the United States.) Breaking Cuba's domestic monopoly of information was an important element of the Reagan administration's plan to put Fidel Castro on the defensive. The explosion of popular discontent in Cuba in 1980 had demonstrated that despite its capacity to project power abroad, Cuba's internal social order was insecure.

But beyond any geopolitical strategy, President Reagan sincerely wanted to supply intellectual nourishment to those in Cuba who suspected their Communist authorities but needed the focus of systematic, objective news and analysis of Havana's foreign and domestic policy. President Reagan's executive order 12323 of September 22, 1981, establishing a Presidential Commission on Broadcasting to Cuba, was accompanied by a statement expressing the administration's belief that breaking Havana's information monopoly would "help the Cuban people to judge the Cuban revolution on its true merits."[10]

The Cubans opted to oppose Radio Marti by raising the specter of a radio war. Cuba's history of interference and its stated intent to expand the capacity to project sound preyed on North American broadcasters, who saw themselves bearing the brunt of Cuba's wrath. The Federal Communications Commission (FCC) estimated that at full power the two five hundred-kilowatt transmitters could be heard in Alaska and Hawaii.

Aware that congressional approval was required to establish and fund Radio Marti, Cuba mobilized opposition. Havana asserted a willingness to discuss radio interference, as long as Radio Marti did not advance. This seeming flexibility was aimed at American radio broadcasters. The Department of State and the FCC, although skeptical of Cuban intent, saw utility in pursuing these technical talks, in which they included representatives of the American broadcasting industry—if only to reassure the latter that no legitimate bargain would be overlooked.

The President's Commission on Broadcasting to Cuba was appointed in January 1982, with F. Clifton White in the chair. The powerful southern Florida influence behind Radio Marti was reflected in the choice of the other members of the Commission's executive committee: ex-Senator Richard B. Stone and, especially, Jorge L. Mas Canosa, president of a new, vigorous interest group, the Cuban–American National Foundation (CANF).

While the National Association of Broadcasters (NAB) looked on the proposed radio with undisguised concern, fearing massive Cuban interference, the South Florida Radio Broadcasters Association, which had experienced the bulk of Cuban radio interference over the years, gave Radio Marti its backing. In southern Florida, the prospect of broadcasting news about Cuba directly to the Cuban people over a U.S.-sponsored radio outweighed the risk of more disruption of AM broadcasting. Moreover, Florida broadcasters were aware that even with no Radio Marti, they would run the risk of enhanced Cuban interference on the AM radio band.

Proposed legislation establishing Radio Marti under the Board for International Broadcasting (BIB), the entity which oversaw Radio Free Europe and Radio Liberty, was enacted by the House of Representatives as H.R. 5427 on August 10, 1982, by a vote of 250–134. The House authorized $7.5 million to establish the new station.[11] It was envisioned that Radio Marti would broadcast at 50 kw on 1040 kHz, on which radio station WHO in Des Moines, Iowa long had broadcast on a "clear channel" to much of the American heartland. The two would not overlap, but the powerful Cuban station on the same frequency could easily interfere with both. WHO was immediately alarmed by this development. It had already appealed, unsuccessfully, to the administration to find an alternative frequency to avoid WHO broadcasts being interrupted by Cuban jamming in response to Radio Marti.[12] Powerful farm lobbies weighed in with Congress on behalf of WHO.

With the Senate Foreign Relations Committee about to take up Radio Marti, Cuba provided a well-timed demonstration of the power of its new transmitters. On the night of August 30, 1982, the Cuban transmitter on 1040 kHz broadcast for several hours at 150 kw (three times the U.S. legal maximum), causing significant interference with WHO's broadcasting and that of four other frequencies.[13] Thus, to their advertised willingness to discuss radio interference, the Cubans added a none too subtle display of their ability to cause it. They were warning Congress against a step that might prove deleterious for one of the most influential U.S. domestic industries.

Congress was listening. The Senate Foreign Relations Committee "markup" of the Radio Marti bill was adopted by an eleven-to-five vote on September 9, but this triumph was hollow. The NAB and its allies mobilized friends in the Senate, and wary Senators knew how to dodge a commitment without appearing to back down to a Cuban threat. On December 21, the Senate defeated by a voice vote a move to call up Radio Marti. Cuba had won the round.

The August 30 radio interference made Cuba's new capacity to cause serious and random radio interference obvious. On September 10, Secretary Shultz asked for a briefing on what countermeasures were available in the event disruptions continued. Little thought had been given to such countermeasures, although H.R. 5427 had included a provision expressing the sense of Congress that the president should establish a task force to analyze the level of interference in the United States and to "seek a practical political and technical solution to this problem."[14]

The Florida broadcasters had thought about this matter. On January 31, 1982, seven months before Cuba's surprise, the Board of Directors of the Florida Association of Broadcasters had adopted a resolution urging the U.S. government to "undertake a project to construct and operate radio facilities that will cause interference to Cuban radio operations, and/or 'jam' Cuban radio operations, until such time that the illegal interference from

Cuba ceases."[15] In May 1983, "senior" administration officials reportedly told commercial broadcasters that a list of forty options was under consideration, including "surgical removal of transmitting antennas," if Cuba began jamming U.S. radio stations.[16]

Neither Radio Marti nor the threat of massive Cuban broadcast interference was to go away. The quest for contingency U.S. countermeasures was only beginning. It would continue through the hectic months and years ahead and delay the eventual startup of Radio Marti. In the newly convened 98th Congress, the administration again brought Radio Marti forward. On March 22, 1983, Assistant Secretary Enders urged enactment before a sympathetic House Foreign Affairs Committee under the chair of Dante Fascell of Florida. In May the Senate Foreign Relations Committee again voted in favor of Radio Marti (thirteen to four).[17] Opponents of the radio, however, were still far from defeated. They raised the same concerns that had stopped Marti in 1982. In the House Energy and Commerce Committee, a rival bill came forward with amendments that changed its focus.

On June 7, Al Sapia-Bosch, adviser for Latin America on the National Security Council staff, called me to elicit "talking points" to use in support of Radio Marti. A Cuban-American had told him that Marti was about to be defeated in Congress. This was by no means an alarmist conclusion, and defeat of Radio Marti would be a serious setback for the Reagan administration's Cuba policy.

Meanwhile, plans were laid for an August discussion on radio interference with a Cuban delegation headed by Ambassador Joaquín Mas Martínez in San José, Costa Rica, even as the Radio Marti bill remained before Congress. By including Joaquín Mas, who had minimal substantive knowledge about radio broadcasting, Cuba was demonstrating that it saw the matter as political. Mas, a former ambassador to Canada who headed the North American office in the Cuban Foreign Ministry, was my approximate counterpart in Havana. The U.S. government sent a four-man State-FCC technical delegation, without Cuba specialists but including radio broadcasting industry representation.

With the benefit of one year on the job, I saw little prospect in these talks since the real objective of the Cuban side—to block Radio Marti—was incompatible with the policy of the Reagan administration. The San José round produced no result, but the Cubans were prepared to meet again, and so were the NAB representatives on the U.S. side. With Radio Marti still hanging in the balance in the U.S. Congress, U.S. agreement to continue the interference talks was aimed at assuaging the NAB, which was nevertheless continuing to lobby Congress against Radio Marti.

In late August, staffers of Senator Paula Hawkins advised of a move in the Senate to alter the character of Radio Marti by subsuming it under the Voice of America. Although Hawkins, a Floridian and conservative Republican, was one of the foremost proponents of the new radio, her staff cautioned that the White House had not convinced friends of Radio Marti in Congress that it was serious. The administration had left advocacy to the Department of State, the staff explained, and that was insufficient. If things were that bad in Florida, it was apparent that there was little stomach in the Senate for Radio Marti in the face of determined domestic pressure groups that feared their interests would suffer if the radio went forward. It developed that Hawkins had approached Senator Lowell Weicker, a foe of the administration bill who had been delaying it by lengthy discussion, to see if some compromise was possible. Weicker agreed compromise was possible.[18] The next step was an amendment developed by Weicker and Senator Zorinsky of Nebraska, another opponent of the administration bill, to place Radio Marti under the Voice of America, where it would presumably not have the impact intended because VOA would not design its Latin American program specifically for Cuba.

In light of domestic political considerations, the administration was tempted by the compromise worked out among Senator Hawkins, Senator Weicker, Senate Majority Leader Howard Baker, and their staffs. The compromise would at least provide for some form of special broadcasting to Cuba, although it was not clear just what this would entail. Moreover, the compromise abruptly and unexpectedly enjoyed the blessing of Jorge Mas Canosa. Mas, the major player in the push for surrogate broadcasting to Cuba, had held out for the original idea of Radio Marti under the Board for International Broadcasting. But he was a new kind of Cuban–American lobbyist—a cool realist with excellent contacts within the government. He had concluded that the compromise would be the best he could get.

On September 13 the Senate adopted Radio Marti legislation by acclamation, establishing it as the "Cuba Service" of VOA (the Voice of America), subject to VOA standards. The "Cuba Service" would use VOA facilities on Marathon Key, Florida and broadcast on 1180 kHz, thereby alleviating the threat of Cuban interference to station WHO in Des Moines. This was an important change. Cuba was critical of Senate action but made no other overt response.

On the following day, an interagency group met in the Executive Office Building to review the situation. The House of Representatives, which had not resolved the problem of its own two incompatible draft bills on Radio Marti, seemed ready to enact the Senate bill as the easy way out. It appeared that Congress was about to enact a solution that might preclude surrogate, home-service broadcasting to Cuba.

That was how the National Association of Broadcasters saw it. NAB President Edmund Fritts called the Senate vote "a major victory for radio broadcasters and the public." *Broadcasting* magazine described the NAB as "euphoric," noting that the bill was not what the administration wanted and was accepted by its supporters in the Senate as the best they could get.[19] *Broadcasting*, like many of the bill's supporters who were cool to Radio Marti, thought that the bill was a death knell for surrogate broadcasting. According to the magazine, Cuba was said to feel that broadcasts by VOA were within the "rules of the propaganda game" but that a separate station would not be.[20]

But the issue was still alive. Marti supporters in the executive branch knew that a radio station broadcasting to Cuba along standard VOA lines would be like a "Cuba Libre" without rum, a voice dealing merely with events and opinions in the United States and the world in general to which few Cubans might listen. But nothing in the bill enacted by the Senate precluded surrogate broadcasting along the lines of Radio Free Europe and Radio Liberty, even if the station were to operate under VOA direction and standards. It might be possible to have both. The legislative record was sufficiently open-ended to allow further creative shaping. What was indispensable to an effective Radio Marti was less the aegis than the determination that it would be a surrogate radio. If so decided, it could speak as a Cuban voice. Rum could still be poured into this brew.

On September 15, Under Secretary of State for Political Affairs Larry Eagleburger approved a memorandum proposing that the administration endorse the Senate bill but clarify and bolster the legislative history by asking Representative Dante Fascell, Chairman of the House Foreign Affairs Committee, to state—for the record and prior to the House vote— that the bill provided for a surrogate, home broadcasting service for Cuba. The White House endorsed this idea. Congressman Fascell, who represented Miami, was happy to cooperate. On September 29, the House of Representatives adopted the Senate compromise bill by a vote of 301–108. During the debate, many opponents condemned the bill in sharp language. Representative Smith of Iowa, chairman of the House Appropriations Committee, wondered just what kind of broadcasting was intended, hoping it would be like that of VOA. But the vote demonstrated that opponents of the bill realized that in addition to with VOA standards, they were adopting a special kind of broadcasting, tailored to Cuba.

It is doubtful that this was the outcome Senator Weicker wanted or expected. It appears that he lost control of his "compromise" on the critical element. His support, and that of other opponents of the original administration bill, however, had made possible the enactment of Radio Marti legislation.

Knowing that Cuban intelligence monitored open-line telephone conversations between myself and John Ferch, chief of the U.S. Interests Section in Cuba, I was careful throughout the congressional debate to refer to legislation pending in Congress as the "Weicker Compromise." Since Havana regarded him as a friend and a strong critic of Radio Marti, I hoped that reference to his support would give the Cubans pause about engaging in any fireworks or special efforts to defeat the bill. While I knew that the Cuban Interests Section was closely following developments and reporting them to Havana, describing the bill as a compromise could not hurt.

On October 4, President Reagan put his signature on the Radio Marti bill without ceremony so as to expedite the appropriation procedure in Congress. Cuba's reaction was delayed, indicating some indecision about an outcome which must have been confusing. In the end Havana's rejection was clear, however. On October 17 Cuba advised that it would not continue radio interference talks with the United States due to the adoption of legislation authorizing radio broadcasting to Cuba. The Cubans had used the talks as a ploy for forestalling this result.

Round two of the radio war had gone to the United States. After two years of effort, the U.S. government had the means to develop surrogate, home-service broadcasting to Cuba. But more rounds lay ahead. Cuba had demonstrated that it could cause serious interference with AM broadcasting in the United States. The development of huge transmitters, the occasional warning blasts they sent, and a very skillful use of intelligence channels would continue to hold Washington's attention. U.S. decisions about Radio Marti would be influenced by the threat of Cuban radio interference and its impact on the U.S. broadcasting industry.

On December 19, VOA Director Ken Tomlinson told an internal U.S. government meeting in the White House Situation Room that the first broadcast of Radio Marti was foreseen for January 1, 1984. I mentioned the need to have appropriate reprisals ready if the Cuban reaction materialized as we feared. No one challenged this proposition. Unfortunately, we were making no progress in developing the sort of countermeasures that would give us a third option between responding to massive Cuban radio interference with a whimper (a protest) or a bang ("surgical removal").

Tomlinson proved premature by more than sixteen months as to the start-up of Radio Marti. There was a need to create a staff of Spanish-speaking, Cuba-oriented persons for surrogate broadcasting in a U.S. government facility. Most of the staff members would be born outside the United States, delaying the security clearance procedures. Aside from the staffing problems and other technical obstacles to a fast start, the threat of a disruptive Cuban response still hung over the new radio. Moreover, 1984 was an election year, the NAB was anxious and prudence would prevail.

THE ECONOMIC WAR—TIGHTENING THE U.S. EMBARGO

Since 1962 the United States had maintained an embargo on trade and financial transactions with Cuba. Critics frequently pointed to the obvious: it had not caused the collapse of the Castro government. Even in the absence of massive Soviet subsidies, it would not have done so. Embargoes on trade and finance seldom have that much effect, and Fidel Castro was not an ordinary leader.

Critics also argued that the embargo drove Cuba closer to the Soviet Union. Yet in the absence of sanctions, Castro, pro-Soviet by choice not compulsion, would have been free to take the best of both worlds. Cuba could and did trade with Japan and Western Europe while remaining a staunch Soviet ally.

The foreign policy purpose of tightening the embargo in 1982 was to add—however marginally—to the burden on Cuba, limiting Havana's options and undermining the attractiveness of the model for other Latin American and Caribbean countries. In view of Cuba's militancy in the early 1980s as linchpin between Soviet power and Latin American revolutionaries, this general restriction on trade seemed to the Reagan administration not only worth maintaining but strengthening.

The embargo, usually and with propagandistic intent called a "blockade" by Cuba,[21] was based upon the Trading with the Enemy Act. As such it had the important benefit of not requiring annual approval by Congress, as did more recently enacted embargoes.

Cuba's serious economic difficulty in 1982 did not stem primarily from the U.S. embargo but from the structural weakness of the Cuban economy and its overcommitment to the Soviet trading bloc. Although the Cubans had sought to expand their hard currency trade with Japan and Western Europe on the basis of commercial credit in the 1970s, Havana was running large deficits with both its Eastern suppliers (in soft currency) and the West

(in hard). At the end of August 1982, almost to the day when t
their powerful transmitters at radio station WHO in Des Moines
were obliged to inform Western creditors that they could no l
payments on their convertible currency debt. They asked Japane:
European banks to renegotiate terms on debt payments due in the next three
years.

Cuba, however, had little prospect of earning sufficient convertible
currency from its export of sugar, nickel, tobacco, and cigars, and from a
negligible amount of tourism—primarily from less affluent Canadians who
frequented the beautiful, almost deserted beaches of Varadero. It was this
bleak situation, in part, which had led Fidel Castro to offer a "dialogue"
with Cuban exiles in the Carter period. The unexpected and disruptive social
consequences of this dialogue for Cuba discouraged Havana from expand-
ing such visits, although other North American visitors would have been
welcome.

Although the administration wished to strengthen the embargo, little
more than moral support was forthcoming from the White House or the
National Security Council (NSC) in the economic context. Coordinating a
more effective program of economic sanctions was neither easy nor popular
in the bureaucracy itself. This was also true within the Department of State,
where conflicting objectives put a brake on change. For example, although
Under Secretary of State for Political Affairs Larry Eagleburger saw opportunity for the United States in the debt rescheduling process for Cuba in
Geneva, it was managed for State by the Economic Bureau, which had little
interest in tightening the Cuba embargo and still less in antagonizing Cuba's
European trade partners.

Though not a member of the International Monetary Fund, Cuba was
given "Paris Club" treatment in the rescheduling of its debt. The creditors
offered Cuba a normal debt rescheduling program in February 1983. In view
of Cuba's declining economic fortunes, however, the rescheduling provided
no real benefit to any of the parties. Cuba became progressively less able
to meet its financial commitments and more of an economic burden to its
trading partners, East and West.

As a technique for channeling interagency resources into embargo enforcement, State sought to establish a taskforce that would unite the intelligence and informational resources of State and CIA with the enforcement
powers of Treasury and Commerce. Although it initially saw its turf
threatened, Treasury ultimately came to increase its enforcement activity in
conjunction with information from other U.S. agencies. Of particular concern were reports of ongoing illegal business being conducted by Cuban

front organizations in Panama and elsewhere. Treasury periodically upgraded its listing of such firms as designated Cuban nationals, after which further business by American nationals would be unlawful. However, the Cubans were adroit at opening new fronts and putting them to good use well before they could be "designated." Since Treasury was open to legal challenge, it was reluctant to designate firms until it had ample public evidence on which to base a defense.

At State's urging and with NSC staff interest, Treasury successfully conducted a series of bilateral negotiations to deter other countries from continuing to buy Cuban nickel. The agreements required the contracting party to certify that its exports to the United States, in their basic shapes or form, contained no Cuban nickel. Third countries henceforth found it more practical to acquire their nickel elsewhere than from Cuba. These agreements also appeared to have an adverse psychological effect on the Cubans, judging by their own comments.

The most important embargo action taken, however, was a successful defense against litigation that would have opened Cuba to general tourism from the United States. Although Cuba lacked the infrastructure for a tourist industry, it might have been able to develop one if foreign entrepreneurs could have counted on a large flow of dollars from American tourists.

The Carter administration, in pursuing normalization of relations with Cuba, had relaxed travel controls under the embargo. In April 1982, the Reagan administration reimposed the same restrictions that Carter had relaxed.[22] Expenditures for travel would henceforth be allowed only for official business, trips by news reporters or academic researchers or for family reunification (i.e., the Cuban-Americans). There was no limit on the use of an American passport for any kind of travel. However, it was lawful to expend funds for transportation to or in Cuba or for expenses there only under certain circumstances licensed by Treasury under the Trading with the Enemy Act. Tourist travel could take place in practice only if the Cuban government were to "host" it fully by paying all costs.

The reinstated controls were challenged in court by the American Civil Liberties Union and a "National Emergency Civil Liberties Committee." District judges refused to grant these litigants an injunction against enforcement of the new rules. On May 16, however, a three-judge panel of the First Circuit Court of Appeals in Boston, including future U.S. Supreme Court Justice Stephen G. Breyer, ruled two to one that the regulations were invalid. The appeals court ordered the lower court to issue preliminary injunctions against the travel restrictions.[23]

Unless challenged, this decision would mean that tourists, including prospective businessmen, could go to Cuba lawfully and spend as they saw fit. Since tourism was virtually the only hope Cuba had for earning convertible currency, this decision was potentially of more value to Havana than nullification of any other element of the embargo.

On June 17, the circuit court of appeals dealt the administration another blow by rejecting a U.S. government request for a rehearing on the embargo travel restrictions. After this decision, State and Treasury strongly urged Justice to appeal the case to the Supreme Court and ask a stay of mandate against the injunction laid down by the appeals court so that travel to Cuba would not be authorized during the inevitably lengthy period the matter remained pending before the courts.

Acting Solicitor General Paul Bator was initially reluctant to make the appeal. Solicitors are jealous of their "batting averages," and this case could go either way. On June 23, however, he decided to honor the State-Treasury request and take the challenge to the Supreme Court, asking that foreign policy argumentation be supplied. The Court granted the administration's request for a stay of the circuit court ruling. The regulations thus remained in force until the Supreme Court decided whether to hear the full appeal or until the appeal was decided.[24]

On April 24, 1984, Bator argued the government's case before the Supreme Court in Regan v. Wald, drawing in part on material State provided. In a decision that *New York Times* reporter Linda Greenhouse called "one of the Reagan Administration's most striking legal victories," the high court found in the government's favor. Greenhouse reported that foreign policy considerations were clearly uppermost in the Court's mind.[25]

There might have been benefits to the United States from unlimited tourist travel—aside from the limits Cuba might have to establish. They would have needed to be balanced, however, against the dollars flowing into the Cuban treasury. In the circumstances of the mid-1980s, given the existence of very close Soviet-Cuban ties and the ongoing conflicts in Central America in which Moscow and Havana were actively engaged, an enhanced Cuba was not in the U.S. interest.

There was no lack of suggestions for getting even tougher on Cuba. For example, ex-Senator Richard Stone of Florida called me on July 6, 1983, urging that we cut off what he said was an annual flow of one billion dollars to Cuba by stopping direct air travel between the two countries. Jorge Mas Canosa weighed in on the same issue one week later, arguing that this step would be welcomed by the majority of Cuban-Americans and offering to provide a public opinion survey that he felt certain would document this prognosis.

Despite these presentations by persons who enjoyed excellent White House connections, the information therein conflicted with other data showing that Cuban-American visitors were spending less in Cuba than suggested. It was open to serious argument whether a travel ban would have been welcome in Miami. Even if I had endorsed the recommendations of Stone and Mas, it would not have been easy to turn them into policy. To maintain public support for a tough overall policy, it was necessary to show flexibility as well as firmness. It was wise to maintain a balance between curtailment of trade and financial transactions with Cuba and provision for humanitarian and other exceptions. In 1985, however, when Cuba made the migration situation far more difficult, we were obliged to reconsider this issue in the light of a new challenge.

THE DRUG WAR—THE COLOMBIAN CONNECTION, PLUS

Narcotics trafficking was a particularly sensitive issue. On one hand, Fidel Castro represented himself as a crusader against drugs. He denied that drug use existed in Cuba. To attest to his rejection of drug trafficking, he pointed to many incarcerated U.S. citizens found in Cuban territorial waters in possession of narcotics. Castro exploited these individuals, whose numbers ranged up to twenty-five, by releasing them from time to time to American congressmen. Americans imprisoned in Cuba for narcotics violations or other common crimes normally served terms of less than two years.

Yet there was evidence of another kind. At times Cuba seemed to facilitate the passage of narcotics from Colombia through Cuban waters to the United States. Documentary evidence was scarce in the Reagan years. Cuban accommodation of narcotics trafficking to the United States was fully verified only in the Bush administration.

In October 1982, the Department of Justice brought charges against four senior Cuban government officials for narcotics offenses in connection with the arrest of Jaime Guillot Lara, a Colombian arms dealer, admirer of Fidel Castro, and supporter of the Cuban-backed M-19 guerrillas.[26] A pungent Cuban diplomatic note of November 12, 1982 denied these charges. Yet intelligence from Havana reported relief that such real keys to drug trafficking as Deputy Minister of the Interior José Abrantes Fernández were not included.

In April 1983 a proclaimed intelligence defector, Mario Estévez González, told federal and New York state law enforcement officials that the Cuban government was conducting narcotics trafficking in New York and Florida.[27] As a consequence of these revelations, James Michel, principal

Deputy Assistant Secretary of State for Inter-American Affairs, testifying on April 30 before a congressional committee in Miami, linked Cuba to narcotics trafficking. Under Secretary of State Eagleburger raised the issue to a higher level, telling the press he found it very difficult to believe that the government of Cuba was not involved in narcotics trafficking.[28]

In September 1983 two members of Congress, Representatives William J. Hughes of New Jersey and Harold Sawyer of Michigan, who wished to go to Cuba to confront President Castro directly about Cuban involvement in drug trafficking, were denied Cuban visas. Although visits by American political figures were normally welcome in Cuba, the Cubans apparently were in no mood to discuss this subject.

Two months later Frances M. Mullen, Jr., head of the Federal Drug Enforcement Administration (DEA), said Fidel Castro and other Cuban officials were involved in distributing narcotics to the United States to raise money for subversive activities in Latin America.[29] Although the accusation against Castro personally went beyond the hard evidence, drug trafficking through Cuba was no doubt taking place. Could it really escape scrutiny by the chief of party, state, armed forces, and government on a small island?

HIJACKING OF AIRCRAFT (AND BOATS)

The first bilateral agreement signed between the United States and Cuba in the Fidel Castro era was in 1973 when the Nixon administration affirmed a five-year accord against hijacking, committing the contracting parties either to punish hijackers or return them to the other party. This reflected Castro's desire to force the United States to acknowledge the existence of his government. The Cubans were also interested in checking the influx of adventurers whose escapades jeopardized lives and brought bad publicity to Cuba. They surely wished to discourage their own citizens from commandeering Cuban aircraft to Florida.

This agreement had not been long on the books, however, when a Cuban airliner was blown up after leaving Barbados in October 1976, with heavy loss of life. The suspected culprit was Orlando Bosch, a Cuban physician convicted and imprisoned for carrying out earlier violent anti-Cuban activities in the United States. Bosch had since violated parole and fled to Venezuela. Although the United States had imprisoned Bosch for earlier crimes, Castro chose to believe that Washington stood behind the "Bridgetown Incident." Cuba gave the required six-month notice so that the agreement expired shortly after the Carter administration took office. Belatedly recognizing hasty judgment but unwilling to concede error, Cuba later announced that it would honor the hijacking agreement as if still in force.

Hijackings remained rare until 1980 but resumed with a vengeance during the Mariel Boatlift as some Cubans returned home by commandeering civil aircraft. In an effort to discourage the practice, a Department of State spokesman announced Cuba had informed the U.S. Government that all recent hijackers had been arrested and jailed.[30]

After still more hijackings, the Cubans announced that perpetrators faced "drastic penal measures" and could be extradited to the United States.[31] Following the hijacking of a Delta Air Lines flight from New Orleans to Atlanta by Crescencio Pérez-Pérez and Juan Adega, Cuba, in an unprecedented action, turned the hijackers over to the United States.[32] They were sentenced to forty years in prison. The severity of this punishment shocked the Cubans and made Havana unwilling to return more hijackers. Hijackings abated, but after mid-1982 the Department of State probed Cuba without success for information about hijackers previously taken into custody.

On May 1, 1983, one day after the narcotics testimony by James Michel and other Department of State officials in Miami, a San Juan–Miami flight was hijacked to Havana. At first there seemed to be a possible connection between the two events. But Cuba returned the plane without delay, and the hijackers appeared mentally unbalanced to other passengers. Hijacking again proved contagious, arousing concern that this could be a Cuban-inspired campaign to remind us of another U.S. vulnerability. However, on June 15 the Cuban Government provided information that the United States had been seeking for over a year on hijackings and the punishment of hijackers between 1980 and 1983. The Cuban diplomatic note asserted that hijackers, most of whom had taken part in the Mariel Boatlift and wished to return to Cuba, had all received prison sentences, which were specified. The sentences seemed to lengthen, as if Cuban authorities were growing tired of these disruptions. In addition to seeking to demonstrate Cuban rectitude, the purpose of the note was to discourage further hijackers, who would henceforth know prison awaited them in Cuba.

On July 20, after two more hijackings within 36 hours, I participated in an ABC "Nightline" broadcast with host Ted Koppel, where I rebutted assertions that the hijackings were a Cuban ploy to force us into negotiations. I cited Cuba's stated punishment of hijackers as a warning to those inclined to emulate them.

The hijackings, nevertheless, continued, causing disagreement between State and the FAA, which wanted hijackers returned for trial in the United

States. State had no problem with this if the Cubans would agree, but pointed out that neither international law nor the 1973 bilateral anti-hijacking accord obliged Havana to do more than punish the culprits. Moreover, State was concerned that it might be placed in a position where Cuba would demand the return of a person who had hijacked an airplane or a boat in order to escape Cuba. This would be a delicate matter, where human rights considerations—not to mention domestic political ones—would conflict with the desire of the aviation industry to discourage skyjacking.

This concern was not hypothetical. On July 21, 1983, a Cuban lobster boat arrived in Florida after being commandeered in Cuban waters by persons wishing to flee to the United States. State arranged with the Coast Guard and the Immigration and Naturalization Service for prompt return of vessel and crew to Cuba. The fugitives were granted asylum and charged with no criminal offense. There had been no bloodshed in the taking of the boat.

On July 28, however, the Cubans were notified that a second lobster boat had reached Florida. The takeover this time appeared to have been less benign. The "boatjackers" reportedly had boasted about having thrown the boat captain overboard. The situation illustrated the hijacking dilemma. Law enforcement and humanitarian considerations might not mesh, and there were foreign policy aspects to be taken into account.

On August 1, FAA Administrator Lynn Helms at a public meeting on hijacking insisted that Cuba be pressed to return hijackers to the United States for punishment. He was assuring Federal Aviation Administration clients that their interests were being forcefully represented.

On August 2, a Cuban diplomatic note demanded that the hijackers of the second boat be punished. Havana conspicuously did not ask that they be returned to Cuba. The note asserted that the boat pilot who had been thrown overboard swam for twelve hours to save himself. State urged Justice to investigate the case carefully in view of the international implications and to bring the suspects to trial if investigation showed they had recklessly jeopardized human life in their escape. In the meantime the boatjackers were hailed as heroes in Miami.

On August 16, Deputy Attorney General Edward C. Schmults chaired a meeting in Justice that included U.S. Attorney in Miami, Stanley Marcus. I argued that if there was evidence of a serious crime, prosecution was important in terms of relations with Cuba on other humanitarian matters of interest to the United States—whatever the outcome of the trial. I stressed that the suspects must not be returned to Cuba, where a fair trial would be unlikely, particularly in view of the surrounding circumstances.

The Justice representatives recognized the dilemma. On the basis of past experience, however, they were skeptical of chances to punish the boatjackers. A federal grand jury in Miami had refused to indict three Cuban refugees who abducted a Cuban boat captain and took his vessel to Florida in 1980.[33] Another venue for a potential trial seemed hard to arrange.

On August 18, the tenth successful 1983 hijacking of a U.S. aircraft to Cuba took place. The FAA hoped the Cubans would return the hijacker, a Jamaican, but his nationality made it even less likely Havana would do so. U.S. leverage with the Cubans, limited at best, seemed to depend in part on whether there was sufficient evidence to prosecute the boatjackers in an American court. In discussing the latest aircraft hijacking, René Mujíca, acting chief of the Cuban Interests Section, pointed out that no one had ever been punished for taking a Cuban boat to the United States. Despite further investigative work by Justice the boatjackers were not brought to trial. The continuing investigation, however, caused Cuban-Americans to protest in early 1985 that the case was still under review.

The spate of aircraft hijackings also faded away in the latter half of 1983. They were not a serious problem in the Reagan administration thereafter. In general, hijacking of aircraft and boats remained relatively free of ideological content and thus represented an area where the two governments saw sufficient mutual interest to avoid linking these incidents to extraneous conflicts.

When Cubana de Aviación, the Cuban national carrier, deviated from the authorized Havana–Montreal route to fly over Griffiss Airforce Base in New York State on two successive flights in early March 1983, State and Defense thought a firm response necessary. Since the overflights of the base seemed clearly intentional, State insisted on suspending Cubana overflights of the United States for two weeks, despite the FAA's concern that this would lead to Cuban retaliation against the far more numerous U.S. airline flights southbound over Cuba toward Central and South America.

To emphasize the air safety—and non-ideological—side of our concern, and therefore minimize the prospect for Cuban retaliation, a senior FAA official was present when I called in the acting chief of the Cuban Interests Section to transmit a protest note on March 21.

The emphasis on air safety worked. On March 28, the Cubans delivered a response which—forgoing customary vitriolic language—acknowledged the civil air violations, said the crews of the aircraft in question had been relieved, and offered the apologies of the airline. There were no subsequent overflights of U.S. air bases by Cubana aircraft in the Reagan-Shultz period.

THE MORAL WAR—VOICES OF THE DAMNED

While his conduct during the 1956–58 civil war featured enlightened treatment of captured Batista personnel, Fidel Castro's post-1959 revolutionary tribunals introduced televised public trials and summary executions. Others received draconic prison sentences. Many persons who ran afoul of the regime were sentenced to twenty-five years or more in prison on political grounds and served full terms, if they survived. In some cases the terms were even extended for unrepentant prison behavior.

Thousands of political prisoners passed through Cuban jails to ultimate release, though seldom to "rehabilitation" in post-1959 society. Many hundreds, however, refused to accept the garb of common criminals. Proudly calling themselves *Plantados*, the firmly rooted ones, they suffered severely. Showing pride was only for the victorious revolutionaries in Cuba. *Vae victis!*

Curiously, the Carter administration, which devoted great attention to human rights violations in various parts of the world, seemed unconcerned about those taking place in Cuba. According to career diplomat Frank McNeil, "Hindsight suggests that the (Carter) administration, initially intrigued by Castro and the illusion of rapprochement, went light on Cuban human rights violations until ten thousand Cubans hit the doorstep of the Peruvian embassy. There wasn't much we could have done except jawbone, but Castro has never been impervious to international public opinion."[34]

Until the 1980s little international attention had been drawn to Cuban treatment of political prisoners. In October 1982, however, a *Plantado* named Armando Valladares was released and expelled from Cuba after coming to the attention of French intellectuals through a book of poetry he managed to smuggle out of prison.[35] The intellectuals had urged French President Mitterrand to appeal to Fidel Castro, who struck a bargain. Mitterrand's gratitude and enhanced cultural ties with France, facilitated by a visit to Havana by Che Guevara's old comrade-in-arms Regis Debray, looked like a success for Cuba.

This time the deal backfired. Castro had released a man seemingly broken in body in prison but who rebounded to help inspire a moral crusade about the injustice he and others had experienced. Valladares flew to Paris to join his wife, Martha, who had met and married him in his prison cell and helped to sustain him in his years of martyrdom. Valladares emerged an unrelenting foe of the regime, and Castro would live to acknowledge his error in releasing a man so determined to illuminate one of the darkest sides of Cuba.

In Cuba, moreover, a very different sort of man was starting what appeared to be a one-man dissident movement. Ricardo Bofill Pages, a former vice-rector of the University of Havana who had been associated with a pro-Soviet faction of the Cuban Communist Party that clashed with Castro's orthodoxy, had gone to prison for his attitude. After his release, almost unknown to the outside world and viewed by many as eccentric, Bofill began bringing to the attention of a startled and none too responsive Western diplomatic community in Havana reports of new oppression, including death sentences. The diplomats were embarrassed to receive Bofill's information, which could neither be easily substantiated nor safely ignored.

Valladares had done his suffering, which he would record in his book *Against All Hope*, prior to November 1982. He conducted his crusade thereafter against the dictatorship in the United States and Western Europe, concentrating on the fortunes of fellow *Plantados* in Cuban dungeons. Valladares came to light in the United States in a presentation on December 14, 1982, at a hearing called by Representative Michael D. Barnes on U.S. policy toward Cuba. His authenticity impressed the committee. Gradually he began to open eyes long shut to human rights violations in Cuba.

Bofill, by contrast, carried on his struggle in Cuba under the close scrutiny of an angry regime, focusing on persons whose fate would otherwise not have troubled the collective conscience, men and women not included on lists of political prisoners that circulated among human rights organizations.

On February 4, 1983, the U.S. Interests Section in Havana relayed an urgent message received via a Western embassy from Ricardo Bofill, then barely known in Washington, reporting the impending execution of five individuals alleged to have tried to form a trade union modeled on the Polish Solidarity. Information was sketchy. Then independent, if incomplete, corroboration came from a chance conversation during a visa interview with a Cuban lawyer, Aramis Taboada, who told a consular officer in the U.S. Interests Section that he had defended persons sentenced to death. The consular officer reported the news without referring to the Bofill accusation, of which he was unaware.

Since the second report seemed to substantiate the first, the information was passed to Amnesty International. Instructions were provided to the head of the U.S. Interests Section in Havana, John Ferch, to discuss it with Western embassies to seek clarification and support. The Europeans were little inclined to become involved in the matter, but the fact that it was no longer a secret apparently stimulated action by the government of Cuba. In early April there was news that the alleged death sentences had been commuted.

In mid-May, *The New York Times* reported that Cuba had commuted alleged death sentences to long prison terms. In view of interest in the issue by the International Confederation of Free Trade Unions, Roberto Veiga, head of the Cuban Trade Union Federation, had been obliged to write, and divulge, a letter to the head of the (Communist) World Federation of Trade Unions. The letter denied the report but conceded that thirty-three persons had been sentenced to prison for "counter-revolutionary activities."[36]

On June 5, the *Washington Post* picked up the story and elaborated it.[37] The principal theme of *Post* reporter Edward Cody, however, was "U.S. isolation" from the Europeans, whom he quoted as calling it "madness, a stupidity" to join the United States in a human rights démarche in Havana. The United States was to find a similar European attitude four years later when it first raised the issue of human rights in Cuba at the United Nations Human Rights Commission in Geneva.

According to Cody's account, there was a "labor disturbance" at a sugar factory in Artemisia on January 25, 1983, which led to a confrontation with the police in which "somebody may have shouted about a new union." Cody asserted, "There were reports of death sentences, but the government of Cuba denied them and nobody knows for sure." Cody also reported that John Ferch had raised the matter with Cuban Vice Minister of Foreign Affairs Ricardo Alarcon and noted that four lawyers were arrested "for defending suspects too vigorously." One of the lawyers arrested was Aramis Taboada. He never was able to use his visa to reach the United States. He died in prison, having been denied medical attention according to a later account by a friend.

In late September, the French Embassy in Havana reported that Ricardo Bofill, who had sought refuge there and was persuaded to leave the premises, had been arrested after having been promised by authorities that he would be able to leave the country.[38] Although the White House favored maximum publicity of Bofill's plight, State preferred discretion, believing it important to keep the French, however reluctantly, in the lead on his behalf. France had far more influence with Fidel Castro than we. Moreover, if the United States became too overtly involved, the French might be tempted to opt out, allowing Washington to take Bofill off their hands.

Human rights in Cuba presented the administration with a temptation and a dilemma. As in the case of probable Cuban connivance with narcotics trafficking, the administration would have been more than willing to reveal Cuban misdeeds, but concrete evidence about violations of human rights was hard to get. Just as some of them had done with respect to the administration's revelations about drug trafficking, critics of U.S. policy would have assailed this merely as an effort to discredit Cuba. At the close of 1983 the administration had achieved some limited success with respect to human rights in Cuba, but it was still a long way from developing an active, effective policy.

CIRCUMSCRIBING CUBA'S REPRESENTATIVES

From his predecessor, Batista, Fidel Castro inherited a small mission to the United Nations in New York. This changed almost at once. With its embassy in Washington out of business after 1961 and its activities as Third World leader on the rise, the size and profile of the Cuban Mission to the United Nations mounted until by 1981 it was one of the largest missions in New York. Equally important, almost all mission employees were on the "blue list" of persons enjoying full diplomatic status, including complete immunity from arrest. This cloak covered dozens of persons whose observed duties never seemed to take them near the United Nations itself. The number of persons on the "white list," with immunity from arrest only while engaged in indicated official functions, was small by comparison.

The size of the mission seemed considerably in excess of Cuba's legitimate needs in New York. Its capabilities to conduct espionage activities or to carry out tasks unrelated to the United Nations were apparent. In addition, since 1977 Cuba possessed an interests section on 16th Street, NW, in Washington, DC. The principal officer in the Cuban Interests Section, Ramón Sánchez-Parodi y Montoto, was officially a counselor accredited, together with his staff of nineteen other expatriates, to the Czechoslovak Embassy in Washington. Sánchez-Parodi, like John Ferch in Havana, was treated by diplomatic colleagues as an ambassador. Although relatively young, he was one of the most senior members of his country's diplomatic corps. Sánchez-Parodi and his section spent little time in contact with State. They concentrated, with considerable success, on developing close relations with Congress, the press, academicians, and influential private citizens. In addition to its component of twenty persons, usually backed by working wives who were not counted on the list, there were at almost all times one or several temporary employees assigned to the Cuban Interests Section.

Sánchez-Parodi's principal deputy in 1982 was René Mujíca, also keen witted and a highly qualified representative of his government. Like all members of the section, each had intelligence backgrounds. Whereas

Sánchez-Parodi could be quick tempered, Mujíca was almost always calm, seldom showing emotion. He had a sly sense of humor that covered an occasional gaff. Once he protested that the garden hose of the interests section had been sliced to bits, but admitted cheerfully one could not preclude that it was an "inside job." Another time he brought in an indignant formal Cuban protest note about a naval vessel that had brazenly interfered with Cuban naval maneuvers, steaming in and out among Cuban ships without regard to maritime safety. When the protest was researched and the offending vessel found to be a ship in the Soviet fleet, Mujíca remarked bravely that the vessel's action was thus all the more worthy of protest.

In Havana the 20-member U.S. Interests Section, more than one-third of whom were U.S. Marine guards, was far more circumscribed in its range of contacts with Cuban society. It was not hindered by formal travel restrictions of the sort that U.S. representatives in the USSR and some parts of Eastern Europe faced, but it was difficult to travel in Cuba without the close observation and, frequently, the cooperation of Cuban authorities. Our principal officer in Havana might have contact with a vice foreign minister, normally Ricardo Alarcón de Quesada, but the dealings of the section were with a relatively small group of Cuban officials trusted by the regime to meet foreigners. In this respect its situation was similar to that of U.S. diplomatic posts in most Communist-dominated societies.

The Reagan administration wished to curb the free range of activity by Cubans in the United States. The Department of State sought to achieve this while preserving—if it could not extend—the operating room of U.S. personnel in Havana. The Cubans were sticklers for reciprocity and could be expected to resist efforts to redress the imbalance they then enjoyed. In part for this reason, State chose to concentrate its efforts on the Cubans in New York, who had no U.S. counterpart in Havana. The Cuban Interests Section was somewhat sheltered by considerations of reciprocity.

The administration also sought to limit the flow of Cuban official visitors to the United States. These voyagers advanced Cuban interests in a wide variety of ways, whereas benefits for the United States from their travel were sometimes difficult to perceive. Restricting such official travel, however, proved to be more difficult than limiting and restricting Cuban officials accredited to the UN or in Washington. Cuban visitors usually had an American client or counterpart to bring congressional or other forms of countervailing pressure against any limitations imposed.

The first restrictive move was directed against the Cuban Interests Section, which was informed that as of January 3, 1983 it would be limited to four entry points: New York (Kennedy Airport), Washington (Dulles

Airport), Houston, and Miami. Although invited to propose alternative points of entry, the Cubans never did so. Obliged to comply under protest with the regulations, they would not dignify them by suggesting amelioration. As in the case of the earlier limitation placed on his own access to top officials of the Department of State, it appeared that Sánchez-Parodi had been counseled in Havana to expect restrictions from the Reagan administration and to tough them out.

On July 19, 1983, State imposed travel, employment and housing restrictions on the Cuban Interests Section. These measures obliged the Cubans to work through the new Office of Foreign Missions, which had been established to seek reciprocity for U.S. diplomats in those countries that required them to deal with government monopolies for their basic needs. These restrictions were applied to the embassies of various countries, not all of them Communist ruled. They did not prevent Sánchez-Parodi or his staff from traveling in the United States as they saw fit, as long as they arranged public travel or accommodations through the Office of Foreign Missions. One effect of this restriction was to ensure that security organs of the United States had sufficient advance notification of the travel plans of the Cuban Interests Section.

The primary U.S. focus, however, was on the Cubans in New York. On April 18, the U.S. Mission to the United Nations requested the Cuban Mission to repatriate two of its members accused of conducting espionage in the United States under diplomatic cover.[39] Then, on April 25, restrictions were imposed on travel by mission personnel, limiting them to a radius of twenty-five miles from the United Nations, where their responsibilities officially lay. The Cuban Mission had enjoyed free travel throughout the United States since the Carter thaw of 1977. Exceptions to the twenty-five-mile limit would have to be approved by my office and were thereafter strictly limited to UN-related business.

Obliging the Cubans to reduce the size of their New York mission and to place a normal proportion of its personnel on the so-called "white list," where their immunities from arrest would extend only to the conduct of legitimate business, was a delicate task carried out by the U.S. Mission to the United Nations. Under pressure the Cubans eventually reduced substantially the number of persons on the "blue list," which subsequently was ratcheted back up almost to its starting point.

Prensa Latina, Ltd., officially a Canadian news agency but unquestionably under Cuban control, had a Canadian citizen as its only employee in Washington. Although there was no doubt of his Cuban connection, the employee enjoyed all the advantages of a Washington press insider. Prensa

Latina, the official Cuban news agency, also had personnel stationed in New York, whereas no American journalists were accredited to Cuba. Those who traveled there were obliged to seek a Cuban visa for each trip. The situation was unbalanced. It was redressed by asking Treasury to designate Prensa Latina, Ltd. as a Cuban national, subject to the embargo. Once Prensa Latina, Ltd. was designated as a Cuban national in January 1984, its one journalist immediately left the United States. He had not been expelled, but had he stayed further dealings between him and his employer would have been subject to the embargo and illegal without specific Treasury license.

Some efforts to limit Cuban activities were more amusing than successful. In late October 1982, a prestigious Cuban delegation headed by the Mayor of Havana, Oscar Fernández Mell, received visas to visit the United States because of a consular error. Rather than accept a *fait accompli*, Assistant Secretary of State for Inter-American Affairs Tom Enders energized Assistant Secretary of State for Consular Affairs Diego Asencio to get the Immigration and Naturalization Service to expel the group. This proved unexpectedly difficult. INS constantly probed where the Cubans had already been. Apparently oblivious to the frantic pursuit, the Cuban delegation went about its business. INS finally caught up with the visitors and expelled them just as they were about to leave the country anyway. (In 1985, while Mayor Fernández Mell was giving me a guided tour of the old town section of Havana, we had a chuckle about surprises we both had during his American visit.)

Visa issuance for Cubans became more controversial within the Department of State after Joan Clark replaced Diego Asencio in the Consular Affairs Bureau in early 1984 and Michael Armacost replaced Larry Eagleburger as Under Secretary for Political Affairs. Asencio and Eagleburger were closely attuned to White House concern about Cuban travelers, whereas Clark was more attentive to congressional attitudes and very disinclined to deny visas. She was generally supported by Armacost.

On one very noteworthy potential visitor State drew a hard line. On August 24, 1983, the National Press Club in Washington advised that Fidel Castro was being invited to speak there. The Press Club either assumed that Castro would come to New York for the fall session of the UN General Assembly (he did not) or had received a feeler from the Cubans that Castro might come to the United States *if* he had such an invitation. The Press Club was told that a visa issued to Castro would be valid only for New York for United Nations business.

No invitation was tendered to Castro. This was not the last time, however, that someone thought a visit from the inevitably romanticized Cuban leader would stimulate interest and attendance at some event in the United States—as it surely would have done. The Reagan administration was willing reluctantly to negotiate with Cuban officials, but there would be no free lunch in Washington for Cuba's leader. In the autumn of 1983 U.S.–Cuban relations were far from chummy and about to become a whole lot less so.

NOTES

1. *The New York Times*, May 16, 1980, I, 31:5. Hereafter cited as *NYT*.

2. By December 1982 there were 12,555 Cubans in U.S. prisons. Dominguez, "Cooperating with the Enemy?" p. 78.

3. *Miami Herald*, January 10, 1983, 17:4. Martinez's source was an assistant secretary of state (*not* Enders).

4. *NYT*, May 20, 1983, I, 15:2. The Cuban-American National Foundation organized the meeting.

5. The number of persons who at that time had been given final orders of deportation by the Department of Justice was 789. In view of the much larger number of persons under detention, the figure was bound to rise. By December 1984, final orders of deportation were issued to 2,746 persons. This was the number Cuba eventually accepted in the Migration Agreement.

6. Shultz, *Turmoil and Triumph*, p. 305.

7. Professor Dominguez asserts: "The Cuban Government, time and again, has forced the U.S. Government to surrender to Cuba some U.S. sovereign prerogatives to set U.S. immigration policies." Dominguez, "Cooperating with the Enemy?", p. 31. The means of pressure were usually Cuban-Americans, but U.S. courts were a complicating factor, as when a judge decided the United States had unlawfully seized thirty-one vessels during the Mariel Boatlift in 1980 and must return them to the owners. *NYT*, January 26, 1984, I, 18:1.

8. *NYT*, June 28, 1983, I, 8:4.

9. In the 1960s, the United States maintained briefly a clandestine radio station, Radio Swan (later Radio Americas), which broadcast partisan material for short-term psychological effect. Until 1974, the Voice of America broadcast a Cuba-oriented daily program called "Cita con Cuba." After that there was no special broadcasting to Cuba by any U.S. government radio station. The Presidential Commission on Broadcasting to Cuba, *Final Report* (Washington, DC: September 30, 1982), p. 4.

10. Ibid., p. 29.

11. *NYT*, Aug. 11, 1982, I, 4:3.

12. Ibid., June 3, 1982, II, 10:1.

13. Ibid., Sept. 1, 1982, I, 11:1.

14. Presidential Commission on Broadcasting to Cuba, *Final Report*, p. 15.

15. Ibid., pp. 58–59.

16. *NYT*, May 7, 1983, I, 5:4.

17. Ibid., May 29, 1983, I, 22:1.

18. *Broadcasting*, Sept. 19, 1983, pp. 33–35.

19. Ibid.

20. Ibid.

21. Embargo is a word of early seventeenth-century Spanish origin, a prohibitory order against ships from leaving port (crossing the *barra*), which has come to mean a "suspension of commerce," either general or particular. Blockade is of French origin. It means to shut up a place by force so as to stop ingress and egress. U.S. action was an embargo because it applied only to U.S. commerce with Cuba. Although the United States sought to discourage third states from trading with Cuba, this was moral suasion. Had the United States imposed a blockade on Cuba, rather than an embargo, the results would have been of a different order of magnitude.

22. *NYT*, April 20, 1983, I, 7:4.

23. Ibid., May 17, 1983, I, 2:3.

24. Ibid., July 7, 1983, II, 9:6.

25. Ibid., June 29, 1984, I, 6:1. Justice William Rehnquist wrote the five-to-four decision, concluding that the 1982 regulations were consistent with federal law and the Constitution and "justified by weighty concerns of foreign policy."

26. *NYT*, Nov. 6, 1982, I, 1:1. A decade later, a reporter, reviewing Cuban narcotics trafficking in the light of subsequent revelations, stated: "Within Cuba, the U.S. indictment produced only a temporary scare and a warning to Cuban officials not to allow drugs onto Cuban soil." Andres Oppenheimer, *Castro's Final Hour: The Secret Story Behind the Coming Downfall of Communist Cuba* (New York: Simon & Schuster, 1992), p. 41.

27. *NYT*, April 4, 1983, II, 1:6; April 6, 1983, II, 4:2; May 1, 1983, I, 30:5. Estévez told a hearing chaired by Sen. Alfonse M. D'Amato of New York that he earned $7 million for Cuba through narcotics distribution.

28. Ibid., May 2, 1983, I, 3:4.

29. Ibid., Nov. 10, 1983, I, 19:1.

30. Ibid., Aug. 23, 1980, I, 7:6.

31. Ibid., Sept. 17, 1980, I, 17:1.

32. Ibid., Sept. 19, 1980, I, 1:5.

33. Ibid., Dec. 14, 1980, I, 26:6.

34. McNeil, *War and Peace in Central America*, p. 97.

35. *NYT*, Oct. 23, 1982, I, 3:1. The book smuggled from prison was called *Desde mi silla de ruedas* (From my Wheelchair). After Valladares' release, the book was originally published in Spain as *Contra toda Esperanza* (Barcelona: Plaza & Janes Editores, S.A., 1985) and then as *Against All Hope: The Prison Memoirs of Armando Valladares* (New York: Alfred A. Knopf, 1986).

36. *NYT*, May 16, 1983, I, 5:5.

37. *Washington Post*, June 5, 1983, 27:a.

38. *NYT*, Sept. 30, 1983, I, 10:3.

39. Ibid., April 20, 1983, I, 3:1. The two were Rolando Salup-Canto and Joaquín R. Penton-Cejas. On the same day, State's Office of Protocol invited Ramón Sánchez-Parodi and his wife to the president's annual reception for chiefs of mission. The invitation was an error, since Sánchez-Parodi was not technically a chief of mission. It had to be withdrawn by an embarrassed deputy chief of protocol.

3

The Tide Turns
in the Caribbean Basin

In autumn 1983, despite congressional enactment of Radio Marti legislation, President Fidel Castro had cause for cautious satisfaction. Contrary to pre-election rhetoric about a naval blockade of Cuba[1] and talk of going to the source, there was no hint of any U.S. military action against Cuba itself, and things were going well in Central America. Castro's protege in Grenada, Maurice Bishop, visited Havana in early October and betrayed no alarm.

THE PROXY WAR—CENTRAL AMERICA

Having helped bring the Sandinistas to power in Nicaragua, Cuba maintained some one thousand military advisers there who assisted the struggle against U.S.–backed resistance forces.[2] Whereas the Reagan administration was finding increasing difficulty in persuading a majority in Congress to help government forces in El Salvador, Soviet and Cuban military assistance flowed to FMLN revolutionaries through Nicaraguan ports and airfields. Honduran guerrillas who would later invade their homeland were in training in Cuba.

Havana was limited in its support of Central American allies by Soviet scruples, its own economic shortcomings, and a general fear of overstepping the line drawn by the Reagan administration in the ongoing proxy war. It heeded U.S. warnings not to put combat troops there, but advisers led by the highly qualified military officer Arnaldo Ochoa Sánchez (later to be executed by Castro) engaged in combat alongside the Sandinistas. Cuba, like the Soviet Union, similarly respected U.S. warnings against introduction of advanced jet fighter aircraft into Nicaragua,[3] but neither Moscow nor Havana was warned not to bring in Soviet-built, Cuban-operated helicopters. They flew combat missions with sometimes severe effects on the resistance.

After more than two decades of staring down the United States, Fidel Castro prided himself on his ability to distinguish tough language from real sanctions. Cuba had grounds to wonder how much military action any president of the United States could take in the wake of the de facto impeachment of Richard Nixon. In those more than twenty years in power he had not yet seen an American soldier.

That was about to change.

THE SHOOTING WAR—GRENADA

In March 1979, Maurice Bishop staged a coup d'etat on the island of Grenada, close to the northeast tip of South America. His "New Jewel Movement" held political prisoners[4] and ruled by force. Bishop had charisma that may have reminded Cuba's leader of his own personal history.

In addition to his friendship for Bishop and his movement, Castro had an additional reason to provide moral and material support to the new regime in Grenada. Its location not only was convenient to South America; it also was a waystation to Africa, where Cuba had assets and unsatisfied ambitions. Thus, Cuban workmen toiled to complete a modern airport facility at Point Salines, which, with a ten thousand foot runway, could support Cuban military operations abroad. Bishop maintained that the airport was for tourism. But such a facility could have multiple uses. It caused heartburn in Washington.

With little warning, the picture changed radically. In October 1983, shortly after his latest visit to Cuba, Bishop returned to Grenada to lose control and his life in a sanguinary struggle with a rival faction of the New Jewel Movement headed by Deputy Prime Minister Bernard Coard. Bishop and some of his followers were slain on October 19 by troops of General Hudson Austin, who was aligned with Coard.[5] This development, although it did not seem to concern the Soviet Union overly, left the Cubans stunned and on their guard lest worse news follow bad. Not only was Bishop dead, but the entire enterprise in Grenada was suddenly at risk. The nearly completed airport might be lost to Cuban aircraft. The Cubans had grave doubts about the new leadership of the New Jewel Movement, but with their investment at stake they groped for a means to forestall the U.S. intervention which they felt sure might follow the Coard/Austin coup.

A Cuban party and government statement on October 20 set forth that, despite Cuba's friendship for Bishop, Cuba had taken a neutral position in the Bishop-Coard dispute out of respect for Grenadian sovereignty. The statement explained that Fidel Castro—in an October 15 message to the Central Committee of the New Jewel Movement, then already in Coard's hands—had expressed grave concern that the "image of the revolutionary process on Grenada, both domestically and abroad, could be considerably damaged."[6] Cuba's October 20 statement also asserted: "Now imperialism will try to utilize this tragedy and the grave errors committed by the Grenadian revolutionaries to sweep away the revolutionary process in Grenada and reduce it again to imperial and neocolonialist domination" and vowed Cuban support for the Grenadian revolutionary process if it succeeded in saving itself.[7]

Although it counted on American public opinion to impede the capacity of any U.S. president to use force abroad, Cuba was aware that there was concern in the United States about a number of American students in a place where power had passed abruptly into the hands of a faction which even Havana had come to distrust. After Iran, the American public was sensitized to hostage taking. What if it occurred to Coard to seize some Americans to forestall U.S. intervention? In the Cuban brainstorming process, even the possibility of such a seizure could be a pretext for the United States to step in.

Cuba came up with a traditional response and an innovation. The first was reflexive: to beef up their small armed force on Grenada by the dispatch of a professional military officer, Colonel Pedro Tortoló.[8] Castro doubtless recognized the futility and risk to Cuba of sending a large force which might only fall into harm's way, but he wanted the Cuban professional soldiers on Grenada to ensure that all Cubans there used their weapons—if necessary—against the expected Yankee invader and in the defense of the Grenadian "revolutionary process."[9]

Cuba also took a less orthodox step. It appealed directly to the enemy, the U.S. government. At 9:00 P.M. on Saturday, October 22, Cuba presented an urgent diplomatic note to the U.S. Interests Section in Havana. The note was totally devoid of the verbal abuse normally directed to Washington. Politely it recounted that each country had citizens on the island. The Cuban citizens all seemed safe. It assumed that the Americans were, too. Cuba suggested that the two parties "maintain contact about this in order to cooperate about whatever difficulty might occur and about the security of these persons."[10] This note was intended to forestall a military move by the

United States that the Cubans realized Coard and Austin had all but invited. But if the Americans missed the opportune moment, Havana may have reasoned, Cuba's enterprise there might still be saved, despite Coard.

Fidel Castro had little confidence that this appeal for cooperation would restrain the United States. The same day he sent a message to Cuban representatives on Grenada, warning of imminent "Yankee aggression" against "our collaborators in Grenada" as well as Cuban forces and personnel in Nicaragua and Angola. If the United States was to send military forces to Grenada, Castro said, "we must defend ourselves energetically as if we were in Cuba, but only if we are directly attacked." He repeated this last condition. If the Americans disembarked only to rescue their own citizens, Castro said, the Cubans should not interfere with them.[11]

Castro's October 22 message instructed Cuban representatives on Grenada to tell General Austin that the Cuban forces there were too few to be a military factor against the United States and could not be reinforced. He urged that the Grenadians give the United States no pretext for intervention, and that they publicly offer and reiterate guarantees of the security of American and British citizens, as well as of facilities for their evacuation.[12] Austin hardly needed this advice, having already said he hoped to meet U.S. representatives to offer "assurances" about the safety of the Americans.[13]

On the afternoon of October 24, twelve hours before U.S. forces arrived, Cuba formulated a message asking the Grenadians to withdraw their military forces from the intersection of the University (where most American students were located) and the airfield (where the Cuban workmen were billeted). This message was supposed to be delivered to the Grenadian authorities at 8:00 A.M. on October 25. By that time the latter were otherwise occupied, and the message was never delivered.[14]

Clearly, Cuba expected U.S. intervention. If it took place, Cuba hoped its personnel on the island could avoid the conflict by hunkering down. But if they could not, they were to fight—not surrender. The Cubans on Grenada were not to engage U.S. forces if they came only to rescue the American students; they were, however, to resist any move for their own exclusion. Yet given the proximity of the American students, and the Cuban workmen, there was little prospect that conflict could be avoided. Castro, the revolutionary strategist, had read the tea leaves correctly but could not prevent what he foresaw. The U.S. government would not ignore the opportunity and the risk which the struggle between Bishop and Coard had created. It was assured of the solid support of the other Caribbean countries, whose concern about events in Grenada had led them to counsel intervention.

In Washington, no thought was given to Cuba's proposed "exchange of views," which was seen as a ploy. Moreover, the threat to U.S. students did not arise from the Cubans, who were themselves in poor position to guarantee U.S. citizens against a possible hostage taking by the unpredictable Grenadian military regime. If the Cubans had not lifted a finger for their protege, Bishop, what would they do for any Americans misused by the Coard faction?

Little thought seems to have been given by those planning the military intervention on how a clash with the armed Cubans on Grenada might be avoided. They appear to have assumed that the Cubans would offer no armed resistance. Describing a briefing he received at Atlantic Command in Norfolk on the day before the landing, General H. Norman Schwarzkopf relates in his autobiography, "The plan . . . called for the Rangers to drive to the Cuban compound and announce, 'We are here to reinstall the legitimate government of Grenada. You will not be hurt. Please stay here while we get this thing over with.' " Schwarzkopf adds, "The thought that kept running through my mind was, *'How do we know the Cubans aren't going to fight?'* " (italics in original).[15] In fact, the United States did not know what the Cubans would do and could not ask. The Cubans did not know that our plans for dealing with them assumed no bloodshed.

On October 22, at the behest of Deputy Assistant Secretary Jim Michel, I had drafted telegrams to the U.S. Interests Section in Havana and to other foreign service posts, providing instructions for action in the contingency that the United States would facilitate the Organization of East Caribbean States in restoring order in Grenada. These messages, like others intended for other overseas posts and the U.S. Mission to the United Nations, were not sent, pending a decision to intervene.

U.S. plans were closely held by Assistant Secretary of State Tony Motley, Enders' successor, who was masterminding the intervention. Motley chaired an October 24 staff meeting in his Inter-American Affairs Bureau (ARA) without betraying any hint of the Grenada operation. Some of us who were witting had not learned of it from Motley, nor was it clear who else in the Department was aware of the plan.

Matters with Cuba were further complicated by communications problems between the Department of State and the U.S. Interests Section in Havana. Telephone lines had been out for several days. The original cause appeared to be local flooding around the interests section, which borders the Caribbean seawall, but the Cubans were dilatory about repairing the lines, despite frequent U.S. requests as the crisis around Grenada deepened. They appeared to believe it to their advantage that rapid communications between the Department of State and the interests section in Havana be hampered. If so, this was shortsighted. Faulty communications to the interests section were to hurt Cuba at least as much as the United States.

I reported to the Department of State operations center at 5:00 A.M. on October 25 (D–Day) to try to ensure that a message get to the Cubans at the earliest possible moment consistent with the safety of our interventionary force. Such a message might head off or limit bloodshed between our forces and the Cuban workmen.

The contingency telegram prepared on October 22 was dispatched, but it was not received by the U.S. Interests Section in Havana, which remained unaware of what was taking place. When it belatedly became clear that the telegram had not been received, I requested authorization to call our principal officer in Havana, John Ferch, at his residence (an unsecured telephone line). I was instructed to defer the call until it was confirmed that our forces had safely landed in Grenada, a confirmation which came well after the event.

I was finally authorized to call Ferch at his residence but did not get through until 8:00 A.M. (7:00 A.M. in Havana). My call awakened him from sleep.[16] I read Ferch our telegram, which contained the text of a démarche which he was to make on the Cuban government as soon as possible. Particularly since I read the message at slow dictating speed on an open line, it was undoubtedly monitored by the Cubans. It told them that the American forces had no wish for conflict with the Cubans, who could be peacefully evacuated.

Circumstances, made more complex by the communications outage, had made a clash with Cuba almost inevitable. Furthermore, since the objective of U.S. and Caribbean forces was to secure the island and not merely to evacuate citizens, the disarming and evacuation of the Cubans was also foreordained. In view of Castro's own objectives, this would probably have led to armed resistance by the Cubans or some effort by them to frustrate our purpose.

In the Cuban account of events, the U.S. Interests Section presented Washington's message at 8:30 A.M. on October 25, one and one-half hours after American forces "attacked" the Cubans at the airport.[17] In an interview with the *Washington Post* on October 26, Fidel Castro asserted that he had received a translation of the U.S. diplomatic note of October 25 at about six in the afternoon—that is, about nine and one-half hours after it had been received by the Cuban Foreign Ministry and about eleven hours after I read its English text over an open line to Ferch.[18]

All accounts, U.S. and Cuban, however, refute a version published in the *Washington Times* on November 9, according to which the Department of State "gave the Cuban government in Havana several hours' advance notice of the attack." The *Times* attributed this assertion to General Schwarzkopf, who it said had announced at a briefing, "We lost the element of surprise." Reporter Bill Kling added, "Schwarzkopf declined to speculate on what might have changed in the planning had commandos known of the State Department's pre-attack notification of Cuba, nor would he indicate what impact it may have had on the results of the fighting."[19]

Other newspapers did not carry this report. In his memoirs, General Schwarzkopf makes no such assertion, noting only that when the Rangers parachuted into Point Salines at 5:35 A.M. by daylight, "the enemy was waiting" and the Cubans were well armed.[20] If the U.S. forces had lost the element of surprise, it was because Cuba sensed in advance what was coming.

In his memoirs George Shultz relates that after he returned from Capitol Hill (i.e., after 7:00 P.M. on October 25) he told Larry Eagleburger to get a message through to John Ferch to tell the Cubans they would be better off to *stop* fighting.[21] Early on October 26, under Eagleburger's instructions, I provided this message to Cuban Interests Section chief Ramón Sánchez-Parodi, offering to facilitate the repatriation of some eight hundred Cuban survivors who were being treated as prisoners of war. Ferch did the same in Havana. Meanwhile in Cuba there were bomb threats against our interests section and anti-U.S. demonstrations.

Cuban resistance finally ended on that day.[22] Fidel Castro appears at first to have assumed that all Cubans on Grenada had died fighting or had been severely wounded. He communicated a melodramatic message that his only request was to have his dead and wounded heroes delivered. Carl Migdail, a veteran U.S. journalist well connected to the Cuban regime, told me a few days later that the Cuban leadership had "panicked" on October 26, thinking their forces had been wiped out.

When Castro learned that his military commander, Colonel Tortoló, was safe and that Cuban casualties were small (twenty-four dead), his relief may have been adulterated by bitter recognition that these men had not fought to the death against the hated Yankee. While the armed workmen had resisted valiantly, Cuban professional soldiers displayed greater survival skills than their commander-in-chief anticipated.[23] Small wonder that the slogan "No one surrenders here" began to appear in Cuba after return of the living and dead from Grenada. And Cubans prominent in Grenada later were reported to be in deep disgrace.[24]

In Washington, no sooner had the guns fallen silent on the island than the Mariel Boatlift criminals were interjected into the Grenada story. On October 27, Senator Chiles of Florida called to say he had written President Reagan to ask that the criminals be taken into account in the return of the Cubans captured on Grenada. He wanted them returned at the same time. A unanimous sense of the Senate resolution was enacted asking that we should seek to link the Mariel criminals to the soldiers and armed workers captured on Grenada. When the White House responded favorably to the Senate's urging, an interagency group was charged with preparation of a plan to have the Mariel Excludables returned to Cuba with the Cuban prisoners from Grenada.

Meanwhile in Havana, Alarcón proposed to Ferch on November 3 that Cuba be permitted to bring out on Cuban aircraft all of its personnel in Grenada, including the unidentified dead (Grenadian as well as Cuban) and Grenadians who had taken refuge in the Cuban Embassy. This proposal was promptly rejected. The U.S. government saw no point in facilitating a macabre triumph in Havana. The fifty-three Cubans in the Soviet Embassy departed on November 4 on a U.S. aircraft to Mexico City, but only after a showdown with the Soviet Ambassador obliged them to abandon their numerous weapons. The remainder of the Cubans would come home in small groups.

The unlikely plan to slip the Mariel criminals into Cuba in the wake of Grenada continued. On November 9 and 10, I chaired interagency meetings (State, Justice, Defense, CIA) on how to implement a presidential decision to have these persons back in Cuba by December 7. Everyone realized that this was infeasible, despite the desire of the president and the whole U.S. Senate. The idea of returning them without Cuban consent, whether by stealth or overtly, was unworkable. There was an understandable reluctance, however, to tell this unpleasant truth to the chief executive.

On November 14, the Justice representatives said that any covert attempt to return the criminals would not be possible under U.S. law. It was clear that they could not be returned overtly to Cuba without the use of armed force. Holding the prisoners of war as hostages until Cuba agreed to take the Mariel criminals would have been a violation of the Geneva Convention on prisoners of war, which precluded their use as a bargaining chip. Therefore it was decided to denote negotiations with Cuba as the first step in the plan for which the president had asked. President Reagan accepted this decision without complaint.

Meanwhile events had taken their course, which ruled out using the prisoners as a means of returning persons from the Mariel Boatlift. By

November 15 all Cuban personnel from Grenada, including the dead, were home. On that day Fidel Castro vented his wrath on the United States in a "funeral oration" for the Cuban dead. He recited "nineteen lies" which President Reagan had allegedly told about Grenada, while a Cuban crowd duly echoed the word *mentira* (lie).

Five days later the Cuban Interests Section in Washington published the Castro speech as a paid advertisement in *The New York Times*.[25] In addition to the questionable wisdom of assailing in print the chief of the government to which it was accredited, this action by the Cuban Interests Section raised a technical question. While the interests section was authorized to draw and spend U.S. dollars for its legitimate operating expenses, calling the president of the United States a liar nineteen times did not appear to be one of them. Upon my request, the Office of Foreign Assets Control of Treasury thereafter specifically denied the Cuban Interests Section the authority to expend funds for purely propaganda purposes.

On November 30, Swiss Ambassador in Havana Armin Kammer, through whom our interests section was accredited to the Cuban government, conveyed to Washington a message from Vice President Carlos Rafael Rodríguez. The message was simply that Cuba would press on with its "internationalism."

Despite this defiant boast, Grenada proved a "marker" in U.S.–Cuban relations. Cuba had to take into account the fact that the intervention had been popular in both the United States and Grenada.[26] The United States had demonstrated that it could use military force under appropriate circumstances. The wind went out of Cuba's sails in the eastern Caribbean.

To add insult to injury, Cuba's erstwhile (and sanguinary) friend in Surinam, Desi Bouterse, acting in the wake of Grenada, obliged it to scale down its diplomatic mission in Paramaribo and to withdraw other Cuban nationals from the country. Its pride wounded, Havana pulled out the entire Cuban representation.

Cuban–Soviet relations also suffered. Fidel Castro was displeased with his ally. Perhaps he thought the Russians had backed Coard without appreciating the greater international appeal of Bishop. Perhaps he resented their fairly restrained reaction to the U.S. move. For whatever reason, the Soviet Embassy in Havana called off its November 7 reception commemorating the Bolshevik Revolution. The British Ambassador in Havana, David Thomas, told me that in his opinion the reception was called off because Fidel Castro would not have attended it, and the Soviets wanted to spare themselves the insult.

NOTES

1. *NYT*, Jan. 28, 1980, II, 5:2. Reagan made the remark on the television program "60 Minutes." A real blockade would have been far different than the embargo measures which Cuba was accustomed to call by that name.

2. Frank McNeil states that Cuban military advisers in Nicaragua were estimated at between 800 and 1,200 in 1982. Estimates rose to 2,500–3,000 in 1986. McNeil believes that the first figure was probably accurate and did not change much. *War and Peace in Central America*, p. 162. McNeil points out that for the Reagan administration in the 1981–83 period the focus was on El Salvador, a crisis, whereas Nicaragua at that point was a "problem" (p. 135). For Cuba, Nicaragua, a bird seemingly in hand, always bulked larger than El Salvador once the Sandinistas attained power.

3. Shultz, *Turmoil and Triumph*, p. 311.

4. *NYT*, June 5, 1983, I, 6:1. Bishop reportedly acknowledged having about forty political prisoners, including six held since his coup.

5. Ibid., Oct. 20, 1983, I, 1:1.

6. *Declaraciones de Cuba sobre los sucesos de Granada: Octubre de 1983* (Havana: Editora Politica, 1983), pp. 1–2.

7. Ibid., pp. 3–4.

8. General Rafael del Pino, a Cuban airman who shot down two antiquated anti-Castro aircraft at the Bay of Pigs in 1961 but later defected to the United States, described Tortoló as a skillful favorite of the regime "with no combat experience." Cuban-American National Foundation, *General del Pino Speaks: An Insight into Elite Corruption and Military Dissension in Castro's Cuba* (Washington: 1987), p. 25. Given the disparity of forces, even General Arnaldo Ochoa Sánchez, who fought in Angola and with the Sandinistas, could not have saved the Cubans once battle was joined. He might have proved even more solicitous about saving the lives of his countrymen whose military position was hopeless.

9. *Declaraciones de Cuba sobre los sucesos de Granada*, p. 6.

10. Ibid., pp. 9–10.

11. Ibid., pp. 7–8.

12. Ibid., pp. 8–9.

13. *NYT*, Oct. 22, 1983, I, 5:1.

14. *Declaraciones de Cuba sobre los sucesos de Granada*, pp. 11–12.

15. General H. Norman Schwarzkopf, *It Doesn't Take a Hero* (New York: Linda Grey Bantam Books, 1992), p. 247.

16. For a time it was assumed in the Department of State communication center that the U.S. Interests Section in Havana had been alerted at 6:15 A.M., but the message did not get through.

17. *Declaraciones de Cuba sobre los sucesos de Granada*, p. 13.

18. Ibid., pp. 20–21.

19. *Washington Times*, Nov. 9, 1983, 1:1. The *Times* liked this scoop so well that it used it anew in early January 1984. The Department of State's press office,

not wanting to give this the mischief the dignity of a denial, ignored it the first time. On the second occasion I was authorized, at my own strong request, to draft for Larry Eagleburger's signature a letter refuting it.

20. Schwarzkopf, *It Doesn't Take a Hero*, p. 250.

21. Shultz, *Turmoil and Triumph*, pp. 336–337.

22. *NYT.*, Oct. 27, 1983, I, 1:5.

23. *General del Pino Speaks*, p. 26. According to Rafael del Pino, only two of the Cuban dead were military officers; the rest were armed workers.

24. *Miami Herald*, May 13, 1984, I, 1:1. Journalist Alfonso Chardy reported from Havana that Colonel Tortoló, former Cuban Ambassador to Grenada Julian Torres Rizo and José Joaquín Méndez Comínches, intelligence and security chief for the Eastern Caribbean and Angola, had all fallen into deep disgrace.

25. *NYT*, November 20, 1983, I, 3:3.

26. A CBS news poll found ninety-one percent of Grenadians surveyed welcomed the U.S. invasion as freeing the island from Cuban influence and preventing construction of a military base. Ibid., November 6, 1983, I, 21:1.

4

1984—In Discourse with Cuba

Despite defeat in Grenada and worsening domestic economic conditions, Cuba could count some positive developments as 1984 began. Diplomatic relations were restored with several Latin American countries, starting with Ecuador. Its conservative president, Osvaldo Hurtado, exchanged ambassadors with Cuba despite a personal appeal from Secretary Shultz. Conservative Latin American politicians seemed fascinated with the evergreen revolutionary in Havana, whose quarter-century in power made him second only to Paraguay's Stroessner as "dean" of Latin American leaders. (He would later far eclipse Stroessner.) They hoped official relations with Cuba would steal the thunder from home-grown leftists.

The idea of a high-level dialogue between Cuba and the United States surfaced again, apparently stimulated by Havana. Senate Majority Leader Baker wrote Secretary Shultz about a Panamanian proposal for talks between Presidents Reagan and Castro. Baker said he told the Panamanians that Cuba must request the talks, but he saw an analogy between such a dialogue and U.S. rapprochement with China in the Nixon administration.

Aside from the fact that Cuba would make no such request directly, the administration did not regard the situation as analogous. Beijing, concerned that Soviet power might be used against China, had possessed grounds of self-interest to talk to the United States. Cuba, perceiving no such danger, urged Moscow to be more assertive in world affairs.

The administration felt no need for intermediaries. The interests sections were available for discussion of substantive issues and to arrange higher level meetings, if deemed useful. On January 5, President Reagan directly addressed the people of Cuba, calling attention to their need for better access to the facts.

In February correspondent Tad Szulc told me over lunch about the ten hours he spent interviewing Fidel Castro for *Parade*. From Szulc's account, it sounded as if he had received the familiar cold-warm treatment by Cuba. Ignored for days, he had left Cuba, but the Cubans invited him back to see Castro. Stung by favorable American public reaction to Grenada, Castro may have been sizing up Szulc to see if he might present a more favorable image. But Szulc's description of his session with Castro, although it implied Havana's willingess for dialogue, gave no hint Cuba would consider substantive policy changes, such as reducing its military involvement in Central America.

As preparations for Radio Marti continued, there was no consensus on what to do if Cuba disrupted U.S. radio broadcasting. The Department of State pressed for development of nonlethal technical countermeasures. The Department of Defense, which saw Radio Marti as a civilian issue, agreed to look into the subject, but no progress was made.

Some mid-level administration officials favored a stronger U.S. response. In separate conversations on April 5, National Security Council staffers Constantine Menges and John Lenczowski expressed to John Ferch and me a preference for military countermeasures if Cuba disrupted radio broadcasting in the United States. A lethal reprisal would require development of no new technology, but had two shortcomings: the risk of overkill (literally) and, precisely because of that, the likelihood that in a crisis higher authority would shrink from using it, in which case there might be no response available beyond indignation.

Cuba played upon U.S. concern that broadcasting interference would be its riposte to Radio Marti. U.S. representatives attending an international radio meeting in Geneva in January reported that Cuban radio specialists boycotted their reception and refused to discuss radio interference. On March 14, Cuba warned anew it would retaliate against U.S. broadcasting if Radio Marti went on the air.

Worried representatives of the National Association of Broadcasters weighed in. On June 15, NAB president Edmund Fritts recommended to State officials that Radio Marti not broadcast before the November election. This cautious view was widely, if tacitly, shared within the administration. Gradually the targeted startup date for Radio Marti receded toward 1985.

Although Congress remained seized with the specter of Cuban narcotics trafficking, hard evidence was elusive. On January 16, Drug Enforcement Administration (DEA) and State officials informed the chief counsel of the Senate Judiciary Committee that their information was either stale or based on sensitive sourcing which could not be divulged in a public hearing.

Congress wanted a smoking gun, although only smoke was available. On February 29, the House Foreign Affairs Committee adopted a resolution condemning Cuba on narcotics grounds. By April, Senator Hawkins was pressing for yet another narcotics hearings on Cuba. There were intriguing reports of mysterious daily flights from the United States to Cuba and of drug smuggling through an air base in Cuba. Years later Fidel Castro would admit the smuggling but deny complicity. The administration, aware that domestic critics debunked earlier exposés as "Cuba bashing," was reluctant to go beyond the evidence.

THE UNITED STATES PROPOSES MIGRATION TALKS

In 1984, Washington wanted to discuss one issue with Cuba: migration. By then Mariel criminals were costing the federal government an estimated $40 million per year merely for incarceration. This did not include costs incurred by state and local authorities.[1] Crime statistics and disturbances in federal detention centers and state and local prisons caught headlines. Domestic pressure to resolve the matter had not diminished.

Nevertheless, members of Congress had a range of mutually inconsistent objectives with respect to Cuban migration. Some concentrated on the problems caused by the Mariel Boatlift, while others like Congressman Peter W. Rodino, Jr., Chairman of the House Judiciary Committee, stressed resumption of processing of immigrant visas in Havana.

In late February, Rodino introduced a bill, section 2 of which would require the Department of State to resume preference immigrant visa processing in spite of the invocation of section 243 (g) of the Immigration and Nationality Act by the Attorney General the previous May. State believed this would undermine prospects for negotiating return of the Excludables, the criminals and mentally ill persons deemed ineligible to remain in the United States whom the U.S. Government intended to ask Cuba to repatriate.

Several thousand former political prisoners and their families remained a separate issue. Most of these "outcasts" were ineligible for immigrant visas and would have to be paroled into the United States. The U.S. Interests Section in Havana lacked staff and facilities for a refugee program, which State believed should be arranged in the context of a migration agreement.

If Cuba refused to discuss a broad agreement, however, State thought it possible to process a few former prisoners without jeopardizing chances for a comprehensive agreement.

Taking into account these considerations and the decent interval since Grenada, the Department of State proposed to Cuba on March 20 that migration talks begin in ten days in New York. Havana flatly rejected this proposal. Undeterred, on April 23 State proposed a meeting in New York, to take place on May 21–22. This time an answer from Havana was slow in coming. It appeared that the Cubans did not want to meet but feared a refusal would cost them sympathy with those who contended Cuba was eager to resolve the Mariel issue.[2] Cuba knew that Rodino's draft legislation would provide much of what it sought (minus the refugee program) without counterconcession. Havana did not respond favorably to the proposal for talks on May 21–22, stating only that it did not preclude such talks *after* the November elections.

Meanwhile, in order to block Rodino's efforts, it was necessary to reason with the influential Cuban–American National Foundation (CANF). Understandably, Cuban-Americans felt greater enthusiasm for northbound migration than for exclusion of the Mariel criminals, but CANF also wanted a tough policy toward Castro and viewed the Reagan administration as a kindred spirit. To persuade CANF to give us time to deal with the issue on terms advantageous to the United States, I stressed to Frank Calzon, its Washington representative, that Cuba could earn $30 million a year by permitting twenty thousand Cuban preference immigrants to enter the United States. American relatives would pay the costs in dollars. This would substantially dent the Cuba Embargo, which CANF wanted strengthened.

On May 9, Jim Michel and I called on Judiciary Committee members. Curiously, there was more sympathy with the administration's dilemma from a key Democrat, Romano Mazzoli of Kentucky, than from Republicans. Ranking Republican Hamilton Fish, Jr., of New York gave little support because he was convinced Fidel Castro wanted an agreement on Mariel. Representative Bill McCollum of Florida was cool, believing we could just force Cuba to accept the Excludables. The Cuban-American National Foundation fortunately did not press for the Rodino bill, which did not advance.

Lack of progress on Mariel negotiations led to reconsideration of the former political prisoners in Cuba. On ethical grounds, it seemed that the United States must resume processing of the "outcasts." Secretary Shultz on June 12 approved my memorandum calling for resumption of refugee processing. While this step could undercut a Mariel bargaining chip, the numbers of persons who would be transferred under a refugee program would be quite small.[3] A bigger program could later be worked into an eventual agreement on migration.

However the Immigration and Naturalization Service, which would have to implement the program, posed objection, especially absent progress on the Excludables. On June 21, INS Commissioner Alan Nelson, who had firm views on Cuban issues, argued that the program could impede passage of the Simpson-Mazzoli bill on immigration which the administration strongly favored. This sounded a death knell for a separate program for Cuban "outcasts."

In view of Cuba's refusal to discuss migration before the November elections and the INS objection to a program for former political prisoners, it appeared there would be no early movement on any migration issue. Then, abruptly, the entire situation was transformed by serendipity. A partisan American opposition political figure, whose objective was to disparage the Reagan administration's Latin American policy, was instead to advance a major U.S. objective with respect to Cuba.

JESSE JACKSON GOES TO CUBA

One Democratic presidential aspirant in spring 1984 was Reverend Jesse Jackson, whose outlook was sharply critical of administration foreign policy, particularly with respect to Central America. In February, Jackson called for the United States to recognize the Cuban government.[4] Soon he became more directly engaged with the Cubans.

On Sunday, June 3, after a 90-minute visit to Ramón Sánchez-Parodi in the Cuban Interests Section, Jackson dramatically announced he had accepted an invitation from Fidel Castro to visit Cuba.[5] According to Cuban sources, the initiative for the invitation came from Jackson.[6]

Jesse Jackson was obviously going to Cuba to promote his candidacy and to demonstrate his differences with the administration's foreign policy toward Cuba and Central America. But just as Lowell Weicker, after a friendly 1983 visit to Cuba, had helped willy-nilly to sponsor Radio Marti, so would Jesse Jackson by his brief visit to Cuba produce results on matters of which he seemed barely aware when he accepted Castro's invitation.

On June 4, I notified Jackson headquarters of travel restrictions under the Cuba Embargo and forwarded pertinent Treasury regulations. Later in the day I spoke on the telephone with Ed Coaxum, a Cleveland attorney who had arranged Jackson's recent Mexico trip. When he learned of the travel restrictions under the embargo, Coaxum commented softly, "We are in deep water."

On June 7, Coaxum, accompanied by a colleague from the Jackson campaign organization, came in for an hour-and-a-half discussion of the planned Jackson trip. Coaxum was a quick study. Having read the regulations, he had correctly concluded that pursuit of humanitarian goals was the best grounds on which the trip could lawfully be justified. At this point, however, the trip appeared to have only political objectives. Coaxum asked for ideas on appropriate humanitarian goals which Jackson might pursue in Cuba.

After reminding Coaxum that Castro had invited Reverend Jackson to Cuba to derive benefit from Jackson's prestige, I said there were two ways in which Jackson could nevertheless promote genuine humanitarian goals. First, he could press Castro for the release of the *Plantados*, the long-term political prisoners who had languished for over twenty years in Cuban prisons. Second, Reverend Jackson could urge Cuba to negotiate on Mariel now, and not await November. This could restore normal processing for immigrants and former political prisoners, benefiting thousands of persons in both countries. Coaxum agreed on the legitimacy of both objectives. He undertook to discuss this with Reverend Jackson. As events demonstrated, Coaxum must have been a persuasive advocate.

The next step came from a Cuba-born Democrat from Miami, where Jackson's intended visit was not popular among Cuban-Americans. Unless the focus were altered, it would augur badly for Cuban–American Democrats. Luis Lauredo, an official of the Carter administration, provided Jackson in Washington with a list of seventeen Cuban–American political prisoners developed by Frank Calzon to give to Fidel Castro with a request for their release. Jackson replied that although he had heard it said there were human rights violations in Cuba, he had never before seen a list of political prisoners.[7] The Calzon-Lauredo action followed my discussion with Coaxum. Cuban-Americans did not contact me about the visit. The common focus on political prisoners was coincidental.

Whether in reaction to the initiative from Miami or intended to preempt such a move, the Cuban government announced the discharge from confinement of a political prisoner, poet Jorge Valls, whose release from Boniato Prison in eastern Cuba was confirmed on June 22. Valls flew to Venezuela and on to France.[8] A press account on Valls' release, the timing of which made it appear a goodwill gesture on the eve of his arrival, identified Jackson as ready to present a list of political prisoners while in Cuba. The article stated that Fidel Castro had already agreed to the request and that a list of twenty-one names had been prepared.[9] This figure strongly suggested a second Cuban ploy to better manage the visit. Since only seventeen names were on the Lauredo list, the twenty-one names prepared by the Cubans seemed a different list. Cuba had a number of American citizens in prison for violation of Cuban laws, primarily transport of narcotics through Cuban waters. It was plausible that Jackson might believe his mission could be termed humanitarian if it served to bring home American citizens incarcerated in Cuba.

In a press conference in Panama, en route to Cuba, Jackson mentioned no intent to discuss Cuban political prisoners but acknowledged, when specifically asked, that he did have a prisoner list. The Mexican-born *Miami Herald* correspondent Alfonso Chardy, reporting from Panama, said newspapermen had the impression that the matter was not high on Jackson's agenda.[10]

Meanwhile Lauredo made his list public, noting that it was led by Eloy Gutiérrez Menoyo, a one-time comrade-in-arms of Castro. Former Ambassador Gustavo Arcos Bergnes, Humberto Noble, the already released poet Jorge Valls, José Pujals Mederos, Angel Cuadra, and Ricardo Bofill were among the prisoners whose freedom Lauredo was seeking.[11]

On June 27, it was reported that Jackson, now in Cuba, had indeed gained a commitment from Castro—but for the release of twenty-two U.S. citizens who were then in Cuban jails. It appeared that he had failed to gain Castro's assent to the release of the Cubans on the list he submitted to the Cuban leader on June 25. According to the same press report, Castro had agreed to discuss the Mariel issue with the United States prior to the November U.S. presidential elections if both the Democratic and Republican parties agreed that the matter "should not become an election issue." Jackson was quoted as saying he had "good vibrations" from his talk with Castro.[12]

The following day, Department of State press spokesman John Hughes noted that the Americans released to Jackson were not political prisoners and that those wanted by American law authorities would be served warrants on their arrival in Jackson's custody.[13] The same day, then Assistant Secretary of State for Human Rights and Humanitarian Affairs Elliott Abrams and I attended Congressional hearings on the administration's unwillingness to issue paroles to Cuban ex-political prisoners. Abrams asserted that only by returning with long-term Cuban political prisoners could Jackson inject a humanitarian purpose into his ongoing visit to Cuba.

Jesse Jackson, traveling as the guest of the inveterate foe of his own country, had compelling domestic political reasons to wish to return from Cuba with some humanitarian success. Release of Americans in jail for transporting narcotics or other common crimes would not do. On the second and final day of his visit, Jackson informed the press that Castro would release twenty-six Cuban political prisoners—but only if the United States would permit them to enter the country and if arrangements could be made to fly them directly to the United States. "The ball," Jackson said triumphantly, "is now in the State Department's court."[14]

It is possible Castro offered this conditional release of prisoners with the thought that the U.S. government might stumble over its own internal conflicts and what he no doubt viewed as Department of State manipulation. This news clearly gave the Jackson visit humanitarian overtones. Yet it was not working out the way the Cubans had hoped. The release of Valls, the plan to free the twenty-two Americans, had not been sufficient. It is reasonable to assume that Castro had wished to focus the visit on a peace settlement safeguarding Sandinista rule in Nicaragua. Now the focus was elsewhere.

On June 26, journalist Carl Migdail, with good Cuban sources, told me the Cuban Interests Section was dismayed about the attention being given to political prisoners. They foresaw the likely impact if anti-Communists in Cuban prisons for over twenty years reached Washington with Jackson.

The ball, Reverend Jackson had said, was in the Department of State's court, but State did not call the shots for the U.S. government on its authority alone. Was it possible that one arm of the United States government could induce Fidel Castro to release long-suffering anti-Communist political prisoners to a mildly enthusiastic Jesse Jackson, only to find that another arm of the same government would refuse them entry? In Washington, anything was possible. How Fidel Castro, presumably, would have enjoyed that bizarre outcome!

The Inter-American Bureau had already appealed, on a contingency basis, for quick acceptance of the political prisoners—if any were released. On June 26, Eugene Douglas, Commissioner for Refugee Affairs, called INS Commissioner Alan Nelson to head off such action on the grounds of inconsistency with normal handling of refugees. Routinely such persons were processed through third countries after careful screening.

I told Under Secretary of State Mike Armacost that this was not a normal refugee matter and required special handling. Armacost, who was responding to a call from Jackson to Vice President Bush, agreed, but Nelson and Douglas stood their ground, insisting that any Cubans released from jail must be screened for entry into the United States through Nicaragua or some third country.

Meanwhile, Jesse Jackson flew from Cuba to Nicaragua on June 27 for a session with the Sandinistas, whom he praised for putting Nicaragua "back on the road to democracy, peace, and reconciliation." He was to return to Havana to pick up the American prisoners and, if possible, the Cubans.[15]

While in Nicaragua, Jackson tried to call the White House and was referred to State. The call was directed to Jim Michel, who told Jackson he would seek a favorable decision but could not guarantee one. Michel then spoke with Vice President Bush, emphasizing humanitarian considerations. Castro had made clear the prisoners would be released *only* if Jackson could take them home with him. Otherwise they would stay in prison. The Vice President accepted Michel's recommendation, perhaps reasoning that to deny them admission would blot the escutcheon of an administration proud of its anti-Communist credentials. There was no further opposition heard in administration ranks to acceptance of these twenty-six men.

As it had in Grenada, the Mariel question popped up anew. State was instructed by the NSC staff to try to get Cuba to accept an equal number of Excludables on the return flight of the Cubana airliner which Castro was insisting upon as the means of transporting the *Plantados* to Dulles Airport in Washington. This proviso, which was not made a condition for accepting the twenty-six, showed again the preoccupation, approaching paranoia, of both the administration and Congress with getting the Excludables back to Cuba. Cuba refused to accept Excludables in return. It was going to be far more difficult than that to get Havana to change its stand.

To ensure that the twenty-six men, fresh from the Cuban gulag, were warmly welcomed, State arranged that the first to greet them should be Armando Valladares, whose book had exposed the brutal conditions in which they had been residing until that day. When Jackson, his party, and the two groups of former prisoners arrived at Dulles Airport in Washington on the night of June 28, the emaciated bodies and vacant faces of the political prisoners attested to the ravages of twenty years or more of physical and psychological oppression with no hope of redemption. Yet there was Valladares, looking hale and fit, sharp in mind and firm in body. For them Valladares was more than a comrade who had shared their suffering; he symbolized the metamorphosis possible even to those bewildered, emaciated survivors of the Cuban prison system.

Another ex-*Plantado* made his mark that night. With the released prisoners was a former Cuban ambassador to India, Andrés Vargas Gómez, who had been released from prison earlier but not permitted to leave Cuba. After Reverend Jackson told the welcoming crowd at Dulles Airport that his trip to Cuba constituted a "moral offensive," he offered the microphone to Vargas Gómez.

Jackson was aware that Vargas Gómez would not agree with his remarks. As the latter subsequently told the *Miami Herald*, he had already told Jackson he could say only what his conscience would permit. "I told him before I spoke, 'I have things in my heart which I must say,' " Vargas Gómez explained. Jackson responded, "Now you are a free man and can say whatever you think."[16] Addressing the crowd at Dulles Airport, Ambassador Vargas Gómez said simply, "To go to Cuba to join in a moral offensive with Fidel Castro is more than morally offensive; it is a moral offense."[17]

Two facts that went generally unnoted would later prove seeds of controversy. One was that the twenty-six persons released by Castro bore little resemblance to the list of seventeen which Lauredo had given to Jackson in Washington. Castro had released only persons he was willing to set free. Eloy Gutiérrez, Gustavo Arcos, José Pujals Mederos, and others would still have a long wait for freedom, and Cuba would follow this tactic in dealing with future lists of prisoners.

Second, the U.S. government had admitted twenty-six men directly from prison, but no thought had yet been given to persons in Cuba who had stood by them in their long years of captivity. Few of these persons could qualify as "immediate relatives" (parents, spouses, unmarried children under twenty-one years of age) of persons who had been in prison for more than twenty years. Hence they did not meet the conditions normally set for refugee admissions. Reunification of these former prisoners and their families in the United States would be an arduous task, protracted by differences between State and INS.

On June 29, Jesse Jackson called on Under Secretary for Political Affairs Armacost. He confirmed having passed the message that the desire to negotiate the Mariel issue was not limited to the administration or to the Republican party. This unlocked the door to negotiations, for Havana could no longer assert that such talks had to await the U.S. national election, still more than four months away, for fear of doing Ronald Reagan a favor.[18]

Jackson explained that Cuba still required a written statement that both the Republican and Democratic parties favored negotiations. The Department of State took the position that the word of the U.S. government was sufficient. Ignoring the impudent precondition, it formally proposed to Cuba that talks be held in New York on July 12–13. Cuba accepted. Migration talks were finally about to take place, some four years after the events which they were intended to redress. Reverend Jesse Jackson was a catalyst in this process. He deserves a full measure of credit for successful advocacy of a proposal the Department of State had laid before Cuba twice earlier in 1984.

SUMMER IN NEW YORK—TALKING MARIEL
WITH CUBA

Had the Mariel talks taken place in 1983, Diego Asencio, then Assistant Secretary of State for Consular Affairs, would have headed the U.S. side. This was intended to deflect criticism from those who opposed any contact with Cuba by underscoring the technical, non-political subject matter under discussion.

Asencio had been reassigned. In his place, Michael G. Kozak, a deputy legal adviser, was selected on Jim Michel's recommendation to head the team. Kozak had participated in the 1980–81 Mariel talks with Cuba and had other negotiating experience. His choice allowed State to call the talks technical, but he was politically astute and—equally important—amenable to guidance on sensitive political issues.

Beside myself, the other member of the U.S. delegation was Craig Raynsford, a young attorney who was associate general counsel of INS. Raynsford was selected by his own agency. State hoped an INS presence might provide expertise on the Excludables, and perhaps facilitate endorsement by INS and the Department of Justice of the results of the negotiations. The delegation was supported by staff from ARA/CCA, the Office of the Legal Adviser, the Consular and Refugee Affairs bureaus, and an excellent interpreter. It benefited from Jim Michel's guidance and backstopping in Washington.

The head of the Cuban team was Ricardo Alarcón de Quesada, Vice Minister of Foreign Affairs for the Western Hemisphere. This underscored that for Cuba these were political talks. Alarcón, former Cuban representative to the United Nations and reportedly a protégé of Cuban Vice President Carlos Rafael Rodríguez, came with a reputation for a sharp and cutting tongue. Experience with him in New York and over the next four years did nothing to put that reputation in question. Yet he was a seasoned diplomat and skillful negotiator who seemed to know how to present his case in Havana, too.

The second-ranking Cuban was José Antonio Arbesu Fraga, Deputy Chief of the powerful America Department of the Cuban Communist Party. Arbesu was deceptively bland in appearance and seemed invariably in a good humor, but he did not leave the impression of making concessions gladly. At the table he said little but observed everything. The U.S. side believed that he and Alarcón worked smoothly together and that Alarcón took Arbesu's views seriously into account.

Other members were Ambassador Joaquín Mas Martínez, head of the U.S.-Canada office in the Foreign Ministry; Olga Miranda Bravo, Legal Adviser in the Foreign Ministry; Ministry of the Interior official García Etenza; Alarcón's personal secretary, and a very good-humored and popular Afro-Cuban interpreter we called Pedro Pablo.

Of these Mas, in particular, was a devoted ideologue. In New York he always seemed a supernumerary, seldom consulted by Alarcón. Olga Miranda also had little evident substantive role. García Etenza, by contrast, seemed to know well the subject of former political prisoners and was consulted by Alarcón.

As in the 1980–81 talks, the U.S. delegation checked into a midtown Manhattan hotel under assumed names. Talking to Cubans was still dangerous business in a city where right-wing Cuban émigrés had recently attempted assassinations. Moreover there was no desire on the U.S. side for publicity.

July 12 brought forth an aggressive opening salvo of propaganda and distortion from Alarcón. He said Cuba would consider taking back to Cuba only those persons who had been in jail *continuously* since their arrival in the United States in 1980, thereby eliminating those who had committed violent crimes after release from custody, that is, the majority of the persons the U.S. government wished to repatriate. This went beyond even a July 9 Cuban note stating that Havana would discuss only the names on the list which Thomas Enders had given Sánchez-Parodi over one year earlier. Alarcón denied that any criminals or mentally ill persons came with the boatlift. He refused to accept the list of Excludables the United States had brought, a list which contained many more names than those provided in 1983. The U.S. side told Alarcón that the number of Excludables might range up to 5,000 persons, the estimate INS provided.

In return, the Cubans wanted an agreement to bar accepting illegal immigration, a proposition which would have required the United States to deny admission to anyone who left Cuba without official permission. They wanted assurances that they could send a minimum of thirty thousand persons per year, a proposal inconsistent with U.S. immigration law.

The Cuban position on the first day seemed unreasonable, even for an opening gambit. There was concern on the U.S. side that the Cubans, having been maneuvered into discussing the subject before the fall elections, might be going through the motions, seeking to cause an early end to the negotiations.

On July 13 things went better. The Cubans said they had received instructions overnight to accept the U.S. list of Excludables "for information purposes." Alarcón largely avoided the rudeness of the first day. The U.S. side said Cuba would have to state whether it would accept the Excludables before the Department of State could consult Congress about the large numbers of former political prisoners whom the Cubans wanted the United States to accept. It was already becoming apparent that Cuba's intense desire to rid itself of these "outcasts" was a main bargaining chip for repatriation of the Mariel criminals.

After it was explained that Havana was out as a locus for subsequent rounds of talks, Alarcón affected to be surprised and distressed. The Carter administration had shown no such qualms. But we felt he had expected this response and that his dismay was diplomatic. New York was easily accessible for the Cubans and offered secure communications through their UN Mission.

Before leaving for home after two days of talks, Alarcón said he was pleased at the "respectful" treatment he and his delegation had received. He did not mind being addressed as "Mr. Minister." While no amount of diplomatic language and behavior would have succeeded in the face of fundamental substantive discord, the two delegations were establishing a rapport which did not wholly vanish throughout the entire troubled U.S.–Cuban relationship in the Reagan administration and which paid dividends in November 1987.

The delegation did not brief the press, but persons in Washington may have felt under no such inhibition. The July 15 *Washington Post* account by John Goshko cited unnamed "U.S. officials" who asserted that the problem for the U.S. side was that the United States could not absorb substantial numbers of immigrants. It would create widespread resentment in Florida, Goshko reported, if the United States "bowed to Cuban demands." If it did not, he added, the administration would anger the Cuban–American community.[19] State did not see this as a problem. The U.S. team stood ready from the outset of the talks to concede Cuba normal migration under the Immigration and Nationality Act if it agreed to take back the Mariel Excludables.

There was also Cuban spin management. Carl Migdail told me of hearing from Cuban Vice President Carlos Rafael Rodríguez that the talks would resume in August and that Cuba would take back the Excludables. Rodríguez made Cuba look reasonable. Should the predicted result fail to materialize, it would appear to be the fault of the United States.

On July 20, the Cuban government advised that it was prepared to resume talking in New York on July 31. In the interim, I returned to New York to make a previously scheduled July 25 address on "Cuba as a Model and a

Challenge" to the Americas Society.[20] My remarks were designed to explain U.S. concerns about Cuba while offering "to resolve those problems with Cuba which Cuba may wish to resolve and for which there is a reasonable basis for mutually satisfactory solutions." I mentioned migration, radio interference, and "perhaps other issues of this nature" where we could make progress if Cuba were interested.

The speech had been vetted and cleared in the Department of State, which was comfortable with the overall approach and printed it subsequently as a government document. The main thrust, however, was that Cuba was a country of paradox: a small island, with the foreign policy and military establishment of a major power, striving for leadership of the "nonaligned" but more closely aligned with the USSR than many members of the Warsaw Pact; an advocate of Latin American unity with a history of intervention in the internal affairs of many states in the region; an economy living off foreign aid that represented itself as a model for others; a country claiming to welcome democratic trends in the hemisphere but permitting not the remotest reflection of such at home.

Miami Herald reporter Alfonso Chardy, a native of Mexico whose outlook on Cuba was very different than that of the Cuban–American community, emphasized what he termed my readiness to make "unspecified concessions" in the talks with Cuba. Moreover, Chardy contrasted my remarks with comments by NSC Adviser Bud McFarlane in Washington, who had just told Cuban exiles that Cuba must bear much of the guilt for sour U.S.–Cuban relations. Chardy took out of context a statement I made expressing willingness to discuss radio interference and added his own twist by calling this "an issue closely linked to Reagan's Radio Marti project."[21] The reader might well infer I was expressing a willingness to make concessions on Radio Marti.

On the other hand, after attending the speech Antonio Navarro, a Cuban émigré businessman under consideration for Director of Radio Marti, called Jorge Mas to recommend it. The conservative Cuban–American National Foundation liked the address well enough to publish it in both English and Spanish as Number 11 in a series on Cuba.[22] The CANF publication bore a preface by Dante B. Fascell, Chairman of the House Foreign Affairs Committee.

Chardy had seen the speech as conciliatory; CANF liked it for being tough. In fact it was both, and thus faithfully reflected the policy toward Cuba which was developing in the fourth year of the Reagan administration: a willingness to solve some issues but to be firm on those where there still was a chasm between Washington and Havana. This was not ambivalence, even though hardliners wanted no contact with Cuba and critics on the left thought us much too firm.

Jim Michel, Mike Kozak, and I shortly thereafter briefed Chairman Fascell on the New York talks. We found him less than enthusiastic. He had voted for the Rodino Bill, he pointed out, but he was concerned at the prospect of a flow of twenty thousand Cubans per year into the United States. Of course, this was the number of nationals of any country who could lawfully enter the United States and would have been available to Cuba under either the Rodino Bill or a U.S.–Cuba bilateral agreement normalizing immigration. The difference was that under Rodino alone, the United States would not have returned any Excludables to Cuba.

The chat with Fascell was an eye-opener. His concern was similar to that of the unknown officials who had briefed Goshko of the *Washington Post*. There was widespread fear that a migration agreement with Cuba might lead to large-scale immigration. Such immigration did not in fact occur, however, and even with a program for refugees would have brought only about one-fifth as many Cubans to the United States annually as came in a few months in the Mariel Boatlift.

Talks resumed on July 31 in New York with a ninety-minute leadership session with Alarcón and Arbesu, which gave no clue whether Cuba would accept the Excludables. The formal talks that followed were full of incisive Cuban questioning about U.S. immigration law and refugee processing. As U.S. law was explained to them, the Cubans could draw their own conclusions about the infeasibility of some of their original objectives.

Although willing to go on talking, the Cubans seemed to be waiting to see how well Walter Mondale's campaign for the presidency was coming. Having given unintended assistance (they thought) to Ronald Reagan's 1980 campaign by the Mariel Boatlift, the Cubans would not make the mistake a second time.

On August 1, the Cubans declared that they needed a great deal of detailed information that would help them to identify the persons whom the United States wished to return. Alarcón evoked a need to be "humane" and to take persons back into Cuban society on a rational basis. While some of this was propaganda, Cuba had a problem in repatriating persons expelled as "scum," whom Castro had promised never to allow back.

On the third and final day of the second round, August 2, the Cubans still seemed undecided whether to take back the Excludables and, if so, in what order and under what conditions. The United States wished the return to be expeditious. The Cubans wanted it to be as gradual as possible. As for the outcasts, the Cubans wanted to send five thousand annually. This was well below the number foreseen by the Carter administration, but in 1984, according to U.S. Coordinator for Refugee Affairs Eugene Douglas, the administration would not have been able to sell such a figure to Congress. They were victims of a hardening general attitude toward refugees.

The two sides left New York agreeing to reconvene the first week in September, but this was not to happen.

CHILLY AUTUMN—HOPING FOR MONDALE?

On August 12, Tomás Regalado of the *Miami Herald* Spanish language edition, *El Miami Herald*, a shrewd observer of the Cuban political scene, used my New York speech to launch a blistering attack called "Un Mensaje para Habana" ("A Message for Havana").[23] Regalado knew the speech was not as conciliatory as Chardy had interpreted it. Regalado accentuated parts critical of Cuba and pointed out that news agencies had taken two or three seemingly conciliatory phrases out of context in what he called "an important work of 22 pages."

Regalado stressed that I had said the New York talks were not "high level" and were strictly dedicated to migration matters. "If Castro doesn't understand it," Regalado concluded, "it is because he doesn't want to understand." This last sentence contained an important kernel of truth and would make even more retrospective sense on May 20, 1985. Anti-Castro Cuban-Americans like Regalado and Jorge Mas of CANF did not welcome any dialogue with Cuba. If there had to be such, they wanted it narrowly confined in subject matter and not at such a lofty rank that Cuba could draw propaganda from the very fact of the talks. We had shaped our delegation to take this point of view into account.

Part of the Cuban purpose in agreeing to discuss the possible return of the Mariel Excludables was to engage the Reagan administration in dialogue. Havana wanted the migration talks to be seen as part of a larger package, as the subject had been in the earlier stages of the Carter administration. Although the Cuban side could derive substantial benefits from a normalization of migration alone, it wanted the talks to lead further. Regalado was putting his perceptive finger on an issue that would become explosive during Reagan's second term.

Soon Cuba had a bone to pick. It protested on August 15 an alleged overflight by an SR-71 reconnaissance aircraft. The protest note asked sarcastically if there were a lack of coordination in the U.S. government. It asked an "explanation" since Cuba claimed to detect an inconsistency of purpose in violating Cuban air space while seeking to negotiate an agreement.

In New York, the U.S. side had been careful to delink migration from other issues. Yet our need to resolve the Mariel problem delivered Cuba a lever. If Cuba was not anxious to reach an agreement before November, the alleged overflight was a convenient pretext for putting on the brakes. Cuba eventually publicized its charge of an overflight. On August 23, the Cubans officially linked this issue to continuation of the Mariel talks.

On September 6, State and Justice representatives met in the Department of State Operations Center to review the talks. Although immediate prospects for further meetings were bleak, the session focused on the number of Cuban refugees the United States might accept. INS Commissioner Nelson, supported by Coordinator for Refugee Affairs Douglas, warned about accepting too many, whereas State representatives supported on humanitarian grounds a larger refugee quota for Cuba. Nelson and Douglas ultimately prevailed.

With negotiations in limbo, Jorge Mas Canosa took the occasion of a September 13 lunch for Dante Fascell hosted by his Cuban–American National Foundation to complain quietly to me that the Cuban–American community had not been consulted prior to the talks. He remarked that the U.S. government would never talk to the Palestine Liberation Organization without first having cleared it with the Jewish lobby. I knew that he was uneasy about the fact that any negotiations with Havana were underway.

Mas, president of Church and Tower, a Miami construction company, had in January 1981 been one of three co-founders of CANF as a "bipartisan organization." It raised over $1 million annually after its foundation. According to its co-founder, Raúl Masvidal, president of Biscayne Bank, "It's the best statement that Cubans have learned to play the game of American politics. It's been more effective than anything old-line Cubans have been able to do crying 'communism.' "24 By 1984 it was apparent that CANF was a far more influential political force than older Cuban groups.

Much as the expert counsel of this group was valued in the Reagan Administration, in my mind no interest group, be it ever so well motivated, should control U.S. foreign policy. So in response, I pointed out that while CANF and the administration were in close accord, there would inevitably be differences because our constituencies were different. Thus each of us put down a marker.

Meanwhile Cuba maintained an ambivalent stance, holding out hope for the talks but refusing to meet. On September 12, Ramón Sánchez-Parodi told me that the framework of an agreement seemed to have been reached in New York. But Cuba still wanted an "explanation" of the overflight, he said.

Two days later he hosted a unique lunch at the Jockey Club in Washington.[25] We discussed plans of his interests section for, among other things, better housing and telex facilities, etc., but his purpose was to seek an explanation for the alleged overflight. My response was that the known differences between the United States and Cuba were deep and serious. We should try to resolve those that we could, as opportunity presented itself. There was now a chance to resolve the migration issue; we should not burden it with extraneous matters. If we failed to do that, neither side would benefit. Sánchez-Parodi was diplomatically non-committal, but the lunch did not resolve the impasse.

A few days later, the well-connected journalist Alfonso Chardy told me after conversations with an unidentified official of the Cuban Interests Section that Cuba was "pessimistic" about the migration talks. The same theme was struck by José Arbesu in Havana. He told Jim Todd, acting chief of the U.S. Interests Section, that my remarks to Sánchez-Parodi had been "inadequate." Separately, Alarcón was quoted as saying he had no intention of going back to New York.

At the end of the month, Fidel Castro told a British visitor that the migration talks were halted "at least for the time being." In view of the delay, members of Congress began to urge accepting former political prisoners without awaiting a migration agreement. Representatives Henry Hyde and Barney Frank, from opposing points of the political spectrum, pushed this argument, which would have impeded completion of a migration agreement.

Outside the context of the stalled talks, the Department of State tried to put pressure on Fidel Castro to release long-term political prisoners. In October it instructed George Landau, U.S. Ambassador in Caracas, I asked that he urge Willy Brandt, then in Venezuela and about to visit Cuba, to make his own appeal on behalf of Cuban political prisoners. Landau did so. This move, however, was unsuccessful. Somehow the Cubans learned of it in advance. When Brandt began to raise the issue during his mid-October visit, Castro cut him off with bitter words about the political prisoners, saying he knew the Americans had put him up to this.

Brandt told the press in mid-October that he had carried some "message" from the United States to Castro. The press misinterpreted this as a message from Reagan to Castro. This was not so. It had been hoped that Brandt, after having heard the harsh facts about the *Plantados* and persons mentioned by Ricardo Bofill, would have made the appeal from his own conscience. He had not been asked to convey a message which could have been given Cuba directly. The Brandt episode was another illustration of how difficult it was to interest West European politicians in human rights issues in Cuba.

As October moved toward its close, election polls forecast the reelection of Ronald Reagan. The Cubans decided the time had come to resume the migration talks. On October 19, after receiving a conciliatory Cuban note on the Mariel talks, the Department of State sent a response for John Ferch to provide to Havana on the note's question as to whether the alleged overflight had been intended to "humiliate" Cuba. Ferch reassured the Cubans that the U.S. government had no such thought and wished the talks to succeed.

On October 29 Ferch was called in by Cuban Foreign Minister Isidoro Malmierca and told that Cuba was disposed to continue the migration talks as soon as the United States was ready. Since Ferch was rarely received at that level, the personal involvement of Malmierca was a message that, whatever the reason for the delay, Cuba was prepared to talk to us seriously about Mariel. Fidel Castro had perhaps concluded that if Havana had to face Ronald Reagan for four more years, it might as well start with an agreement.

There was an underlying difference between the objectives of the two sides. The United States simply wanted to reach an agreement on migration which would enable it to return the Mariel Excludables to Cuba. It was willing to open Cuba to normal immigrant processing procedures and to establish a refugee program for the former political prisoners there. It was unwilling to offer any concessions outside the framework of the agreement. The Cubans, then and later, hoped and may have assumed tacitly that an agreement on migration would lead the United States to alter its foreign policy toward Cuba, particularly with respect to plans for Radio Marti. However, they never raised such issues in the negotiations.

There were also differences between State and the Immigration and Naturalization Service. On November 7, INS questioned our negotiating posture and presented its ideas for a Cuban–U.S. agreement. They were discussed the following day in State's operations center, with Michael Armacost of State and Alan Nelson of INS leading the respective agencies and with Robert Kimmit of the NSC staff in the chair. INS sought to oblige Cuba specifically to agree to (a) accept Excludables indefinitely, in addition to those names on the lists we had presented, (b) pledge that there would be "no more Mariels," and (c) cooperate with us in blocking illegal immigration through third countries.

State did not believe Cuba could be brought to accept the first condition, even though it could be induced to honor it in practice by the implicit threat of reinstatement of U.S. sanctions. The Cubans had made their "principles" quite clear on this. We intended to finesse them, not make them eat their words. State viewed an agreement on migration in itself to be a strong safeguard against a "second Mariel." If Cubans could come to the United States under the same terms as persons from third countries, there would be less incentive for their government to stimulate mass departures, as at the real Mariel. State doubted Cuba would renounce an option to announce that anyone wishing to leave Cuba could do so. It argued that the U.S. government itself could prevent a new mass influx of Cubans by controlling the indispensable U.S. carriers.

State objected to the third point on grounds that it was improper to interfere with emigration from Cuba other than to ensure that entry into the United States was orderly and lawful. Cooperating with Cuba to block Cuban emigration into third countries when we were arguing with the Soviet Union about the right of its citizens to emigrate would, at a minimum, represent discord in our own policy. It would have been inconsistent with our global emphasis on human rights.

INS never withdrew its objections, but authorization was given by the NSC to proceed into a second round of talks along established policy lines. On the eve of resumption of these talks, there was a human rights issue to address: the processing of the kin of the twenty-six men who had come in June with Jesse Jackson. We had informed Cuba on September 7 that we were prepared to take the immediate relatives of the twenty-six men at once. On November 21, Havana responded that it was prepared to begin processing family members for travel to the United States.

The Cuban green light led to internal disagreement within the U.S. government between those who favored a positive response and those who objected to the fact that many of the kinfolk of the former prisoners were not immediate family members. It was a kind of replay of the June debate, which Vice President Bush had decided in favor of by permitting an exceptional admission of the prisoners. But this time the profile of the issue was lower. The deadlock went unbroken. The ensuing delay would eventually subject the Reagan administration to sharp criticism.

A FAIR BARGAIN, FAIRLY STRUCK—
MARIEL RESOLVED

The third round of talks began on November 28. This time the locus was the magnificently appointed "Perez de Cuellar" suite of the UN Plaza Hotel, amidst breathtaking views—enhanced by well-situated mirrors—across Manhattan to the Hudson River and New Jersey, down to New York Harbor, and across the East River far out on Long Island.

The Cubans, still formally noncommittal on taking back the Excludables, had been "identifying" the names we had provided during the summer. On November 30, Ricardo Alarcón introduced a draft agreement, which he claimed to have written the previous night but which looked as if it had come from Havana. After consultations on the U.S. side, Kozak told Alarcón privately that if the Cuban draft were seriously intended, the talks were in deep trouble. Alarcón then partially backed away from his text while keeping his options open.

Thereafter the delegations sparred over the shape of a possible agreement. The U.S. side endeavored to convince the Cubans that no minimum number of visas could be guaranteed for Cuba and that under U.S. immigration law Cuba would have the same right as any other state but no special category. This meant a maximum of twenty thousand preference immigrant visas in any year, assuming such persons were otherwise qualified under U.S. immigration laws.[26] In addition, immediate relatives of American citizens (spouses, parents, unmarried children under the age of twenty-one) could be processed without numerical limitation if they met all legal requirements. Since there were about one million Cuban exiles and their families in the United States, it seemed likely that nearly twenty thousand preference immigrants would be processed in most years. Subsequent experience showed, however, that Cuban immigration would be much lower.

The United States offered to accept up to three thousand former political prisoners and families as refugees in the first fiscal year. No specific U.S. commitment for future years could be made because of the need for annual consultation with Congress, but Cuba was assured that we would be as open as our worldwide responsibilities permitted.

On December 4, a few important issues remained, such as the order and rate of return of Excludables. A number of points were "bracketed" (unresolved), as a marathon session was ending at 11:30 P.M. Alarcón announced unexpectedly that his delegation would have to return to Cuba for instructions. While agreement seemed near, there was danger in another break for consultations in capitals. Some unsatisfied party might try to raise the ante, or an extraneous event might set back chances for agreement. One such event had just narrowly been avoided when a ship under lease to the U.S. Navy escaped from a Cuban Coast Guard towline and was able to resume its course.

Despite the fact that it was well past midnight after a harrowing day of talks, Kozak, stressing that the remaining differences could be overcome, persuaded Alarcón to call Havana immediately. After some hesitation, Alarcón agreed to call Vice President Carlos Rafael Rodríguez. At 3:00 A.M.

on December 5 Alarcón awakened Kozak in bed with the response: "Carlos Rafael agreed with you."

Agreement to go on talking did not guarantee agreement on the substance. One key dispute hinged on the U.S. desire to be able to "catch up" if it were to start slowly in returning Excludables—as actually occurred. Federal courts or other outside factors might mean initial delays even after agreement was reached. The Cubans also wanted the easiest cases (for them) to be returned first, whereas the U.S. side insisted—ultimately with success—that it should decide the order of return. In the end a balanced bargain was struck. On the following morning, December 6, the U.S. negotiators brought to Washington an agreement containing virtually every major U.S. objective. Most important from the U.S. perspective, the Cubans agreed to accept all 2,746 persons whose names had been provided to them.

In view of the fact that most of the additional work would fall to the United States, the Cuban side also agreed to permit an increase of ten persons in the size of the U.S. Interests Section in Havana. No increase was authorized for the Cuban Interests Section in Washington despite vigorous Cuban argumentation. In return it was agreed that Cuba would be treated as all other countries in so far as legal migration was concerned. There would be a program for former political prisoners and families, of whom the United States agreed to accept three thousand in the first year. It committed itself to maintain at least this number in future years.

This agreement provided for orderly return of the Mariel Excludables to Cuba in a way which U.S. courts would sanction as consistent with American law. It conceded only measures which Congress, in the absence of an agreement, would have taken anyway. The biggest gainers were Cuban-Americans, who could look forward to a rapid influx of immigrants and former political prisoners.

Despite general satisfaction in Washington, INS Commissioner Nelson felt that the agreement reached was unsatisfactory. He asked for a cabinet meeting to review the accord. Nevertheless, on December 11, President Reagan approved the recommendation of the Department of State, supported by the NSC, that he authorize signature of the U.S.–Cuba Migration Agreement, rejecting the counterargument that the United States should seek additional concessions.

On December 13, the final details and comparison of discrepancies on the list of Excludables were worked out in the "State Suite," a bare room on the mezzanine of the old (Theodore) Roosevelt Hotel, the only space available in New York on short notice. Final confirmation from Havana came after midnight.

AFTER-HOURS DIPLOMACY—A THRUST FOR HUMAN RIGHTS

Near the end of the eighteen hours during which the respective delegations painstakingly compared lists of names in the "State Suite," Kozak and I invited Alarcón and Arbesu for a drink in the somewhat more presentable "Governor's Suite" on the 13th floor of the Roosevelt Hotel. Our chat began slightly after 2:00 A.M. and lasted the better part of an hour. After some small talk, I invited the attention of our guests to a deplorable condition that harmed Cuba's image, the existence of several hundred persons who had spent as much as a quarter of a century in prison for their opposition to the system. I urged that they rid themselves of this burden by releasing the prisoners. If they did, Cuba could be assured we would see to it that under our new agreement the *Plantados* were put at the top of the list of "former prisoners" and taken quickly to the United States.

After a considerable silence, Alarcón responded that I must have been speaking of some persons of interest only to Amnesty International and such groups. He added that U.S.–Cuban relations were not yet good enough for Cuba to be able to contemplate such a concession. I responded that I was not speaking in the context of bilateral relations and did not regard the action suggested as a concession to the United States. As long as the *Plantados* were suffering a cruel, protracted imprisonment, the world would condemn Cuba. It was in Havana's own interest to take this action voluntarily, without outside pressure. In other words, it was not a proposed deal. It was just a way for Cuba to help itself.

Further discussion of this point led to no meeting of minds. Arbesu, especially, seemed almost apoplectic about discussion of the *Plantados*, whom he described as CIA agents or worse. Alarcón, less emotional, stuck to his position that Cuba could not go so far at present.

We hoped that we had planted a good seed. Heretofore Fidel Castro had allowed the *Plantados* liberty only in response to campaigns on behalf of specific captives, e.g., Armando Valladares by French President Mitterrand, and the twenty-six "given" to Jesse Jackson. It was our objective, as it had been in the unsuccessful effort to energize Willy Brandt, to make the Cubans realize that such celebrated releases of prisoners only called greater attention to the fundamental injustice of the prison sentences.

It was difficult to say what impact this presentation had. Within a month, however, Fidel Castro would accept a list of political prisoners from a visiting group of American Catholic churchmen and interrelease some of them, along with a larger group which he himself selected.

And a few days after that I would have the opportunity to remind Castro of it personally during a chat in Santiago, Cuba.

WHAT THE AGREEMENT MEANT AND DID NOT MEAN

The welcome conclusion of the first (and only) bilateral agreement between the United States and Cuba in the Reagan administration on December 14, 1984 raised questions about its portent. Some administration supporters, especially in the Cuban–American community, wondered if we would now be led astray with respect to Cuba. They wanted to get tougher. There was no support in the administration itself for a softer line toward Cuba and a good deal of concern about loss of conservative backing if one agreement led to more negotiations.

On December 17, I addressed this issue at the "Face-to-Face" program of the Carnegie Endowment for International Peace in Washington.[27] I asserted that Cuban conduct in international affairs lay at the root of our differences. By maintaining the largest armed forces in Latin America, engaging in combat far from Cuba, aligning itself with Soviet power, and supporting revolutionary forces wherever and to the extent possible, Cuba obliged the United States to defend its own interests. I confirmed that negotiations with Cuba had been "strictly limited to migration issues" and attributed the successful negotiations to the fact that our objectives had been limited and realistic.

The speech in Washington deliberately did not mention, as did the one in New York in June, other possible areas of agreement between us. First we should implement successfully the bargain which had just been concluded. If that worked well, it would argue for additional negotiation on practical concerns that we and Cuba shared as neighbors. I had mentioned that there was room for constructive diplomacy in our relationship.

Senior Reagan administration officials had no desire to move quickly to new areas of negotiation with Cuba, particularly since none looked promising. The year 1983 had ended in the afterglow of the serious reverse which the United States had handed Cuba on Grenada. The year 1984 was ending with a prospect that a somewhat more constructive relationship might be carefully carved out on selected bilateral issues. However, the United States intended to keep Havana on the defensive in major international conflict areas such as Central America.

This was a delicate course, which not everyone would understand, but it was worth a try. It would require judicious restraint on the American side, especially with reference to timing, and a realistic comprehension by the top Cuban leadership of the limits of American flexibility. But judicious restraint in Washington and realistic comprehension by Cuba would not be conspicuous in early 1985. Coming events would make it seem as if we had plowed in the sea.

NOTES

1. Dominguez, "Cooperating with the Enemy?" p. 79.

2. Ibid., p. 80. Professor Dominguez's otherwise admirable account of U.S.–Cuban migration history accepts the thesis that "bureaucratic lobbying" for negotiations with Cuba succeeded in 1984 only because it was an election year and because "the Reagan administration felt vulnerable to the charge that it could make peace with no one." This overlooks the negotiating history of 1980–81, when Cuba said it would take back only those who wished to return voluntarily. Even in early 1984, Cuba showed no eagerness for talks when the United States proposed them. In hundreds of hours spent discussing these negotiations in the Department of State and with other agencies of the U.S. government, I never heard any view which would corroborate the assertion that the Reagan administration needed the talks to show it could "make peace" with Cuba. That was furthest from the mind of the administration and especially of its hardliners. Only Cuba seemed to harbor the illusion that Reagan needed to talk to Havana before the election.

3. The Office of the U.S. Coordinator for Refugee Affairs had budgeted to take seven thousand former political prisoners and their families in fiscal year 1980. After the opening of Mariel Harbor for the Boatlift, the Office raised the number of Cuban refugees expected in FY-1980 to 10,500 and in FY-1981 to 12,000. Dominguez, "Cooperating with the Enemy?" p. 62.

4. *NYT*, Feb. 19, I, 34:1.

5. Ibid., June 3, I, 32:1.

6. *Miami Herald*, June 3, 1984, 1:1, cites a spokesman for the Cuban Interests Section in Washington as saying Jackson had solicited the invitation, which Castro quickly provided.

7. Ibid., June 15, 1984, 1:1.

8. Ibid., June 23, 1984, 1:1. *NYT*, June 25, 1984, II, 8:2.

9. *NYT*, June 24, I, 1:2.

10. *Miami Herald*, June 24, 1984, 1:2.

11. Ibid., June 25, 1984, 1:4.

12. *NYT*, June 27, 1984, I, 1:1.

13. Ibid., June 28, 1984, I, 4:3.

14. Ibid., June 28, 1984, I, 1:4.

15. Ibid., June 29, 1984, I, 1:1.

16. *El Miami Herald*, June 30, 1984, 1:1.

17. *NYT*, June 29, 1984, I, 1:1.

18. Professor Dominguez refers to this as "Jackson's election year intervention." Dominguez, "Cooperating with the Enemy?" p. 64. Arguing (p. 85) that "Ideological Phobias" paralyzed Reagan administration policy on the Cuban migration issue between 1981 and 1983, he leaves the impression that Jackson pushed the administration into negotiations in 1984, whereas Jackson was the catalyst the Department of State used to induce Cuba to expedite the talks. Another catalyst in moving Cuba was probably the shock of Grenada which made it inadvisable just to say no to proposals for negotiations.

19. *Washington Post*, July 15, 1984, I, 9:1.

20. Kenneth N. Skoug, Jr., *Cuba as a Model and a Challenge* (Washington, DC: U.S. Department of State, Bureau of Public Affairs, Current Policy No. 600, August 1984).

21. *Miami Herald*, July 16, 1984, 1:5. The headline of the story said the United States "gives ground." Antonio Navarro had written a book, *Tocayo*, on his own experiences in the anti-Castro underground in the first months after Castro's seizure of power. He would head Radio Marti after 1989.

22. Published with the original English title, *Cuba as a Model and a Challenge*, and in Spanish as *Cuba como modelo y desafío*, (Washington, DC: The Cuban-American National Foundation, 1984). Calzon told me CANF intended to distribute 10,000 copies.

23. *El Miami Herald*, August 12, 1984, 9:1.

24. *NYT*, May 20, 1983, I, 15:2. The third co-founder of CANF was Florida Realtor Carlos Salman.

25. It was unique in that it was the only time in my six years as Coordinator for Cuban Affairs that Sánchez-Parodi ever invited me to share a meal in Washington.

26. The Hart-Celler Act, in effect since 1969, had set a maximum of twenty thousand as the limit on persons who could immigrate in one year from any one country. A 1976 amendment applied this restriction to Latin America as well. Edward H. Dixon and Mark A. Galan, *The Immigration and Naturalization Service* (New York: Chelsea House, 1990), pp. 63–64.

27. Kenneth N. Skoug, Jr., *The United States and Cuba* (Washington, DC: U.S. Department of State, Bureau of Public Affairs, Current Policy No. 646, 1984.)

5

1985 (I)—From The Mariel Agreement to Radio Marti

A bizarre skyjacking on the final day of 1984 started the new year with a portentous ill omen. Ishmael LaBeet, a convicted multiple murderer being transported from the Virgin Islands to New York, drew a gun on three accompanying sky marshals and diverted the aircraft to Cuba.[1] Following the Mariel Agreement, it seemed possible that this felon was one hijacker Cuba might return, but it did not.[2] LaBeet, a black, may have claimed to be a victim of U.S. racial injustice to bolster his appeal to Fidel Castro.[3]

The new year revealed that the United States and Cuba were proceeding from radically different assumptions about the new agreement. Washington, viewing the accord as discrete, focused on its implementation. Justice prepared to return the Mariel criminals. State located and assigned temporary personnel to expand the cadre in the U.S. Interests Section in Havana and began a major communications upgrade to permit, *inter alia*, faster processing of large numbers of preference immigrants and former political prisoners.

Cuba looked at the big picture. As Tomás Regalado had forecast, Fidel Castro believed what he wished about the Migration Agreement. Appealing directly to American public opinion, he exploited the settlement to hint at the utility of new talks. In the back of his mind was the intent to head off Radio Marti.

Castro met foreign press, congressmen, Cuban and American religious leaders and diplomats—projecting an image of readiness to discuss Cuba's relations with the United States, especially bilateral issues. In all his pronouncements and dialogues he made clear, however, that improvement in U.S.–Cuban relations would not affect Havana's close relations with the USSR or its support of revolutionaries in Central America. But that was central to the dispute.

In Washington, pressure mounted to start Radio Marti. Interagency meetings discussed progress, or lack of it, on sanctions the United States could use if Castro disrupted U.S. radio broadcasting when Marti began. Despite instruction from higher authority, the Department of Defense neither developed nor revealed its technical capabilities. State felt this issue should be resolved before startup. The President concurred. Despite the anxiety of the U.S. Information Agency and its Voice of America to start broadcasting—and the fact that the 1984 election was two months in the past—President Reagan on January 18 decided that Radio Marti should not begin until technical (non-lethal) contingency countermeasures were in place. The Voice of America, responsible to Congress for the funding of a still silent voice to Cuba, pressed for a May 1 start. This seemed reasonable, if the contingency countermeasures were ready.

There were two dangers in this situation. The Cubans believed the delay in the start of Radio Marti was evidence of the correctness of their assumptions, despite what they were being told by the Department of State. They thought their strategy could keep the station off the air. On the other hand, Castro's appeal for a dialogue could be mistaken as a sign that Cuba would pay dearly to have one. Just as General Haig had once read the Cubans as "anxious," others might now arrive at a similar conclusion.

State hoped to make one more diplomatic effort to convince Cuba that Radio Marti was not as dangerous as Havana thought. This would be undertaken once there was a firm startup date for the radio. State thought it had time.

IMPLEMENTING THE NEW ACCORD

In Washington, an internal dispute over interpretation of the new accord arose in January. Cuba had agreed to take back 2,746 persons from the Mariel Boatlift whom the United States had determined to be excludable. Yet there were many more Mariel Cubans in U.S. jails, and the number was increasing. In late February, Senator Alfonse D'Amato of New York asserted there were nearly two thousand Cuban nationals in state prisons whose names were not on the list given to Cuba.[4] Governor Graham of Florida raised the same question.

The U.S. negotiators had given Cuba a list of all persons for whom Justice had given final orders of exclusion at the time of the agreement, but there were many more potential Excludables. Cuba had agreed to take back a maximum of one hundred persons per month; thus the United States would be occupied for at least twenty-seven months in returning the persons to whose repatriation Cuba had specifically agreed. Unless there were to be "substitutions," persons not on the list would not be returnable to Cuba until at least the twenty-eighth month.

The Immigration and Naturalization Service argued that Cuba had agreed to accept *any* Cuban the United States identified as excludable. This was an objective Commissioner Nelson felt should be in the agreement. But Cuba did not agree to it during the negotiations. It would accept persons only on a case-by-case basis. The fact that the Cubans accepted *every* name the United States presented made agreement possible but did not eliminate the difference of principle.

When INS made its position public in a letter to Governor Graham, Cuban Vice Foreign Minister Alarcón at once responded that Cuba would take back only those persons whom it had specifically agreed to accept. If the United States had any new names to offer, Alarcón indicated, it would have to be discussed. Alarcón was right, but the Cubans had been put on notice by Kozak about U.S. law, particularly section 243 (g) of the Immigration and Nationality Act. If the United States were to ask Cuba to take names of new Mariel Excludables, and if Cuba were to refuse to accept them, the United States could again apply the legal sanctions which were in effect before the agreement was signed.

The issue of new names was theoretical in 1985. The immediate problem for Justice was to begin returning the 2,746 persons Cuba had agreed to accept. A major step forward came when the federal appeals court in Atlanta stayed a decision by Judge Marvin Shoob of the federal district court there and ruled that Justice could repatriate hundreds of Cubans held in Atlanta Penitentiary.[5] On February 1, Justice William H. Rehnquist of the U.S. Supreme Court ruled that the United States could begin returning the Mariel Excludables to Cuba.[6] The first thirty-three Cubans were repatriated on February 21.[7]

Cuba, too, had a false interpretation of the new agreement. On January 15, an NBC correspondent advised that the Cuban Interests Section was arguing that the United States had violated the month-old agreement by not sending back a pair of shipwrecked Cubans from Tampa. The Cubans did not wish to go home.[8] Nothing in the Mariel Agreement obliged the United States to return a Cuban to Cuba. The U.S. government would not agree to

Havana's wish that persons who left Cuba illegally should be returned there by the United States.

THE "PEACE OFFENSIVE"

Fidel Castro launched his campaign in a series of meetings with visiting American and other public figures, including conspicuous interviews with the press and a meeting with American Roman Catholic bishops. The Cuban leader first spent some thirty-seven hours in January with Congressmen Bill Alexander of Arkansas and Jim Leach of Iowa, who traveled with a large delegation of American businessmen billed as "advisers" to Alexander. Upon their return, Alexander and Leach asserted that the United States should negotiate with Cuba to improve bilateral relations.[9]

Castro later told *Washington Post* reporters that the climate of the Alexander visit was "really good" and asserted that it reflected a "certain frame of mind in some sectors." Castro claimed that the U.S. administration "did not view the trip negatively."[10] It is possible that he drew this favorable, but misleading, conclusion from something the congressmen told him. In fact, I had informed Alexander in advance of the visit, under instructions from Assistant Secretary of State Tony Motley, that the Department of State did *not* look with favor upon his business-oriented delegation.[11] Alexander was a strong opponent of the embargo who had visited Cuba in August 1984. His delegation of prominent businessmen bordered on deliberate violation of U.S. law.

If the congressmen or their group had received encouragement from the executive branch, those who gave it kept it a secret from the Department of State. According to a press account, Alexander, after returning from Cuba on January 17, called Secretary of Defense Weinberger to say Castro wished to normalize relations with the United States. Alexander said Weinberger promised to take this up with the president and with George Shultz.[12] Alexander's own slant may have strengthened Castro's basic misconception.

With hypersensitive Cuban–American antennas raised as a result of the Migration Agreement, the Reagan administration was on its guard against "euphoria." White House press spokesman Larry Speakes stated shortly thereafter that lines of communication between the two governments were open, but he noted fundamental disagreements over Cuban subversive activities in Central America, large Cuban troop deployments in Africa, Cuba's close allegiance to the USSR and the violation of human rights in Cuba.[13] President Reagan's own response was, "We've heard this before. Early in my administration there were signals sent of this kind, and we took them up on it. And we have tried to have some meetings with them, and nothing came of it. Their words are never backed by deeds."[14]

It was not, however, a matter of contradictory words and deeds. Castro's words, when analyzed, in no way suggested he would modify any policy, much less alter his principles. Although willing to discuss bilateral technical matters, Castro foretold nothing new in the major conflicts that gave U.S.–Cuban relations their adversarial character.

On January 28, Castro gave an interview to three *Washington Post* editors which set forth many themes on which he would dwell until mid-May. Although there were no bilateral problems between the United States and Cuba as important as migration, he said, others such as Coast Guard matters (safety of life at sea), anti-hijacking cooperation, radio interference, and fishing allocations could be discussed. Castro also acknowledged that the Reagan administration had not encouraged illegal departures from Cuba and had taken measures against terrorist elements in the United States (Cuban–American extremists who had attacked Cuban diplomats in 1980).[15]

Castro explained that he could not say Cuba would discuss Central America with the United States. Describing Latin America, perhaps hopefully, as a "powder keg," he was coy about Cuban assistance to the Salvadoran FMLN, but confirmed that Cuba had taken steps to toughen the mix of its forces in Nicaragua by selecting personnel "who had the physical conditions to resist any invasion there . . . to take on the kind of struggle that might be waged there."

Castro acknowledged that the fugitive American financier Robert Vesco had been in Cuba, where he had received "medical assistance" for "humanitarian reasons." Claiming not to have had dealings with Vesco, himself, Castro said he knew his "people" had talked with Vesco because "he has information and knowledge about many things in this world." At the time, the U.S. Marshals Service was trying to arrange repatriation of Vesco, whose children were identified as attending a school for foreigners in Havana. The celebrated swindler had been living in Cuba, at least intermittently, for at least three years.[16] The marshals believed that the Cubans had soured on Vesco because he had cost the Cuban trading corporation CIMEX a great deal of money through bad or corrupt business practices. Despite Castro's disclaimer, the admission that Vesco was free to use Cuba in his activities was a blot on Cuba's notebook. The Cubans never turned Vesco over to the U.S. Marshals, who speculated he might know too much about drug trafficking.

In January, Castro also welcomed visiting American Catholic bishops. The meeting fit well with his public relations campaign and was consistent with a carefully crafted "opening" toward the Cuban Catholic church. Having taken note in Nicaragua of the role played there by several Catholic clergymen who were also prominent Sandinistas, Castro offered a guarded opening to the church in Cuba.[17] He was studying whether some relaxation of control over religious life in Cuba could be turned to his advantage, increasing his regional appeal without weakening his authority. He even toyed with the idea of a papal visit, although this would have to be structured so that Pope John Paul II did not become a focal point for resistance to the regime or combine the visit with a stop in south Florida.[18]

The U.S. bishops, perhaps inspired by Jesse Jackson's example, brought a list of 146 long-term political prisoners whose release they sought. Castro accepted the list, saying that those with a "real health problem" would be studied, but he heaped contempt on them. Release of the "counter-revolutionary prisoners" to the United States "would only swell the ranks of those who are working against Cuba, carrying out acts of sabotage or other crimes against our country." He could not release "individuals who would later become new instruments for the United States to use against Cuba."[19]

After the bishops departed, just as he had substituted names on the list brought by Jesse Jackson in 1984, Castro created a "counteroffer" of seventy-five prisoners, including only thirty-one from the bishops' list and adding many former Batista personnel whom he had long wished to expel. It was this "counterlist" of persons which INS later interviewed in Cuban prisons in 1986.

Castro probably had Armando Valladares in mind as a "counter-revolutionary" whose release had come back to haunt him. Even though most lacked the literary skill and impressive presence of Valladares, almost all of the released prisoners were like him in outlook. Castro reserved for these men his special hatred, matching their determination with his own. Although he continued to play the prisoner release game with advantage, it might have been in Castro's interest to release them all in early 1985. Among other things, it would have lent substance to his "peace offensive."

A VISIT TO CUBA

On January 28 I visited Cuba, in part to discuss implementation of the Migration Agreement. The Cuban Interests Section told NBC it was a "high level" visit, a benign exaggeration intended to support Havana's public relations blitz.

The Migration Agreement, at Cuban initiative, contained provision for review sessions on implementation. On January 29, Vice Minister Alarcón suggested that the first such session be scheduled two months after all three main elements of the agreement (Excludables, immigration, and former political prisoners) had been put into effect. That way there would be some experience with each element to review. This was reasonable. Unfortunately, since the return of political prisoners began only on May 20, the timing of the review session was set back. It would become an aborted opportunity.

On January 30, the sensitive issue of Radio Marti came up during a lunch for Alarcón, Arbesu, and Joaquín Mas hosted by the principal officer of the U.S. Interests Section, John Ferch, at his magnificent official residence. Conversation was largely social until Ferch's deputy, Jim Todd, asked aloud what would happen when Radio Marti came on the air. This introduced a long moment of guarded silence as each side awaited the other's comment.

The Cubans seemed under instruction to keep their lips buttoned on this matter. I felt something needed to be said and recalled that the new station was U.S. law and would soon be broadcasting to Cuba as a service of VOA. Noting that the radio was committed by the enacting legislation to conform to worldwide VOA standards for accuracy and objectivity and that VOA had been broadcasting to Cuba for many years without incident, I urged that this long foreseen event not be exaggerated by Cuba. In response, Alarcón said only, "But for 14 hours a day?" None of the three Cuban officials made other comment or offered any hint as to what Cuba might do when this happened. Probably they did not yet know. They were unwilling to discuss the matter, even in the relative informality of that room. However, any self-deluding Cuban hopes that the United States would not put Radio Marti on the air were nourished from other fountains than statements from the executive branch of the U.S. government.

At lunch with Ferch and me on January 31, José Luis Padrón, for several years a special conduit to Castro for the U.S. Interests Section, presented the Cuban case for a dialogue. Padrón was well connected. He headed the Cuban delegation at the 1980-81 migration talks and was an interlocutor for Ferch at the time of Grenada. They had discussed Angolan issues, without evident result. Padrón handled a number of Cuban business dealings, including management of some of the trading entities used by Cuba to circumvent the embargo. The care and nourishment of Robert Vesco may have been one of his many assignments.

At the lunch, Padrón was insistent that the importance of Castro's pronouncements on international affairs not be missed by the United States, but he did not go beyond the careful generality of his chief. Ferch and I listened with attention, but when Ferch referred to Castro's ideas as a "peace offensive," the normally suave Padrón became highly agitated. I inquired what was to be achieved in light of Cuba's continuing deep differences with the United States, which Castro had not addressed. Padrón, who seemed to feel under pressure, appeared anxious to elicit a more favorable reaction. Only when assured that we were not rejecting anything but wanted to hear more substance, did he seem to relax. He promised to be back in touch.

The subject of Radio Marti, conspicuously, did not arise at this lunch. This seemed to confirm that the Cubans had instructions not to raise the subject and to keep the United States guessing. From the U.S. standpoint, there was nothing to add to what had just been said to Alarcón.

Padrón implied that he intended to speak to Fidel Castro and then supply more information. But events took another course. Later, Padrón was reported to be in serious trouble with his own superiors for business transactions, possibly involving Vesco, that had gone awry. This may have contributed to his agitation when his presentation of Castro's new approach elicited less enthusiasm than he had hoped. Although he remained influential inside Cuba, Padrón did not figure again as an intermediary for Fidel Castro in the Reagan administration.

On February 4, while I was traveling with Jim Todd and his wife, Evelyn, in eastern Cuba, Ramón Sánchez-Parodi, head of the Cuban Interests Section in Washington, unexpectedly greeted us at the gate of the Moncada Barracks in Santiago, where Fidel Castro had staged his famous July 26, 1953 attack on the Cuban Army. I knew Fidel Castro had just flown to Santiago on party business. Sánchez-Parodi's presence at Moncada was a sure sign that Castro wished to see me.

After much sightseeing, during which he seemed to be waiting for me to take the initiative, Sánchez-Parodi finally made the pitch as we sat in twilight beside Santiago's old Moro Castle overlooking the Caribbean: the Cuban leader would like to talk with me that night if I were interested. Of course I was, but I asked Sánchez-Parodi to inform President Castro in advance that I had no instructions from my government for such a meeting and was in no position to get them (it was by that time around 9:00 P.M.). That was agreeable to Castro so I informed Ferch in Havana by telephone. It would be the Cuban leader's first meeting with an official from Washington since Vernon Walters in 1982.

A WEE HOURS DIALOGUE WITH PRESIDENT CASTRO

At 12:30 A.M. on February 5, Sánchez-Parodi's automobile appeared at our motel and conducted Jim Todd and me through the darkened streets of Santiago to a well-guarded installation on the edge of town. Once inside Sánchez-Parodi, Todd and I were shown to a vigorously air-conditioned room (we were wearing the light *guayabera* shirt that suited Santiago's sultry weather) to await the meeting.

At about 1:00 A.M. President Castro entered, accompanied by his aide José ("Chomi") Miyar. Castro was wearing a neat and well-pressed olive green military uniform, looking younger and more physically fit than I expected. Although his beard was gray, his skin color was fair. He coughed three or four times during our conversation of over three hours—in which he did at least ninety percent of the talking—but gave no other sign of any health problem that may have obliged him to quit smoking his famous cigars. During our meeting he took no alcoholic beverage nor did he offer one. When he wished to make a point in the conversation, Castro would jab at me for emphasis with his index finger, but he was careful to keep it two or three inches from touching me.

Two years later Cuban propaganda would seek to portray the atmosphere in this meeting as confrontational, but in fact it was polite and conciliatory. Castro apologized courteously for keeping me waiting. (In reality he had been punctual.) He asked if I were comfortable with his speaking Spanish, there being no interpreter present. I found his diction clear and crisp. He asked if I were enjoying my visit, the details of which he seemed to have encyclopedic knowledge. He said he had been told that I was anti-Communist, but he enjoyed having discussions with persons of different points of view. (At that I reflected silently that Cuban citizens with different points of view than his could easily get into deep trouble for expressing them, especially if they persisted.)

I was surprised to hear the head of the Cuban state and government and of its Communist Party and armed forces name all the senior Cuban officials who would be having lunch with me two days later in Havana. Noting that the restaurant where we would be eating was a new one, he asked Miyar if he were sure it was of adequate quality. Miyar responded that they had "checked it out."

Castro inquired about the coming departure of Ferch, who had been named ambassador to Honduras, and courteously offered to receive Ferch—who had never met with him—for a farewell visit. I told him that Curtis Kamman was coming from Moscow, where he had been deputy chief of mission, to replace Ferch. "Ooh," said Castro, who may not have been surprised by this information, "is that a promotion for him or for us?"

Castro then turned to the Mariel Agreement, complaining pointedly but politely that we had not returned the persons who had been shipwrecked off Tampa. I stressed that our new agreement on migration did not mean that we would turn away those Cubans who arrived under their own power in the United States and wished to stay. After some further debate, Castro remarked with good humor, "Well at least we won't have to send each other more diplomatic notes about this matter." He had clearly been personally engaged in the matter.

He contended that no misfortune came to persons who had been returned to Cuba by the United States. I saw this as an opportunity to raise the case of Andrés Rodríguez Hernández, a young Cuban who had reached Florida as a stowaway in January 1982 and had been returned involuntarily to Cuba by INS.[20] This event, which antedated by several months my arrival in Cuban affairs, had ignited an explosion of resentment in Miami. After his forced repatriation, diplomatic efforts were made to ensure that Rodríguez Hernández would not be imprisoned for illegal departure from Cuba, compounded by having embarrassed the Cuban government (not to mention the U.S. government). He was at first reported to be "safely back with his family in Havana."[21] However, Tomás Regalado of the *Miami Herald* had informed me of reports that Rodríguez Hernández was nevertheless in jail.

With this background in mind, I told Castro I was aware of a case where a person we had returned in error was currently in prison. He reacted in surprise, but, obviously well aware of the case, quickly said, "Well, he didn't have impunity." Castro quietly directed Chomi Miyar to look into it.

To anticipate the outcome of this case, on February 7, just prior to my departure from Cuba, Sánchez-Parodi called to say the stowaway had been jailed six months after his return for "some crime" (i.e., in about July 1982) and had been sentenced to four years in prison. Such a sentence would have been twice the usual term for leaving Cuba illegally, no doubt because of the embarrassment he had caused the Cuban government. So much for Cuba's concern with the previous diplomatic representations in Havana on the stowaway's behalf. Sánchez-Parodi added that Rodríguez Hernández had been released from prison that same day—after having served eighteen months of his sentence. Some time later in Washington, Sánchez-Parodi advised that Rodríguez Hernández could be processed for travel to the United States. The story has a happy ending because he did subsequently come, without fanfare, to Miami. This was a small but satisfying victory for "quiet diplomacy."

Castro inquired if I would like to discuss multilateral issues. I responded that I had no instructions on that point. In fact, I was well aware of his views and did not believe any meeting of minds on these issues was possible. I would merely have been subjected to an harangue, and I was feeling the fatigue of a very long day. Castro's conversational style was to engage in a monologue, which I could interrupt only when he paused for breath or to interject a question. It was by now nearly 3:00 A.M., but Castro seemed to be in his element, an aspect of his personality which the *Washington Post* editors had also observed. Castro had no objection to foregoing discussion about multilateral issues, noting that his views had been communicated to the *Post* editors and to the Catholic bishops who had visited Cuba in January.

I said I did wish to raise one matter with him, prefacing my remarks with a reference to the informal discussion Kozak and I had conducted with Alarcón and Arbesu in the Roosevelt Hotel as we concluded the Mariel Agreement. After reiterating humanitarian concern for the plight of long-term political prisoners in Cuba, I said that the release of the *Plantados* would be in everyone's interest. I stressed, as I had in New York, that we could put their names at the top of the list of refugees and take them immediately out of Cuba.

Upon my use of the term *Plantados*, which is what the unbroken political prisoners called themselves, Castro changed expression. He obviously was not accustomed to hearing that word uttered in his presence but knew very well to whom I was referring. He appeared to be as disturbed by mention of this subject as had been Arbesu in the Hotel Roosevelt. Without abandoning his polite tone, however, Castro observed it was well I had made my remarks in the context of the Migration Agreement, since otherwise the subject would have been unacceptable. These individuals were a domestic matter of concern only to Cuba. He fulminated at length about their nefarious activities and just punishment. They could be released from prison when they completed their terms or possibly for reasons of health. I noted that according to evidence I regarded as authentic, some of these persons had already completed their terms and yet were still in prison. Castro said Miyar could look into this.

As he vented his scorn on these helpless individuals who had been brutalized so long in Cuban prisons, some of whom were suffering at that moment in Boniato Prison, not far from Santiago, there came to my mind Shakespeare's adage that the abuse of greatness is when it disjoins remorse from power. Despite Castro's agitated response, I hoped I had laid down a marker in a good cause. I felt that unrelenting pressure was necessary to persuade him that continued suffering of these victims would have a growing political cost.

Perhaps because he was stung by the reference to the *Plantados*, Castro then turned to the two interests sections, favorably contrasting the one in Washington with ours in Havana. Whereas their interests section was scrupulous in obeying U.S. law, Castro argued, ours engaged in reprehensible behavior, which he did not describe and of which he cited no examples. He said the day might come when its transgressions would be made public. Since I was unprepared for this charge and was hearing it for the first time, I asked Todd to respond. Todd, as puzzled as I, said he was aware of no improper behavior.

Despite the hour (well past 3:00 A.M.) Castro appeared livelier than ever, as a man who either needs very little sleep or had caught a cat nap. He continued vigorously discussing his life, dwelling on various purported attempts to assassinate him, directing his comments to no one in particular, and seeming to anticipate no response. I listened with a sense for the ironic as he in part ascribed the 1980 mob attack outside the U.S. Interests Section to inappropriate behavior by the then principal officer, Wayne Smith, who since his retirement in 1982 had become a relentless critic of U.S. policy toward Cuba.

As this wee hours monologue continued unabated, I realized that the man still possessed enormous and self-generating rhetorical capacity and needed neither notes nor a response to go on talking incessantly. If his forensic powers had been greater in the past, they must have rivaled those of Demosthenes. Just as I was beginning to wonder if the dawn would overtake us there, Castro concluded his remarks around 4:30 A.M., shook hands courteously, and departed briskly with Miyar, leaving Sánchez-Parodi to escort Todd and me back to our hotel.

Castro never referred to Radio Marti during this extended conversation. Since I was sure that my comments to Alarcón and Arbesu had been reported to him, I did not repeat them. In retrospect, I felt strongly that I erred in not doing so for additional emphasis. At that time, however, we had no anticipated startup date for the radio, and there was nothing specific I could add to what had been said to Alarcón. In early February Castro was still hoping Radio Marti would go away. The action he would take in May might not yet have occurred to him.

In Havana on the morning of February 6, after cabling Castro's remarks to the Department of State, I told Ferch about the puzzling passage on misdeeds of the U.S. Interests Section. Ferch was equally baffled. Also, on February 6, a conversation with José Arbesu and Alfredo García Almeida of the America

Department of the Cuban Communist Party to discuss Central America was unexpectedly expanded to include a personage rarely seen by foreign diplomats—Manuel Piñeiro Losada, known as "Barba Roja" (Red Beard), head of the department and a prime mover of Cuban policy in the Western Hemisphere.[22] In our conversation, "Red Beard" (it was gray by then) left no doubt that Cuba would oppose the United States and work for revolution throughout Latin America as it saw fit. He said bluntly that Cuba had as much right to support revolutionary forces in El Salvador and Guatemala as the United States did to uphold the respective governments. But he did not reject totally the case I tried to make for the region's future as a hemisphere of democracy. After ninety minutes of polite intellectual combat, he escorted me courteously to the door of the party central committee building. "Red Beard" had underscored the message of Carlos Rafael Rodríguez after Grenada—Cuba's "internationalism" would go on.

My report to Secretary Shultz upon returning to Washington concluded that while Castro's public relations campaign was based on Cuba's economic and security requirements and revealed no intention to alter Havana's basic approach to foreign policy, the U.S. government should continue to listen carefully to what he was saying, keep lines of communication open, and examine whether progress were possible. Harry Shlaudemann and Tony Motley told me that Shultz liked the memorandum. On February 19, I was asked to do a one-page summary for Bud McFarlane of the National Security Council.

THE PEACE OFFENSIVE CONTINUES

On February 11 and 12, WETA-TV carried Robert MacNeil's interview of Fidel Castro.[23] MacNeil quoted twice from my Carnegie Endowment speech, in which I had expressed doubt that Cuba would change the thrust of its foreign policy. In response Castro reasserted his principles, including the Soviet alliance and world revolution. He praised the "very close relations" with the Soviet Union and asserted that he would not change a single one of his principles "for a thousand relations with a thousand countries like the United States." Castro indicated that whatever the United States might do, it would remain a threat. He hypothesized that the United States might become a Marxist–Leninist country "more Communist than the USSR and China," but Cuba would not disregard its defenses.

This statement must have stung his apologists. It strengthened the impression that no American conduct, be it ever so conciliatory, would lead to relaxation of Castro's revolutionary vigilance, since the very existence of the United States posed a threat to Cuba. Nothing could be done to change that.

Castro conjured up an early revolutionary situation in Chile. (It was perhaps in trying to make this a self-fulfilling prophecy that a large Cuban arms shipment was later was found by Chilean authorities.) This was no more surprising than Piñeiro Losada's statement to me. Cuba's 1976 Constitution, Article 12 (c), provided that Cuba "considers that its help to those under attack and to the peoples that struggle for their liberation constitutes its internationalist right and duty."[24] Those who read this as rhetoric misunderstood the Cuban reality.

Castro freely acknowledged to MacNeil that Cuba had political prisoners. "Yes, we have them. We have a few hundred political prisoners. Is that a violation of human rights?" He went on to say that the two hundred or so such prisoners were "potentially dangerous." If released, they would prepare attacks.

Fidel Castro's expansive interviews continued. In a February 13 discussion with the Spanish news agency EFE, he described the Sandinista strategy in Nicaragua as "perfect" because it would implement "socialism" gradually. He did not want Nicaragua to make some egregious miscalculation that would open the door to U.S. armed intervention. Castro also encouraged Tad Szulc to write what he undoubtedly hoped would be a relatively friendly biography.[25]

Having passed up a visit to Moscow for the funeral of Konstantin Chernenko in March, Castro denied in an interview with Dan Rather of CBS that this was a signal to the United States. Soviet–Cuban relations were better than ever, he said. While declaring that Cuba was the "most independent country in the world" because it did not depend, "not even the slightest," on the United States, Castro nonetheless expressed a belief that bilateral relations could be improved. Castro denied that drugs were transiting Cuba to the United States and said Cuba had proved it wanted to stop airline hijackings.[26]

The April 14 visit by new Ecuadorian President León Febres Cordero showed that Cuba was escaping hemispheric isolation.[27] Reestablishment of diplomatic relations with other South American countries would follow, strengthening Havana's prestige in the region even as its growing economic problems were making it less attractive as a trading partner to Western Europe and an increasing burden for the Soviet Union and Eastern Europe.

The Cubans probed to see if the Migration Agreement would lead to benefits in other aspects of their relationship with the United States. Generally the answer was no. Partly at Cuban urging and partly for commercial reasons, International Telephone and Telegraph sought authorization to upgrade significantly existing telephone and telegraph communications with the island. With hundreds of thousands of Cuban exiles in Florida alone, an upgrade would have permitted a quantum leap in the number of calls placed, but this would have been a financial windfall for Cuba. The Department of State authorized a modest upgrade, balancing humanitarian against foreign policy considerations.

The Office of Technology Assessment undertook to arrange a visit to U.S. facilities by a group of Cuban doctors. The Department of State objected to the visit in light of Cuba's continuing assertions that the United States had spread dengue fever in Cuba.

Cuba offered to send a twelve-member delegation to a meeting of the Latin American Studies Association (LASA) in Albuquerque, New Mexico. LASA was supportive of this offer, but the FBI objected to some delegation members. The Department of State was prepared to grant visas to the rest, but Cuba took an all-or-nothing stand. No Cuban went to Albuquerque.

A potentially high visibility gain for Cuba was involved in a May 14 request from the Commissioner of Baseball for State's assent to a baseball game between the New York Yankees and a Cuban team. Nothing would have been likelier than such a game to convey the impression that we were now chummy with Havana. It would have been hard to contain Cuba Fever if the Cuban nine met the Bronx Bombers on the diamond. The United States, the Department decided, could scarcely have persuaded anyone that it took Cuban transgressions seriously if this game had been played.

The Cuban peace offensive even inspired Treasury's Office of Foreign Assets Control to suggest a more relaxed enforcement of embargo controls on Cuban-directed corporations in third countries such as Panama. Commerce also found the moment propitious to urge relaxation. State took the position that the embargo was addressed to Cuban conduct in international affairs, arguing that it was irrational to relax the rules just because Fidel Castro was exposing himself to the U.S. communications media.

State authorized the U.S. representative in Havana to maintain his conversations with Padrón, however, and to call on President Castro prior to his departure from Cuba. Although circumspect in responding to Castro's public relations campaign in early 1985, the administration wished to keep the lines of communication to Cuba functioning.

Radio Marti was still silent. The range of contingency countermeasures against disruptive Cuban broadcasting was no better. A State communications specialist appealing to Fred Ikle in Defense to develop a credible response other than use of force was told, "Don't rule out missiles." Suzanne

Garment, who had just visited Cuba, asserted in the *Wall Street Journal* that Radio Marti was still silent "because Congress will not face Mr. Castro down when he threatens to jam U.S. radio stations in retaliation and will not spend the extra money to get around the problem of technical means."[28] Mrs. Garment was correct that the "problem of technical means" was not yet resolved. It never would be.

A "SATURDAY SEMINAR" WITH SECRETARY SHULTZ

April 27 brought a rare opportunity to brief George Shultz on Cuba. The occasion was one of the "Saturday Seminars," which he later described as a trademark of his time as Secretary of State.[29] He used these sessions to brief himself on important issues on which he might have to make key judgments. At this session, Shultz stated, more as confession than complaint, that he was "not up to speed" on Cuba. This was a surprise since we had been providing him memoranda on Castro's public relations campaign and other developments. In addition to a ten-page memorandum upon my return from Cuba in February, I had sent him a shorter document on a Cuban "non-paper" received March 22.

Responding to a personal initiative undertaken by John Ferch in Havana, the Cuban "non-paper" expressed willingness to discuss an "agenda" of subjects to be worked out between the U.S. Interests Section in Havana and the Cuban Foreign Ministry. The "agenda" had been Ferch's own notion, which the Cubans accepted. My memorandum suggested that instead of an "agenda," we should propose talks on radio interference. I specifically excluded negotiation on Radio Marti, feeling that the administration would not accept this. Under Secretary for Political Affairs Mike Armacost, who was anxious to discuss Cuba in a speech scheduled for Baltimore, amended my draft to leave room for high level talks in the second half of 1985 and for discussion of Radio Marti. However, the Armacost Cuba speech was never made, and we would never propose to Cuba a discussion of Radio Marti.

Shultz had returned my memo, as modified by Armacost, marked "O.B.E." ("overtaken by events"), leaving the inference that we had responded to the Cuban non-paper in some undisclosed manner. No one in ARA, however, knew what the Secretary meant by this comment.

After reading the article by Suzanne Garment in the *Wall Street Journal* recommending a more nuanced policy toward Cuba (the same one in which she mentioned Congress withholding funds for Radio Marti countermeasures), Shultz on April 22 had requested our comment. Since we did not know what his "O.B.E." meant on the earlier memo, however, we had been hard pressed to respond.

On April 27, the Secretary said we ought to be doing more than we were with Cuba. He immediately explained, however, that he was not in favor of engaging Havana on a broad agenda since that would allow third parties to draw incorrect conclusions. This was actually not too different from the line Fidel Castro was taking—that we could negotiate about specific bilateral problems even though there was no agreement between us on ideological questions.

As an aside, Shultz remarked that President Reagan and NSC Director Bud McFarlane hoped it might be possible to "turn Cuba around." He explained that he did not share this view. However, he fully endorsed probing Castro's "peace offensive" to see if it contained exploitable elements. His expectations seemed to me sober and realistic. In particular, Secretary Shultz endorsed Mike Armacost's recommendation that John Ferch be instructed to mention substantive issues during his farewell call on Fidel Castro.

Bud McFarlane of the NSC had been little involved with Cuban bilateral issues. One of his senior staffers had mentioned that McFarlane thought Castro badly needed a dialogue with the United States and would presumably pay well to have one. Conceivably, he and/or his aides may have concluded from Castro's public statements that we had "leverage" because the Cuban leader seemed so eager to talk to the United States.

The thrust of the Reagan foreign policy had been to limit Cuba's options and demonstrate that it was no model for emulation. This was prudent but no way to "turn around" Cuba. Since there was no turning Cuba around without also turning Fidel Castro, whose celebrated "principles" were immutable, this was a romantic notion but not an attainable objective.

Ironically, Castro's own public relations campaign may have strengthened unrealistic hopes. Apparently he believed he could head off Radio Marti by suggesting trade and talks on bilateral issues. He was looking for benefits for Cuba at little or no cost to him. He was not at all about to be "turned around."

As a result of the meeting with Secretary Shultz, a blind memorandum was sent to Havana for John Ferch to hand Padrón. A May 8 message to Havana proposed that the first review session of the Mariel Agreement be held in June. That would be a chance for diplomacy, including an attempt by Kozak and me to encourage Havana not to overreact to Radio Marti. The Cubans accepted.

In late April and early May 1985, both parties were still on an upbeat tack. The United States proceeded with plans to increase its staff and to upgrade its technical facilities in Havana. The Cubans were planning to do the same on 16th street in Washington where they still owned property.

April brought reports that approximatley 150 Cubans serving time in New Jersey prisons and facing deportation hearings had to be segregated from other prisoners because that some were planning to kill their guards.[30] Even in detention the Mariel Excludables were a danger to American society. A number of U.S. prisons and detention centers could attest to that in the five years since the boatlift. At least now there was a lawful and orderly means by which they could be returned to Cuba.

At the Saturday Seminar, no one had asked Secretary Shultz what he meant by writing "O.B.E." on the memorandum on Cuba's non-paper. Unforeseeably, the "honeymoon" with Cuba, such as it had been, was drawing to a premature close. Curiously, it would soon all be "O.B.E."

But it would be overtaken by events that had yet to occur.

NOTES

1. *NYT*, Jan. 1, 1985, I, 1:2. LaBeet was out of prison to pursue a civil suit in the Virgin Islands, the locus of the homicides for which he had been sentenced. His innocent guards let him use the bathroom, from which he emerged armed.

2. Cuba wanted back two 1980 hijackers whom Havana had returned but whose punishment by a U.S. court the Cubans thought barbaric. Justice was unprepared to seek release of the two convicted hijackers from detention so that they could serve out their term in Cuba.

3. In June 1985, Representative Mickey Leland of Texas, an Afro-American on good terms with Fidel Castro, informed me of a plan to visit Havana, where he would seek to correct any misunderstanding the Cuban leader might have about LaBeet. Whatever Leland said to Castro was of no avail.

4. *NYT*, Feb. 25, 1985, I, 11:1.

5. Ibid., Jan. 17, 1985, I, 1:1.

6. *Washington Post*, Feb. 2, 1985, I, 4:3.

7. Ibid., Feb. 22, 1875, I, 10:1.

8. Emotions had been aroused in Havana by misleading Florida press reports that the pair wished to return but were not being allowed to leave. Whatever they may have said, possibly to protect their families in Cuba, in fact they wished to remain in the United States.

9. Ibid., Jan. 31, 1985, I, 7:1.

10. Quoted from *Washington Post* transcript of Castro interview, published Feb. 3, 1985, 1:2 and 1:4.

11. When he had learned of Representative Alexander's travel plans, Tony Motley ordered me to "read him the riot act" for undertaking what was clearly an extravaganza completely out of keeping with U.S. policy toward Cuba. I carried out Motley's instructions on January 7 with all appropriate discretion, having long ago learned congressmen were disinclined to take unsolicited advice from the Department of State and could be controlled only by their committee chairmen or party leaders. Alexander was a very senior Democrat. I expressed to him strong skepticism about his anticipated trade bonanza and reminded him of U.S. law. However, I did not tell him whom he could take as "advisers."

12. *Washington Post* transcript.

13. *Washington Post*, Feb. 5, 1985, I, 10:5.

14. *NYT*, Feb. 12, 1985, I, 1:6.

15. *Washington Post* transcript. The articles are by Leonard Downie, Jr., and Karen De Young jointly and by Jim Hoagland, supplanted by additional articles on days following Feb. 3, 1985. Hoagland gives the flavor of the *Post's* own slant, stating that "the Cuban revolution has taken on the form of the quixotic but apparently mellowing comandante." Castro indeed had something of Don Quixote in his makeup, but there was no indication he was "mellowing."

16. The U.S. Interests Section in Havana first detected Vesco's presence by developments observed in the school itself. Frank McNeil states that Costa Rican President Luis Alberto Monge, inaugurated in May 1982, stopped Vesco from entering the country, "bouncing him back to Managua and Havana." *War and Peace in Central America*, p. 167. In 1983 Jack Wolf, an Assistant U.S. Attorney, identified Vesco as living in Cuba and as instigator of a plot to smuggle U.S. goods into Cuba. *NYT*, November 15, 1983, I, 3:4.

17. Frei Betto, *Fidel and Religion: Castro Talks on Revolution and Religion with Frei Betto*, trans. Cuban Center for Translation and Interpretation (New York: Simon and Schuster, 1987), p. 237. The interviews with the sycophantic Brazilian liberation theology priest Betto, whom Castro first met in Nicaragua, took place in February and May 1985. Also see *NYT*, Jan. 29, I, 3:1.

18. Betto, *Fidel and Religion*, pp. 219–220. Castro told Betto the bishops were "concerned about and opposed to the interventionist policy in Latin America."

19. Ibid., p. 230.

20. *NYT*, Jan. 16, 1982, I, 7:5. According to *The Times*, Rodríguez Hernández was the first Cuban refugee deported from the United States to Cuba.

21. Ibid., Jan. 22, 1982, I, 12:6.

22. Rex A. Hudson, *Castro's America Department: Coordinating Cuba's Support for Marxist-Leninist Violence in the Americas* (Washington: Cuban-American National Foundation, 1988), p. 70. Arbesu laughingly presented us with the remark, "One Columbia man, meet another." Piñeiro Losada and I both had been there in the early 1950s, I in Columbia College and he to study business administration.

23. Quotations from transcript of MacNeil interview of Castro.

24. Pamela Falk, "Cuba, 1974–78," in *Constitutions of the Countries of the World*, ed. Albert P. Blaustein and Gisbert H. Flanz (Dobbs Ferry, NY: Oceana Publications, 1979), p. 7.

25. Tad Szulc, *Fidel: A Critical Portrait* (New York: William Morrow and Company, 1986). Over lunch on February 22, 1985, Szulc told me he would be doing the "first objective biography" on the Cuban leader. Although Castro had originally welcomed Szulc to Cuba for the project, his ardor may have cooled when he learned that Szulc's daughter was on a U.S. news team "staking out" Robert Vesco in Cuba.

26. "CBS Evening News with Dan Rather," March 15 and 19, 1985.

27. *NYT*, April 15, 1985, I, 7:1.

28. *The Wall Street Journal*, April 19, 1985, 28:3.

29. Shultz, *Turmoil and Triumph*, p. 39.

30. *NYT*, April 6, I, 23:6.

6

1985 (II)—Radio Marti; Cuba Strikes Back

Two years after President Reagan signed the Radio Broadcasting to Cuba Act of 1983, Cuban-Americans were anxious to have Radio Marti commence broadcasting. Part of the delay was attributable to the need to hire a staff whose knowledge of Cuba and the Spanish language qualified them to conduct surrogate radio broadcasting. Almost all were Cuban expatriates, and the procedure for them to become U.S. government employees was lengthy.

The other reason for delay was the same concern that troubled Radio Marti in Congress in 1982 and 1983—fear of Cuban interference with U.S. domestic radio broadcasting. Cuba had demonstrated the means to do it, and CIA sources in Cuba warned that this was the likely Cuban response to Radio Marti.

Thirty months after George Shultz asked about U.S. countermeasures to deal with disruptive Cuban radio broadcasts, the option of technical electronic measures still seemed missing. Despite NSC instructions, the Department of Defense apparently had not produced them. Instead, administration hard-liners spoke of "taking out" offending Cuban transmitters.

President Reagan in January 1985 had determined that a full range of countermeasures must be ready before broadcasting commenced. State, aware that satisfactory countermeasures were absent, assumed the President's decision would prevent a premature start. State wanted first to use diplomacy to discourage a disruptive Cuban response. Having reached a beneficial agreement on migration, it planned to use the consultative mechanism built into that agreement to inform Cuba in advance when Radio Marti was to begin. The review session was scheduled for June.

Another thesis in existence, though of unclaimed parentage, held that Cuba's anxiety for talks could be utilized to forestall or halt a disruptive response by Havana. In a mid-March discussion of countermeasures, a Department of Defense official told Deputy Director John Modderno of the Office of Cuban Affairs in State that a State official and an NSC staff colleague who specialized in international communications and information had come up with a notion called "preemptive negotiations" with Cuba. This idea was said to be based on the assumption that Cuba badly needed a dialogue and with one in progress or about to start would not overreact to Radio Marti.

On March 15, Jim Michel and I, together with the State officer mentioned by the Department of Defense (DOD) as coauthor of the "preemptive negotiations" thesis, briefed Deputy Secretary Ken Dam for a Communications Policy Planning Group session that would discuss Radio Marti. Michel mentioned "preemptive negotiations" as a DOD idea, as it may have been since the State official roundly denied authorship. Dam voiced scorn for the concept.

A BELATED VOICE TOO SOON

In mid-May, a rumor reached State that Radio Marti would begin broadcasting on May 20, Cuban Independence Day. Such reports had been heard in the past, but from persons who did not know that the president insisted on having technical countermeasures in place in advance. But this time the rumors were true. A plan to start Radio Marti on May 20 had been communicated to Acting Secretary of State Dam with the proviso that he keep the information to himself. Dam insisted that Secretary Shultz, who was outside Washington, be consulted but did not otherwise divulge the news.

According to the subsequent account of Constantine Menges, then the NSC staffer for Latin America, the impetus came from Jorge Mas Canosa through U.S. Information Agency Director Charles Wick. Menges wrote: "Finally Jorge Mas found the ally he needed: Charles Wick," who used his friendship with President Reagan to bring the station to life.[1] Perhaps the move was intentionally made when Shultz was not in Washington. With Dam's lips sealed, it caught State by surprise.

Upon Shultz's return, the Department worked feverishly to gain a sufficient delay so that Cuba could be informed diplomatically and confidentially in advance of our intended action. The Department suggested that a July 4 start would be appropriate for an American radio station. This would also give additional time to develop technical countermeasures to answer massive radio interference.

Despite State's appeal for delay, President Reagan decided on May 18 to go ahead with Radio Marti. According to Menges, who was not present (nor was I), Reagan cut Shultz off when he voiced the State's concerns about the timing, asking Wick if everything was ready for startup. Wick supposedly replied, "Everything is ready for Radio Marti to go on the air within two days."[2] The die was cast.

The NSC staff seems not to have supported Secretary Shultz's caution. Possibly they felt the start, premature in one sense but long overdue in another, was no risk because the Cubans needed a dialogue. "Preemptive negotiations," perhaps, had become "contingency negotiations."

It was my view that Castro's statements, which had cost him nothing, were aimed at freezing the status quo and deterring us from starting Radio Marti. Once it began, Castro would probably end his so-called "peace offensive" and resume his customary tone toward the United States, just as Cuba terminated radio interference talks in 1983 once Congress authorized Radio Marti.

On May 19, a Sunday, a task force on Radio Marti was established in the Department of State and placed under my direction. At its first session an NSC staff representative argued that if the U.S. population became angry over expected Cuban radio interference with United States' AM band broadcasting, President Reagan would have more options for dealing sternly with Cuba. I found it difficult to imagine what the United States could do to Cuba in response, unless it was prepared to use violence.

At the request of NSC Adviser McFarlane, I prepared a paper on Radio Marti and U.S.–Cuban bilateral relations. He was said to want the paper to show that the United States had leverage over Cuba. My paper argued instead that the Cubans were offering a dialogue in part to head off Radio Marti; since the tactic had failed, it would be discarded.

We soon learned Cuba already knew, from clandestine sources, about the decision to start Radio Marti. The Cuban response to the announcement of its start was indeed disruptive but not at all what they had led us to expect. At 2:00 A.M. on May 20, the acting principal officer in the U.S. Interests Section was summoned to the Cuban Foreign Ministry to receive a diplomatic note stating that Cuba had "suspended" implementation of all aspects of the Migration Agreement and canceled permission for Cuban-Americans to enter Cuba.

A few hours later Radio Marti began its long delayed transmission with the historic words "Buenos días, Cuba" ("Good morning, Cuba"). Those words came after Castro had already bade the freshly negotiated Migration Agreement good night. A major achievement of the administration with respect to Cuba had been lost only 167 days after it was gained.

No one in Washington had expected Cuba's response. No intelligence analyst had forecast it. No one came forward to say "I told you so." Washington was blindsided. Radio Marti had been authorized, as the Cubans well knew, one year before the migration talks began and sixteen months before they ended. The subject had never come up in those negotiations.

The Cuban response was similar to Castro's cancellation of the 1973 anti-hijacking agreement after sabotage of a Cubana airliner in 1976. In each case, reacting emotionally and reflexively to an exogenous event, he nullified a signed commitment, supplying ammunition to those who thought negotiating with Havana a waste of time.

At a senior coordinating committee meeting at 1:30 P.M. on May 20, the NSC representatives still seemed to assume that Castro, recently so eager to talk, would accommodate himself to the new radio. But the "peace offensive" was over. Castro concluded that the United States, by starting Radio Marti, had spurned him. Now it could have the back of his hand. Havana quickly made clear that suspension of the Migration Agreement logically canceled the June review session as well. A potentially useful communications channel was thus aborted before it could be utilized. José Luis Padrón found no time to receive John Ferch in Havana, and Ferch would not be granted the final courtesy call which Fidel Castro had said in February he would be glad to receive. The Department of State had sent Ferch substantive talking points which went unused with Castro—or anyone else.

According to a mid-August report from Havana by Joseph B. Treaster in *The New York Times*:

Soon after the start of the broadcasts an American diplomat was sent to mollify the Cuban government, according to foreign diplomats stationed here. His message was that the United States also felt the immigration agreement represented an improvement in relations and hoped the "technical discussions" that led to it could be continued, moving on to such issues as commercial radio interference and Coast Guard rescue operations. But the Cubans refused to receive the American, the diplomats stated.[3]

This report may have been based on Cuban disinformation or produced by the diplomatic rumor mill in Havana, which in turn had bought something dangled by Cuban agit-prop. State was aware of no such diplomatic mission, which could only have brought further embarrassment on the United States.

Admittedly, it is likely that a short delay in the startup of Radio Marti and a confidential advance word to Havana through diplomatic channels would *not* have stayed Castro's emotional reaction. But it would have cost little aside from time. At a minimum, the Department of Justice would have been able to return more Excludables to Cuba, thereby saving federal, state, and local governments millions of dollars. More ex-political prisoners and preference immigrants could have come to the United States.

By an ironic stroke of luck, the first former political prisoners to leave Cuba under the Migration Agreement flew from Havana to Miami on the morning of May 20. These fortunate individuals found freedom even as Radio Marti was broadcasting its first messages and after suspension of the agreement that had made their flight to the United States possible.

It soon became clear that Cuba, while its broadcasting could be heard in the United States, was not conducting massive interference. Cuba had supplied disinformation to U.S. intelligence. Had it been ready to pay the price for beaming the huge transmitters long hours to the United States, U.S. options would perhaps have been limited to using force or protesting. But for reasons best known to him, Castro decided not to use the weapon—illegal under international law—which he had been developing, advertising, and occasionally testing for at least five years.

Just as with Congress in 1982, the Cuban threat to disrupt U.S. radio broadcasting worked as an effective delaying device. The Cubans had outsmarted us. We had spent many quarrelsome hours developing no answer to a question they did not pose. The real Cuban response—suspension of the Migration Agreement and strict limits on travel by Cuban-Americans to Cuba—was designed to hurt precisely the warmest supporters of Radio Marti, the Cuban-Americans. By blocking movement between Florida and Cuba, the Cuban government aimed at embarrassing the Cuban–American National Foundation in the eyes of the *comunidad*, which learned that Radio Marti would come at high cost in terms of family separation. CANF could easily catch the blame for this situation. It would have to be prepared to deflect the blame on others if things got too hot.

Havana cut the number of Cuban-Americans who could visit Cuba monthly from about eight hundred to one hundred.[4] This restriction introduced competition for limited places. Cuba would exploit the pinch by finding various hoops through which would-be travelers would have to jump.

Cuba's response to Radio Marti was clever. But it betrayed evidence of having been conceived in haste and wrath.[5] In suspending all aspects of the Migration Agreement, Cuba eliminated those which involved self-interest and which carried much appeal to Cuban-Americans: the outflow of former political prisoners and preference immigrants. Havana *wanted* those people to leave. It wished their departure so badly that it had been willing to accept the despised Excludables in the bargain. Now it would prevent us from returning Excludables, but it could not rid itself of a heavy economic and social burden. Cuba was forgoing millions of U.S. dollars by denying itself lucrative earnings from the high-cost transfer of refugees and immigrants to the United States. As it stood, the Cuban–American community would be angry at Havana, not at CANF for its zealous pursuit of Radio Marti and not at the U.S. government for putting the station on the air.

It did not take Castro long to recognize his error. On May 22, there were reports that Cuba might allow refugees and immigrants to travel through *third countries* to the United States. Although Ricardo Alarcón told Jim Todd in Havana flatly that the two sides were back to December 13, 1984—the *status quo ante* Migration Agreement—the Cubans had thought how to have their cake and eat it, too.

On May 24, the Cuban Foreign Ministry informed the U.S. Interests Section that refugees henceforth could leave via third countries for the United States. Cuba was backing away from its original position and preparing to allow its "outcasts" to travel. It would stand to gain economically and politically from this more nuanced approach. As Havana was aware, the U.S. government would be at odds with the Cuban–American community if it failed to process these persons.

To accept Havana's terms would give Cuba the main benefits of the Migration Agreement without the part of most interest to the United States—the exclusion of the Mariel criminals. It would nevertheless have been a good bargain for Cuban–American activists, happy to have Radio Marti in action and willing to finance the flow of immigrants. Havana thus threw down the gauntlet for the U.S. government, knowing that it must either accept Cuba's terms or expect some Cuban-Americans to condemn the administration.

On May 28 the Radio Marti Task Force disbanded. The anticipated crisis had not materialized. Cuba's action required no interagency task force. The U.S. government was again confronted with the issue it had been dealing with since the 1980 boatlift. Now, however, a solution to that problem would be even harder to achieve.

Early June brought verification that Cuba was authorizing the departure of would-be immigrants to the United States through Mexico. We had to deal with Cuba's plan to have the benefits of the Migration Agreement without cost. An interagency meeting on June 11 ratified State's decision to stop issuance of preference immigrant visas and refugee documents in Havana at the end of the week. Word of this decision leaked at once. State and INS were bombarded with telephone calls.

One significant call came my way. The Washington representative of CANF, Frank Calzon, complained that State was punishing innocent Cubans for Castro's behavior. He argued that Cubans ought not be denied permission to enter the United States, regardless of the Excludables. Calzon had been an effective lobbyist for Radio Marti and a tireless advocate for Cuban–American causes. Yet his view on the migration question was in close accord with that of his worst enemies in Havana.

Calzon exploited his telephone call to arouse Miami. He informed *El Miami Herald* of what he termed his "private conversation" with me. On June 12, the *Herald* ran his version of our telephone conversation incorporated into a story by Alfonso Chardy. Calzon no doubt hoped that strong early reaction from the Cuban-Americans would force Washington to rescind its decision. Whether it did so or not, CANF had found a place to deflect the blame.

The U.S. government's first formal response to Cuba's suspension of the Migration Agreement came on June 18, when it ceased processing preference immigrant visas in the U.S. Interests Section in Havana. Processing of former political prisoners and family members was also temporarily suspended. The primary U.S. objective henceforth became to oblige Cuba to end its suspension of the Migration Agreement. Cuba swore it would never do so as long as Radio Marti was broadcasting. The Reagan administration would not compromise on Radio Marti. These were to be the parameters for the next two and one-half years.

GROPING FOR A RESPONSE

After May 20, 1985, the United States broadcast daily news, commentary, and programs of interest to Cubans over Radio Marti. The radio was under the direction of Ernesto Betancourt, who had been the representative of Fidel Castro's 26th of July Movement in the United States while Castro was conducting his fight against Batista. Radio Marti gave the Cuban government no reasonable grounds to protest its content, although such reporting as interviews with key Cuban defectors would eventually get under Havana's skin.

Radio Marti operated under the mandate of the U.S. Congress to meet VOA standards. It provided reliable news for Cubans about their own country. Although monitors detected a hum that interfered with reception in Havana, Cuba did not attempt to jam reception to the station as the USSR and East European states did with broadcasts of Radio Liberty and Radio Free Europe.[6]

Bilateral relations took a sharp turn for the worse as soon as the new voice was on the air. Cuba applied pressure by such means as publishing on July 12 a Notification to Airmen, requiring a twenty-four-hour advance notification for flights through their offshore air control zone in the Gulf of Mexico. This occasioned a dispute between State and the Federal Aviation Administration which, pleading air safety, argued insistently for negotiations with Cuba on the Notice and even discussed with Mexico possible tripartite talks.

On July 18, Cuba tried the tactic again, announcing an aviation closing in Guantanamo province on July 26. This province surrounded the territory of the U.S. naval base, where U.S. naval aircraft operated subject only to guidance from the base. Although the Cubans specifically and pointedly "exempted" U.S. "naval military" aircraft from the ban, assertion of an authority to "exempt" our aircraft might be followed by a closing with no such exemption.

In response, the Department of State pointed out that U.S. rights to fly into the naval base at Guantanamo could not be affected by Cuba. This was akin to what we had done when Soviet air controllers sought to "exempt" Allied aircraft from some asserted prohibition on flights in the Berlin air corridors.

The main battleground involved the former political prisoners and families, whom the Cubans in New York the previous summer had estimated at about thirty thousand. Reinstitution of Section 243 (g) of the Immigration and Nationality Act precluded issuance of preference immigrant visas in Havana now that Cuba was again refusing to take back its citizens at U.S. request. The law did not prevent the United States from taking ex-prisoners as refugees, but this had been a part of the agreement now suspended by Cuba. State increased to six thousand the number of refugees who could be taken in one fiscal year—with the proviso that this figure, double the number in the Migration Agreement, would apply to Cuba *only* if it ended its suspension of the agreement.

In addition to this carrot, a new stick was made ready. Aside from establishment of full diplomatic relations and an end to the embargo, there was no objective Cuba pursued more assiduously than visits to the United States by Cuban officials or employees to receive technical assistance or to engage in advocacy activities. The Consular Bureau, under congressional pressure, was reticent to deny visas merely because of membership in the Communist Party. To skirt this problem but deny Cuba ready access to the United States, State recommended that the president prohibit travel of Cuban government or party officials to the United States under section 212 (f) of the Immigration and Nationality Act. This was expeditiously implemented.

Proclamation 5377 of October 4, 1985—called "Suspension of Entry as Nonimmigrants by Officers or Employees of the Government of Cuba or the Communist Party of Cuba"—suspended indefinitely the entry of such officials unless for the exclusive purpose of conducting official business at the Cuban Interests Section in Washington, the Cuban Mission to the United Nations in New York, or the United Nations itself, except as the Secretary of State or his designee might decide.[7] Proclamation 5377 gave State a flexible means of pressure, one that could be modified if Cuba withdrew the decision which had generated it.

Limits were imposed on the generosity toward Cuba of the Pan American Health Organization (PAHO), which was seventy-five percent funded by the U.S. government. Admission of Cubans to the United States to take advantage of PAHO stipends was thereafter strictly limited. Heretofore Cuba had been one of the most active users of PAHO benefits.

At the instance of State, Treasury agreed to tighten enforcement of the Cuba Embargo. In particular, State hoped Treasury's Office of Foreign Assets Control would act more quickly against Cuban-controlled organizations in Panama and elsewhere that engaged in illegal trade activities .with U.S. firms.

The question of long-term political prisoners in Cuba was raised anew in August during a visit to Washington by the Papal Nuncio in Havana, Monsignor Giulio Einaudi. He confided that Fidel Castro had reiterated his earlier willingness to release seventy-five persons from prison if they would be taken into the United States. These included thirty-one of the individuals on the list of 146 names the U.S. Catholic bishops had given Castro in January, supplemented by forty-four officials or officers of the Batista regime whom Castro wanted to expel from Cuba.

On September 11, three Cuban Catholic bishops, permitted to visit the United States as a token of Castro's cultivation of a better relationship with the church, told Elliott Abrams, newly named Assistant Secretary of State for Inter-American Affairs, and me that the Cuban government would permit an aircraft to fly the seventy-five political prisoners and their families directly to the United States. Abrams promised the bishops we would process the prisoners.

The seventy-five prisoners and their families caused more disagreement within the administration. INS Commissioner Nelson sought to link their acceptance to Cuba's ending its suspension of the Migration Agreement. An NSC staffer said that Nelson convinced Rear Admiral John Poindexter, the new National Security Adviser, that he and Attorney General Meese should devise a strategy, based on "public diplomacy," to induce Cuba to withdraw its suspension of the agreement.

Nelson believed Cuba's willingness to release political prisoners was a bargaining chip for restoring the Migration Agreement. INS spelled its ideas out in a widely distributed memorandum arguing that State's "piecemeal" approach would not exploit Cuba's assumed need for a face-saving way to restore the agreement. The memo demanded, with unconscious drollery, that we "open up a void."

Also in September Representative Peter Rodino resurrected his earlier plan to require the issuance of preference immigrant visas in Havana, despite the Attorney General's invocation of Article 243 (g) of the Immigration and Nationality Act. His initiative was pressed by the Cuban–American lobby.

At the same time, ironically, State was asked to respond to Rodino's questions about what it was doing to get Cuba to resume the Migration Agreement. One thing was clear. Legislation such as his would remove one of the few genuine bargaining chips which the United States still possessed. Hence, as in early 1984, one thing State could do to get Cuba to repatriate the Excludables was to resist legislation like that proposed by Rodino.

MAKING MISERY PAY—CASTRO SEIZES THE UNPAYABLE DEBT

After May 20, Fidel Castro spoke no more about a dialogue with the United States but turned to themes of confrontation. He focused on a problem he had mentioned even during the "peace offensive," the "unpayable" foreign debt afflicting many developing countries. Three years had passed since Cuba notified Western creditors it could not meet debt payments. The "Paris Club" restructuring had not saved the day. Aside from continuing to supply oil in excess of Cuban needs—oil "reexports" had become Cuba's chief source of hard currency—the USSR was disinclined to provide the means for Cuba to trade with the West. Cuba was already a sufficient burden for the Soviet citizen.

In early 1985, CANF published a secret National Bank of Cuba report to Western creditors recommending increased energy efficiency, new export products for convertible currency markets, better attainment of commitments to Soviet Bloc countries, accelerated programs of tourism, and more emphasis on meeting foreign trade objectives.[8] It was a litany of what was wrong in Cuba.

Fidel Castro characteristically sought to turn adversity into political advantage. He had no thought of economic rationalization for Cuba, but he saw the value of the foreign debt theme as a means of strengthening Cuba's already improving ties to the Third World and for undermining the United States. Notwithstanding its close military ties to Moscow and its highly trained cadre of personnel that made it seem in some respects more like a developed country than not, Cuba was still paramount among the "non-aligned." Castro now exploited the debt issue to assert Cuban leadership of the downtrodden. In late May he told a Brazilian interviewer that "the rich countries are sucking the blood of the poorer ones without consideration or remorse." He charged that the Federal Reserve Board of the United States was the "rattlesnake of the world economy" and asserted that the United States was exporting revolution in the form of inflation, recession, rebellion, and subversion.[9]

At the end of July, Havana entertained 1,000 politicians, writers and academics from seventeen Latin American states at a five-day conclave. Latin American and Third World guests applauded Castro's harsh rhetoric, even though neither they nor Cuba itself were prepared simply to renounce the debt. It was good theater. The aborted dialogue had become a monologue. But it did not serve Cuba any better than the "public relations campaign."[10]

ENTER THE RUSSIANS—FRANK, BUT NOT COMRADELY

In Moscow, Mikhail Gorbachev had supplanted the rigid, almost senile leadership of Leonid Brezhnev and his two short-lived immediate successors. While sharp differences remained, U.S.-Soviet relations began to improve. As part of the strategy to promote a Reagan–Gorbachev summit meeting, the Department of State, driven by the European Bureau and without the knowledge of ARA, invited the USSR to "consult" on regional problems, including Latin America (though not Eastern Europe). Moscow accepted.

ARA Assistant Secretary Abrams was unhappy at the prospect of "consulting" with those whose military assistance supplied the Sandinistas and the FMLN and who monitored American communications and patrolled the Atlantic Coast from Cuban facilities. Although it was the Soviet–Cuban alliance that jeopardized U.S. security in the Caribbean Basin, we knew the Russians would refuse to discuss Cuba.

Overriding the European Bureau's protests, Abrams insisted on reading the riot act to the Russians, including the role played by Cuba. He asked me for themes for the October 31–November 1 session. The objective was to keep it short, give the Soviets a firm message on Central America, and not be drawn into any "understanding" that could inhibit U.S. freedom of action in the region. I knew the Russians reasonably well from having spent three years in Moscow (1976–79), as counselor of embassy for economic and commercial affairs. I also knew personally the Soviet representative at the talks, Ambassador Vladimir Kazimirov, from his time as Soviet Ambassador to Venezuela a few years later. While the Soviets indeed would argue strenuously that Cuba must not be discussed, their delegation stopped in Havana en route to Washington. Foreign Minister Shevardnadze and Kazimirov were in Havana on October 28 when *Granma*, the Cuban Communist Party newspaper, ran a particularly vicious personal attack on Abrams, the timing of which could not have been coincidental.

The Washington "consultations" were of the kind Soviet jargon would describe as "frank." The Soviet guests could escape discussion of Cuba only by shutting their ears. For his part, Kazimirov complained that Abrams had even discussed Cuban domestic affairs. He asserted that he had to forgo presenting a "conciliatory message" because of Abrams' tactics, but he nevertheless later conveyed the message, which the U.S. side did not find reassuring.

Kazimirov, having made favorable mention of the "Contadora" proposals for a Central American settlement, was maneuvered by Abrams on the second day into declining to endorse all of the Contadora points, which included democracy. He also refused to provide the numbers of Soviet and Cuban military personnel in Central America, asserting that he was not a "prisoner of war" under interrogation.

Since the first U.S.–Soviet consultations on the Caribbean Basin were so "frank," ARA hoped that the Russians would see no more value than we in such sessions. The opposite was true. Moscow liked the idea of discussing Latin America with the United States. Although the Russians no doubt would have preferred different U.S. interlocutors, they accepted the ones they found. The dialogue was the thing.

The first Reagan–Gorbachev summit meeting took place in Geneva later in November. Their joint statement endorsed "periodic discussion of regional issues."[11] Accordingly, we would be meeting again, and often.

DOWNHILL

While the Russians were in Cuba, Havana denounced what it asserted was a U.S. surveillance overflight. On November 1, as the Washington talks ended, there was a huge demonstration outside the U.S. Interests Section in Havana.[12]

Later in the month we sought to resume quiet diplomacy. Mike Kozak and I lunched with José Arbesu, who was attending the UN General Assembly session in New York. We hoped to enlist Arbesu—intelligent, a senior party apparatchik and personally affable—in our quest to break the post-May deadlock.

Arbesu flatly said there would be no resumption of execution of the Migration Agreement as long as Radio Marti remained on the air. Whereas the three Cuban Catholic bishops had hinted in September in Washington that a change of name might help—the Cubans claimed to be especially insulted that the station was named for a Cuban patriot—Arbesu was categorical in his rejection.

Kozak and I expressed regret at the decline in U.S.–Cuban relations as a result of Cuba's overreaction to Radio Marti. We cautioned that things could become worse if we did not restore the Migration Agreement, which both sides continued to call fair and balanced.

Arbesu acknowledged that the United States had never during the migration talks made any statement about Radio Marti. (Suzy Garment of the *Wall Street Journal* said Ricardo Alarcón had claimed Cuba was assured during the talks that Radio Marti would not come on the air.) The lunch, however, had no positive effect on a deteriorating situation. Moreover, on November 15, Curtis Kamman, our new principal officer in Havana, reported having heard from Alarcón that the Migration Agreement would not be restored as long as Radio Marti was on the air.

While stonewalling Washington, Cuba sought to drive a wedge between the U.S. government and Cuban-Americans. It permitted thousands of Cubans to leave for Panama, whence they hoped to enter the United States. This earned dollars for both Cuba and Panama because Cuban-Americans paid for the travel, the fees, and in many cases the bribes of government officials. Since most of these persons were ineligible for U.S. visas, they were stranded in Panama.

Intelligence sources also reported Cuban plans to bolster Havana's weak financial situation by permitting Cuban-Americans to visit the island for $5 hundred apiece. The visitors would also have to accept nominal membership in some sort of Cuban-sponsored front if they wished to be permitted to enter Cuba.

Cuba also began, cautiously, to disrupt U.S. radio broadcasting. A Federal Commmunications Commission official on December 10 informed a senior coordination committee on Radio Marti of several violations of U.S. air space.[13] But Radio Taino, with 500 kilowatts, sufficient power to disrupt a clear channel radio station in Salt Lake City, had not yet caused significant interference.

For the United States, the primary policy tool to persuade Cuba to resume implementation of the Migration Agreement remained refusal to process preference immigrant visas or former political prisoners in Havana. The other main sanction was strict limitation on travel by Cuban officials in the United States. These controls evoked a relatively low amount of criticism of the Department of State from U.S. institutions. The Cubans hoped that these protests would weaken Washington's resolve, whereas State reasoned with academics that restoration of the Mariel Agreement was in their interest as well.

Late in December, Elliott Abrams and I met with the Cuban–American National Foundation's Washington representative, Frank Calzon, to discuss how the United States might deny funds to the Cuban government while responding to humanitarian questions. Abrams was particularly sympathetic to the situation of the former prisoners.

Calzon acknowledged that Cuba would benefit financially from the travel of Cubans to the United States via third countries. Like Abrams, he seemed primarily interested in helping the former political prisoners living on the margin of Cuban society. Judging by what the Cubans had told us in New York, there were over thirty thousand such persons in Cuba. Since only about sixty thousand refugees worldwide were authorized by Congress to enter the United States in any given fiscal year, there could be refugee numbers for no more than to six thousand Cubans in any single year, even if Cuba were to end its suspension of the Migration Agreement. A program, if any, for former political prisoners in Cuba would have to be modest while the agreement remained suspended.

Thus, a criterion was essential for rank-ordering any processing of these thirty thousand or so outcasts. I suggested that we might start with those who had served ten or more years in prison. Calzon responded favorably. INS, however, worried that any program would weaken pressure on Cuba to resume accepting Excludables under the Migration Agreement. The Cuban–American position and that of the U.S. government were growing further apart. Were its own conditions not deteriorating so fast, it was an American dilemma Cuba could have relished.

NOTES

1. Constantine C. Menges, *Inside the National Security Council: The True Story of the Making and Unmaking of Reagan's Foreign Policy* (New York: Simon and Schuster, 1988), p. 219.

2. Ibid. Menges identifies the Department of State as leading the "faction" that "seemed intimidated by the Cuban threats." He says he was elated by Reagan's "good judgment and decisiveness." Castro did not carry out his threats, Menges added. His book makes no reference to what Castro did do.

3. *NYT*, Aug. 20, 1985, I, 10:1.

4. Dominguez, "Cooperating with the Enemy?" p. 65.

5. Ed Gonzalez and David Ronfelt comment that Castro miscalculated in believing he could influence Reagan administration policy with the Migration Agreement and a media blitz. *Castro, Cuba and the World*, p. 119.

6. *NYT*, August 27, 1985, I, 12:1. Joe Treaster reported from Havana that ordinary Cubans had become more relaxed in discussing Radio Marti with foreigners. Everyone followed the soap opera saga of Esmeralda, a poor blind girl who won the heart of a rich young man. Treaster said the radio had many listeners despite efforts by local block wardens to discourage it.

7. *United States Code: Congressional and Administrative News*, 99th Congress, 1st Sess. 1985, (St. Paul: West Publishing Co., 1986), vol. 3, pp. A112–113.

8. Cuban–American National Foundation, *Cuba's Financial Crisis: The Secret Report from the National Bank of Cuba* (Washington, DC, 1985), pp. 3–5.

9. *Folha de São Paulo*, June 2, 1985, pp. 14–18.

10. Gonzalez and Ronfeldt noted that Castro had "great difficulty" manipulating the Reagan administration and political process to Cuba's advantage. *Castro, Cuba and the World*, p. xii.

11. Shultz, *Turmoil and Triumph*, p. 606.

12. *NYT*, Nov. 2, 1985, I, 10:4 reported 200,000 protesters.

13. Radio Rebelde, broadcasting at 100 kw on 710 kHz, was disrupting WOR in New York. It was responding to a Cuban–American station called Radio Mambi, broadcasting on the same frequency.

7

1986—From Bad to Worse

Little light was left on the horizon for U.S.–Cuban relations as 1986 began. Cuban support for the Sandinistas and the Salvadoran guerrillas was unflagging. Fidel Castro spoke of keeping troops in Angola until the end of apartheid. Despite its belligerence and its sagging economy, Cuba made progress in Latin America. It was admitted to the Latin American Parliament just as if its parliamentarians had been freely elected. Havana's influence in the nonaligned movement seemed as great as ever. Castro's denunciation of the "unpayable" foreign debt had resonance among debtors.

The symbiotic relationship with Moscow remained close, but now he had to live with the new style of Mikhail Gorbachev, whose *glasnost* and *perestroika* launched the USSR on a path Castro surely would not have recommended and decidedly would not follow. Already Moscow, more aware of economic costs and less devoted to strategic advance, worried about Cuban economic performance. Castro had no mind to relax central controls. He was determined to "rectify" Cuba by reducing market factors and stressing moral incentives instead.

The administration pressed ahead. Radio Marti was getting through. The majority of Cubans could hear it, albeit slightly jammed in Havana. Cuba's media had to deal with issues which they might otherwise have ignored.

Travel of Cuban officials—virtually every Cuban bearing an official passport except those going to the Cuban Interests Section, the Cuban Mission to the United Nations, or the UN—was restricted. The primary U.S.

objective in bilateral relations was to oblige Havana to end its suspension of the Migration Agreement.

But Cuba believed it was winning this tug of war. While its chief aim—to force Washington to withdraw the new radio—had not been achieved, the United States seemed stuck with the Mariel criminals. If Cuba could live with Radio Marti, the new standoff might suffice from Havana's point of view.

The number and costs of Excludables mounted. Cubans, comprising under five percent of the prison population in the Atlanta Penitentiary, accounted for over half of inmate-to-inmate assaults and one-third of assaults on guards. Representative Kastenmeier urged the administration to shut down Radio Marti and reopen negotiations with Cuba to expel as many undesirables as possible.[1] A March 12 *New York Times* editorial urged scrapping Radio Marti to save the agreement. (The *Times* shortly thereafter retracted this recommendation.)

THE ECONOMIC BATTLEGROUND

When Fidel Castro opened the Third Cuban Communist Party Congress in February, declining living standards could no longer be ignored. His response to shortages and growing indebtedness was a "rectification" campaign where Cubans would be stimulated by moral incentives to raise quality and quantity of output. Not for Cuba the Soviet approach to a "socialist market" or the more substantial changes introduced in Eastern Europe. They were inconsistent with his ideal of a new socialist man, motivated by ideology, not material interests.

The party apparatus passed more tightly into the hands of Fidel Castro and brother Raúl, whose status as designated successor was strengthened.[2] Castro appointed himself chief critic of economic performance—pointing, warning, and punishing. If the system was failing to achieve its objectives, he attributed this to rectifiable human error and weakness.[3]

At the deferred final session of the Third Party Congress, Castro would say:

What has never crossed my mind is to use the standard of living as motivation for the masses. . . . it is not what motivates . . . revolution-aries. . . . If we spoke only of living standards—and I have never even liked the term—we could unleash a terrible national selfishness. Marxism–Leninism is internationalism. . . . If the masses are taught only in terms of living standards, then they will never have an internationalist awareness because everything that you do to give to another, you are taking away from yourself.[4]

This voice was out of harmony with the drift of the Communist world, but it was the voice of the man who determined Cuba's course. Castro strengthened his political grip but could not alleviate Cuba's economic distress. The belt grew tighter. Ration lines grew longer, and coupons brought fewer goods. Castro criticized the "laziness" of Cubans.[5] He halted the free markets that were a small window for the profit motive which he was no longer willing to tolerate.[6]

U.S. policy was to try to tighten the screw. By 1986 the Office of Foreign Assets Control in Treasury had negotiated several agreements encumbering Cuban nickel sales for convertible currency. State urged U.S. trading partners, and prominent recipients of U.S. economic assistance, to buy their sugar from other suppliers than Cuba. In March, Egypt was dissuaded from a large dollar purchase of Cuban sugar.

In April, yielding to State's pressure, Treasury made a further commitment for more expeditious action against Cuban front companies, especially those registered in Panama—the majority. This followed agreement by Secretary of the Treasury Baker to give Customs substantially greater resources for dealing with embargo violations. Customs was eager to cooperate.

THE MIGRATION STALEMATE

Suspension of the Migration Agreement denied Cuba its two chief practical benefits—a source of dollars and the departure of unhappy Cubans. A partial remedy was to route emigrants to third countries like Panama. Cuban–American relatives would finance their movement. They hoped the emigrants could enter the United States quickly. Many, however, at least temporarily ineligible for admission under U.S. immigration laws, became "stranded" in third countries. Cuba offered to allow former political prisoners to come to the United States, but only through third countries, outside the framework of the agreement. It mobilized influential Cuban-Americans, many of whom sympathized with these measures, against the U.S. government for refusing to cooperate.

The main public pressure on the U.S. government, however, still was to expel the Mariel criminals. There were again bizarre proposals for doing so. On January 3, a well-known attorney whose client claimed to be close to Raúl Castro told Jim Michel and me that for $2 thousand a head and return of his U.S. passport, the client could use his connection with Castro to get twenty-five hundred to three thousand Mariel Excludables to Cuba. The client wanted no publicity. Michel told the attorney that under the U.S. system of justice this would be impossible. Courts would insist on the facts. The attorney went away, and no more was heard of this scheme. (Implausible as the scheme seemed, it might have been a bargain to return three thousand Excludables for $6 million.)

More disincentives were needed to persuade Cuba to end its suspension of the Migration Agreement and to keep it from enjoying its benefits by sending Cubans through third countries. New restrictions would anger Cuban-Americans, however, so State had to take into account the pressure they would generate through contacts in both the executive and legislative branches.

I believed that the best way to maintain pressure on Cuba while keeping Cuban–American support for U.S. policy would be to balance restrictions on immigration with a well-prioritized program for former political prisoners in Cuba, taking first those who had suffered longest. Elliott Abrams and I had suggested late in 1985 to Cuban–American National Foundation representative Calzon a program that began with former prisoners who had served over ten years.

A program for ex-prisoners required support from the Immigration and Naturalization Service, but INS saw it as undercutting efforts to restore the Migration Agreement. Disagreement focused on two issues. First, on humanitarian (and political) grounds, State wanted Cuba to release long-term political prisoners *currently in detention*. It wished to accept them *at once*. They were relatively few in number and their plight especially serious.

The top INS leadership opposed this approach. It regarded current prisoners as no different from former political prisoners in Cuba. INS tended to see any Cuban prisoner as a potential bargaining chip for the United States. Hence they should be taken only if we could obtain something in return. This outlook was akin to the position the administration had taken when it sought to return Excludables to Cuba in exchange for the twenty-six persons who came with Jesse Jackson and to put Excludables alongside Cuban prisoners of war being repatriated from Grenada. But the administration had fortunately not insisted on a *quid pro quo*. Cuba did not agree to a "swap."

The other difference concerned State's proposal for a small, prioritized program for *former* political prisoners and family members living on the margin of Cuban society. Like INS, State knew that Cuban desire to expel these outcasts to the United States proved a valuable tool in the 1984 negotiations. But whereas INS wanted to build up the pressure by refusing to open this sluice until Cuba restored the Migration Agreement, State felt domestic support for a tough overall policy could not be maintained if we did not begin to take these persons. If Cuban–American unhappiness became too great, State foresaw, Congress might force the administration to yield across the board. By being too rigid, Washington would lose all. Cuba would gain the benefits of the Migration Agreement without its obligations. In addition, by prioritizing the former prisoners, the program would make it more difficult for Fidel Castro to set counterpriorities.

State wanted to maintain the dam by letting a little water spill over. It did not want the dam to break. It dealt with all Cuba-related issues, whereas INS concentrated on migration. State had to maintain public support for Cuba policy. INS just wanted to repatriate the Excludables. Foreign policy was not its business, but its power over action had important policy implications.

Since INS controlled admissions procedures, its point of view prevailed. The only exceptions were high-profile current prisoners with public relations impact, where State could appeal to the White House. On January 24, I sought during a dinner conversation in Miami to convince INS Commissioner Alan Nelson of the value of a small, selective program for the outcasts in a package of new sanctions against Cuba. Nelson, a thoughtful and earnest man with firm views but open to discussion, seemed to accept my reasoning that this program would not fatally undermine our position on the Migration Agreement. But doubts must have crept back in. INS did not change its position. Moreover, internal differences were cropping up in State. Some, like Richard Schifter, new Assistant Secretary for Human Rights and Humanitarian Affairs, began to argue for taking all former prisoners and immigrants as well. Our new principal officer in Havana, Curtis Kamman, cabled on April 4, urging that we resume processing of preference immigrants. He predicted Cuba would not take the criminals and felt State should accept this "reality."

The first half of 1986 saw no progress on freeing the 75 current prisoners offered to the U.S. Catholic bishops or on bringing up the families of the 26 men who arrived in June 1984 with Jesse Jackson. It also saw no movement on a program for former political prisoners.

Another risk was that public pressure for exceptions to restraints on Cuban official travelers would undermine our special sanctions. Reflecting this pressure, the Bureau of Consular Affairs argued for a more liberal visa policy.[7]

There were valid arguments on both sides of each issue. If the shoe were to pinch the Cuban foot, however, there had to be sanctions which State could apply or relax, depending on Cuban behavior. In contradistinction to failure to establish a more flexible policy on Cuban political prisoners and their kin, the line was held on official visitors.

A HERO'S RETURN—AND A PROPOSAL
FROM FIDEL CASTRO

During the second U.S.–Soviet consultations, in Moscow on May 19 and 20, Abrams and Vladimir Kazimirov again debated but closed no gap. There was, however, a useful aside in Moscow. During post-luncheon conversation at the U.S. Residence (Spaso House), I told Kazimirov we were perplexed that Cuba was still suspending an agreement which Fidel Castro in his Third Party Congress speech in February mentioned with favor. Kazimirov replied that Havana realized it erred in suspending the agreement since Radio Marti was not having as bad an effect as anticipated on Cuba. Although we suspected this might be the case, confirmation of it by a knowledgeable Soviet official was worth many hunches.

Meanwhile, Cuba was about to send a man and a message about the Mariel Agreement that seemed to accord with Kazimirov's revelation. In May, Fidel Castro offered to release Ricardo Montero Duque to Senator Ted Kennedy. Montero Duque commanded Cuban émigré forces at the Bay of Pigs a quarter-century earlier and had been in prison ever since. Kennedy intended to send a staff member, Gregory Craig, to Havana to bring him back.

This plan led to a short squabble between State, which supported the idea, and INS, which initially opposed letting Montero Duque enter the United States with an aide to Kennedy. INS Commissioner Nelson on May 30 insisted that this should have the prior concurrence of the Secretary of State, the Attorney General, the Vice President, and possibly President Reagan. I stressed the moral imperative—and political realism—of admitting Colonel Montero Duque at once.

Fortunately, INS saw the light. On June 4, Nelson and his deputy, Tom Ferguson, joined me in Kennedy's office to brief Craig and two other staffers and to ask that Craig make a strong pitch for restoration of the Migration Agreement. This resulted in good cooperation within the U.S. government. Defense made available Homestead Air Force Base, near Miami, to receive Montero Duque. Craig Raynsford of INS and I welcomed him to freedom on June 8, along with Ambassador Andrés Vargas Gómez and Jeb Bush, son of the Vice President.

Fidel Castro had another motive. He sent a message with Craig, to whom he had granted an interview. Craig would not tell me what it was. Only Ted Kennedy could divulge, and he would tell only the Secretary of State. On June 12, Senator Kennedy called on Secretary Shultz, who received him without Abrams, Michel, or myself. Castro's proposal, we learned, was based on a paper the United States had given Cuba at the time of Radio Marti's startup in May 1985. It voiced no objection to Cuban broadcasting to the United States if done in accordance with international agreements on frequencies and if it did not pose interference problems for U.S. stations.

The implication seemed clear. Cuba, looking for a way out of the impasse, wanted to broadcast to the United States and in return would end its suspension of the Migration Agreement. Cuban broadcasts had been heard in the United States for many years. It sounded as if the dilemma might soon be resolved. Secretary Shultz on June 17 approved an approach to Havana.

Unfortunately, Cuban–American sensitivities had been aroused rather than soothed by the release of Montero Duque, in part because a Department of State press statement distinguished between him and thousands of former political prisoners still in Cuba. Led by the *Miami Herald*, they assailed the putative "new doctrine," which seemed callous to the fate of thousands.

Yet the *Miami Herald* also criticized the administration for failing to gain Cuban agreement to restore the Migration Agreement. On June 10, 1986, it editorialized: "It's imperative that the Administration do as Gregory Craig, Sen. Kennedy's foreign-policy adviser, did in his recent talks with Cuban officials: Reiterate the *urgent need for Cuba to restore the immigration and refugee agreement that it suspended in May 1985*."[8] (Italics mine; this would make most interesting reading in November 1987.) Greg Craig's urging in Havana, of course, had been my counsel to him before he departed Washington.

Cuba quickly agreed to meet on July 8–9 in Mexico City to discuss the Mariel Agreement and Cuba's desire to broadcast to the United States. The Department's optimism was further stimulated when Cuba did not allow the June 26 arrest of an employee of the Cuban firm Cubalse—caught trying to smuggle thirty-one suitcases of electronic equipment plus two ounces of cocaine out of Miami—deter it from a new dialogue.

State consulted closely with the Federal Communications Commission to see what broadcasting pattern might be suggested to Cuba. FCC Chairman Mark Fowler authorized an FCC specialist, Wilson La Follette, to attend the Mexico City talks in an expert capacity. Along with State's

William Jahn, we would have an experienced team to discuss any technical issues the Cubans might raise.

Then *The New York Times* on July 3 carried a damaging leak on the fact, locus, and date of the talks.[9] The account seemed sourced to an administration insider knowledgeable of closely held details and sympathetic to émigré concerns. By providing advance assurance against U.S. concessions, the leak was intended to reassure Miami, but it provoked Havana.

Citing "Reagan administration officials," the article stated:

> They expected Cuba to agree to reviving the immigration accord, the most important agreement between Cuba and the United States. They also said there was no likelihood that the United States would halt its broadcasts over Radio Marti. . . . They said the Cubans had decided it was in their interest to revive the immigration accord to improve relations not only with Washington but also with Cubans in both Cuba and the United States who had resented the cutoff in travel between the two countries.

The article, citing an "administration official," said that Senator Kennedy had played an indirect role in getting the negotiations on track. An aide to Kennedy, it explained, got a letter from "Cuban authorities" in which the idea of restoring the agreement was broached. "It was unclear what concessions, if any, the United States might make to the Cubans. Officials insisted Radio Marti would not be given up."

The Cuban Interests Section presented a strong protest before the day was out. However, Cuba's only request was that the first session take place in its embassy in Mexico City, rather than ours. We had no problem with that.

FALSE DAWN—THE MEXICO CITY TALKS

The U.S. delegation came to Mexico believing Cuba wanted face-saving egress from a mutual dilemma. Radio Marti was not hurting it all that much. Yet it had lost substantial benefits by suspending the Migration Agreement. In hurting the United States, the Cubans were hurting themselves—perhaps more.

The Cubans came believing that the U.S. government, under siege from Cuban émigrés in Miami and desperate to rid itself of the Mariel criminals, might be ready (and able) to grant Cuba substantial concessions in broadcasting. They perhaps hoped to sell us, as supplicants, the old package at a much higher price.

Michael Kozak and I met with Ricardo Alarcón and José Antonio Arbesu for three and one-half hours on July 7, on the eve of formal negotiations. The problem emerged at once from our chat. Alarcón stated that Cuba wanted two things from the talks: the same way of broadcasting to the United States as we had to Cuba, recognizing that it would be difficult for us to arrange, and a change of name for Radio Marti. Alarcón thought the second item would be less difficult for the U.S. government.

Kozak explained that broadcasting frequencies in the United States were limited and in constant demand. Although we had worked carefully to see how Cuban stations could broadcast to very substantial numbers of Americans without causing interference, he said, our flexibility was limited. While we did not yet know what Havana sought, it would be hard to offer much of substance.

On July 8, Carlos Martínez Albuerne, director of electric radio frequencies in the Cuban Ministry of Communications, presented a grandiose, unrealistic proposition for four "clear channels" to the United States—on frequencies to be decided by Cuba—to be supplemented by leased time broadcasting to cover the Pacific Coast region of the United States, which could not be adequately reached even by the most powerful Cuban radios. "Clear channels," a concept no longer used by the FCC in allocating radio frequencies, would have required that U.S. stations on these frequencies be denied broadcast rights for as far as the Cuban stations could be heard.

The U.S. note fourteen months earlier had welcomed a "free exchange of ideas" with Cuba. The choice of language had been more grandiloquent than carefully considered. It was intended to persuade Cuba not to engage in disruptive broadcasting. The Cubans were now relating what they understood by such an exchange.

Alarcón called formally for a name change for Radio Marti which indicated that Cuba could live with the radio. But the Cuban proposal for broadcasting was so non-negotiable that the name was irrelevant.

In response, Kozak, referring to recent (and disputatious) talks between the delegations of the two countries in Geneva at a regional meeting of the International Telecommunications Union (ITU), confirmed that the U.S. position had not changed. He inquired if Alarcón wished to hear from Bill Jahn, State's communication expert, the position that the latter had set forth at Geneva. Alarcón declined.

After the session the U.S. delegation, principally communications experts LaFollette and Jahn, worked on a response which would state our principles and offer Cuba a way to broadcast to millions of Americans with minimum interference. There was no way to offer Cuba as large a percentage of the American public as Radio Marti had in Cuba. The laws of nature precluded such a ratio. The U.S. radio experts calculated that the Cuban proposal, if accepted, would put off the air or adversely affect up to forty U.S. radio stations.

On July 9, Kozak, supported by Lafollette, made a careful exposition of how Cuba could reach the maximum audience without major disruption to U.S. broadcasting patterns. He made no offer to take U.S. stations off the air so that Cuban broadcasting could replace them. Lafollette explained that broadcasting opportunities for Cuba were limited, but he offered to provide ideas on how Cuba could best broadcast without interfering with U.S. stations.

The Cuban side expressed polite interest. José Arbesu asked for a copy of the map which Lafollette and Jahn had drawn up the night before to show how much of the United States could be reached in this manner, a valuable document from the Cuban point of view. Arbesu's request, which was at once granted, was a prearranged signal for Alarcón to authorize Martínez to launch a nasty diatribe about U.S. broadcasting and our failure to meet minimal Cuban conditions.

An evening meeting in the U.S. Embassy produced grossly offensive presentations by Martínez and Alarcón. When it was Kozak's turn to respond, Alarcón and Arbesu found something amusing to discuss between themselves, obliging Kozak to ask for their attention so the session could continue.

By 10:00 P.M. it was clear that there was no point in extending the talks. The unrealism of the Cuban proposal and the rudeness with which it was presented led Kozak to tell Alarcón that he disagreed with much that the latter had said but was in full concurrence that further conversation would be a waste of time. On this note, the Mexico City talks ended in failure.

There were two possible explanations for this outcome. Either the Cubans came with vastly exaggerated views of U.S. vulnerability to Cuban sanctions and/or U.S. capacity to meet Cuba's radio broadcasting aspirations, or else they wanted to probe areas where the United States might permit Cuban broadcasting. Jahn and Lafollette had seen the Cubans recently in Geneva, where the heat of the debate between Jahn and Carlos Martínez was thought to be greater than ITU officials had ever witnessed. In Jahn's later view, the Cubans came to Mexico City fully aware of the unacceptability of their demands and interested only in probing the U.S. tolerance level for increased Cuban broadcasting. Since the U.S. side supplied valuable data, the Cubans, negotiating in bad faith, went away after a successful communications espionage foray.

The other possibility was that Cuba, having consulted mainly sympathizers in Washington and having listened to Cuban–American grievances about U.S. sanctions, was overly confident that the U.S. side would offer significant concessions to regain implementation of the Migration Agreement.

Whether they negotiated in good faith or not, the rude Cuban behavior throughout the talks supports the conclusion that Havana wanted either major gains or a speedy end. The United States stood firm, so Cuba called off the talks. There is some reason, however, to wonder whether the Cubans intended the session to end quite so precipitously. Their probe of U.S. vulnerability may have led them to anticipate some counteroffer of broadcasting rights. This self-serving explanation came forth from Havana in conversations the Cubans knew would get back to us. It was supplemented by anecdotal evidence.[10]

For State and Justice the results in Mexico City were deplorable. Cuban-Americans, especially those close to Radio Marti, were less concerned. Radio Marti had not been touched, nor had Cuba received any concessions about radio broadcasting. As for increased migration northward, efforts would be intensified to bring this about outside the framework of the Migration Agreement. State had no choice but to strengthen the sanctions it hoped would eventually cause Cuba to resume implementation of the agreement. The failure of the talks in Mexico City meant that both sides would play hardball.

THE AFTERMATH—BETWIXT AND BETWEEN

In the wake of the failed negotiations, State was more determined than ever to expel the Mariel Excludables. It planned special sanctions strong enough to make Havana change its mind. Specifically, measures would be taken to prevent Cuba from eluding the effect of Section 243 (g) of the Immigration and Nationality Act by directing Cuban immigrants to the United States through third countries.

Since these measures would cause outcry among influential Cuban–American groups, there was a question whether the administration would be able to take the heat long enough to make Cuba yield. In order to win Cuban–American understanding and support for this sanction, the Department of State wanted to end the deadlock over travel by current Cuban political prisoners whom Castro had offered to the Catholic bishops and to French oceanographer Jacques Cousteau. It also wanted to start a small, prioritized program for the ex-political prisoners and families in Cuba. State pressed INS to take out the current political prisoners promised by Castro a year and a half earlier, together with their families and the kin of the twenty-six who had come with Jesse Jackson in June 1984. It also requested that INS begin processing those former political prisoners who had suffered the longest.

Meanwhile there began to appear in print invective from partially informed pundits who assailed delays, real and imaginary, in processing Cuban political prisoners. A July 18 op-ed piece in *The New York Times* by Michael A. Ledeen, assailed State for allegedly refusing to grant "visas" to seventeen political prisoners whom Castro had promised to Jacques Cousteau in appreciation for Cousteau's favorable references to him in a documentary film. According to Ledeen: "The . . . group of 17 is being held hostage by the State Department which insists that it will not grant asylum to Cuban political prisoners until Cuba agrees to take back approximately 2,000 criminals."[11]

This assertion turned the facts upside down. State had never placed any condition on accepting current political prisoners, such as the ones Castro had offered to Cousteau. In the case of the twenty-six who came with Jesse Jackson and in that of Montero Duque, the Department had battled for their admission. It used every opportunity to pressure Cuba to release political prisoners.

Ledeen was on stronger ground in asserting that seventy-five relatives of the twenty-six political prisoners who came with Jesse Jackson two years earlier were being denied admission to the United States. Without explanation, Ledeen blamed Attorney General Meese for this stonewalling. Ledeen quoted President Reagan as saying on June 14, "I would like to know if there's been any case where there's been a release and they haven't been admitted to the U.S." The president was quite correct in the strict sense of this assertion, including the words "where there's been a release."

The nub of the matter was that there were current political prisoners in jail in Cuba whom Castro refused to "release" until the United States agreed to accept them. Although the United States had accepted the twenty-six men with Jesse Jackson without processing—over the objections of INS and the Coordinator for Refugee Affairs—INS insisted on processing the prisoners offered to the Catholic bishops and Jacques Cousteau in Cuba to ensure that they were eligible for admission to the United States under U.S. law. This was a defensible proposition, but INS had failed to send personnel to do the processing, leaving these persons prisoners in their cells in Cuba.

On July 21, Secretary Shultz lunched with Armando Valladares, whose activism was beginning to affect even persons long willing to overlook Cuba's grim prisons. Valladares made a strong impression on Shultz, especially with respect to the *Plantados* still in jail in Cuba. Shultz reportedly told Valladares the United States planned to accept all *former* prisoners held more than eight years.

Meanwhile Representative Gus Yatron was calling for new hearings on human rights in Cuba. Knowing that the executive branch was likely to come in for criticism for not having moved current political prisoners in Cuba, State succeeded in having the hearings postponed until September in order to process Cuban prisoners.

On July 24, an interagency meeting chaired by Peter Rodman in the White House Situation Room approved State's recommendations. It dealt both with new sanctions and a humanitarian approach to the prisoner question. Elliott Abrams successfully utilized Secretary Shultz's new special interest in the *Plantados*. The session approved a decision to send INS inspectors to Cuba to process the prisoners and family members. State's proposal to halt the inflow of Cuban immigrants through Panama and elsewhere was approved, together with its plan for a small, prioritized refugee program to break the logjam on the former political prisoners without destroying U.S. leverage for restoring the Migration Agreement.

By July 29, someone leaked the outcome of the July 24 White House meeting to the *Miami Herald*, which referred to a "compromise" between State and INS on the prisoner issue and quoted Frank Calzon as saying it was "not enough." The leak in this case may have come from State's Bureau of Humanitarian Affairs, which was particularly close to the Cuban-Americans.

The new sanctions included better enforcement of the Cuba Embargo. With Mike Lane in a deputy assistant secretary slot in Treasury, Customs began checking more carefully the small charter aircraft which conducted almost all of the passenger traffic between Miami and Havana.

Next came restrictions on immigrant travel to the United States through third countries. On August 22, 1986, after consultations had been held with Florida Senator Paula Hawkins and influential Cuban-Americans, acting White House press spokesman Charles Redman announced Presidential Proclamation No. 5517 called "Suspension of Cuban Immigration," limiting it to immediate relatives of U.S. citizens or those preference immigrants who could demonstrate they had left Cuba prior to the date of proclamation.[12]

After June 1985, Cubans could no longer be processed for preference immigrant visas in the U.S. Interests Section in Havana. That is why the Cuban government had been directing them to Panama. The new proclamation meant

Cubans would henceforth derive no advantage by going to a third country. The effect was to deprive the Cuban government, as well as unscrupulous officials in third countries, of a significant source of convertible currency.[13] Together with the Proclamation of October 4, 1985, restricting Cuban official travel and the stricter enforcement of the embargo, this measure put Cuba under greater pressure to restore the Migration Agreement.

Despite the prior consultations with Cuban-Americans, they were not pleased with the travel restrictions. In a meeting with Elliott Abrams on September 11, Mas and a South Florida group criticized the new proclamation. To my astonishment, Abrams agreed with Mas, saying: "We goofed." Abrams was being tugged two ways by his anti-Communist views. He did not wish to give in to Havana on the Migration Agreement, but his heart was with Mas and Calzon, who could not be tough enough on Havana, except when it came to bringing Cubans to the United States.

Havana's representatives sometimes hinted that the United States and Cuba were not as far apart as it appeared. On August 25, René Mujíca, acting chief of the Cuban Interests Section, told me the Cubans had been just as "frustrated" as we by the results of the Mexico City migration talks. He thought the door was not closed.

Upon his return from Havana, Ramón Sánchez-Parodi told *Los Angeles Times* correspondent Don Shannon that the United States and Cuba agreed in principle on bilateral issues (i.e., the ones like migration, radio interference, etc.). Shannon apparently failed to ask Sánchez-Parodi why the Migration Agreement had not been restored if that were the case.

EL DÍA DE LA LIBERTAD—FREE AT LAST

The administration was finally in position to deliver belated redress on the political prisoner issue. A senior INS inspector, Perry Steele, supported by skilled Department of State legal, consular, and refugee specialists, was dispatched to the U.S. Interests Section in Havana, to interview 111 current political prisoners and family members for admission to the United States.[14]

Fidel Castro at once threw yet another hook. He insisted that the United States take *all* persons on the list, or else no one would be released. This would deprive the U.S. government, specifically INS, of the right to decide who would enter the United States as a bonafide refugee. The majority of persons on the list had been inserted there by the Cubans—not the American Catholic bishops, as commonly assumed. Most of them, as Steele later reported after the interviews, had been soldiers in Batista's army. Some had committed offenses which might conceivably have disqualified them from consideration as refugees. Steele and the State experts recognized the long, brutal incarceration these persons had suffered and were liberal in deciding acceptability of the prisoners. After careful review of their deeds, none was rejected.

On September 14, a delegation from Washington flew to Miami to arrange an airport arrival ceremony much like that for Jesse Jackson's group of prisoners twenty-seven months before, except that it would be warmer because of the enthusiastic Cuban-Americans.

September 15 was "El día de la libertad" (Freedom Day) for 110 souls[15] who had suffered so long. They arrived at 6:30 A.M. on an Eastern aircraft jet leased by the ABC Charter Company. (Castro did not insist on flying them on a Cubana plane into Miami.) The liberated prisoners—almost all aged, infirm, bewildered, and largely drained of emotion—were greeted by Ricardo Montero Duque, who had been welcomed only three months before at Homestead Air Force Base. Jorge Mas Canosa, Jeb Bush, and State and INS officials from Miami and Washington stood in line. Success had many fathers.

Elliott Abrams and I were most struck by a few youngsters in the group. The older people could only spend the twilight of their lives in tranquility, but for these children romping through the airport it would mean growing up free.

On the morrow of Freedom Day the press was full of quotations from government officials. The *Washington Post* cited Secretary Shultz as saying that the refugees were an exception and not a change in policy. *New York Times* Miami correspondent Jon Nordheimer quoted me that the U.S. government would now take in prisoners more expeditiously if Castro would release them.[16] Jorge Mas was quoted as crediting President Reagan for having shaken up policy by saying at a news conference that he would make any effort to help former prisoners. (If the President played any role, I was not aware of it, but he did favor taking prisoners released by the Cubans.) Elliott Abrams was cited as saying we hoped to bring out prisoners in larger numbers. Craig Raynsford was quoted as saying INS was "fairly confident" the refugees were who their reports said they were.[17]

On September 18, the error of January 1982 was belatedly corrected when INS approved the travel of Andrés Rodríguez Hernández, the young stowaway the U.S. government had returned to prison in Cuba.

Elliott Abrams on September 24, addressing the Human Rights Subcommittee of the House Foreign Affairs Committee, acknowledged administration responsibility for not processing the prisoners more expeditiously. The session was conspicuous for attacks on the administration's policy on Cuban political prisoners. Although Abrams prudently refrained from attributing the delay to INS, *The New York Times* nevertheless reported he had done so.[18] I called Tom Ferguson, Nelson's deputy, to assure him that Abrams had not singled out INS. Ferguson commented that Attorney General Meese had just asked him about it.

A SPOTLIGHT ON CUBA—ILLUMINATING THE DUNGEONS

Ricardo Bofill, whom the French had once talked out of seeking asylum in their Havana Embassy, took refuge there at the end of August.[19] On September 23, the French Embassy in Washington delivered a letter from Bofill to President Reagan. The official who did so left the impression that France would not force Bofill to leave sanctuary again. However, the French sought to induce him to leave voluntarily, denying him permission to communicate with his wife in the United States despite representations on her behalf.

Bofill's flight to the French Embassy presaged harder times for lonely human rights advocates in Cuba. On the same day as the House subcommittee discussed human rights in Cuba and criticized the Reagan administration, the Cubans arrested three persons close to Bofill. They also expelled foreign correspondents of AFP (Agence France Presse) and Reuters who had shown too much interest in the existence of a small group of dissenters in Havana. After Tomás Regalado of the *Miami Herald* called me with the news, I informed George Gedda of Associated Press, who asked for additional information at the noon press briefing in the Department of State. In this way, the news went out to the nation and was not limited to southern Florida.[20] In such cases, notoriety was normally helpful to those arrested.[21]

On September 27, I met with Bofill's wife, María Elena, at Regalado's home in Miami. Hilda Escalona and the wife of Elizardo Sánchez Santa Cruz, who had just been arrested in Cuba, were also present. The discussion convinced me it was necessary to devote more attention to the deterioration of human rights in Cuba. There remained a need to explain to concerned members of Congress why circumstances precluded processing all former political prisoners and family members in Cuba. Few were aware the Cubans had suggested in New York in 1984 that there might be thirty thousand such persons.

On September 29, Jim Michel and I urged Representative Henry Hyde, a conservative Republican from Illinois, not to push a resolution in Congress that would call on the U.S. government to take all such persons, regardless of Cuban action. We emphasized that a decision to take all would permit the Cuban government to decide the order in which these persons would travel to the United States and would deprive the United States of the right to set workable priorities consistent with its own values. Hyde was receptive to this approach.

Then, for the first time, we heard that Fidel Castro himself had expressed scorn for the Migration Agreement. On October 20, Kennedy staffer Greg Craig—who had visited Cuba to escort Román Conde Hernández, the last Bay of Pigs prisone, to the United States[22]—told Craig Raynsford and me of spending four hours with the Cuban president. Castro had mocked the Migration Agreement, saying he could understand why the United States wished to resume it. He would do nothing to help elect a Republican in 1988, Castro told Craig. Thus the old, misbegotten Cuban notion was resurrected that the Republicans would gain from an agreement for normal migration with Cuba.

On October 22, I tried to train a spotlight on Cuba with a blunt speech to the St. Louis World Affairs Council in which I mentioned Fidel Castro's crackdown on the Cuban population since the Third Party Congress in February, including his favorable reference to the Soviet practice of capital punishment for so-called economic crimes.[23] I cited Cuba's recent crackdown on the Cuban Committee on Human Rights—including arrests, the death of young Antonio Frías Sosa in police custody, and the prison death of attorney Aramis Taboada—who had earlier told a U.S. consular officer of defending persons sentenced to death on political grounds.

A sign of growing Cuban sensitivity on the subject of human rights violations came when it denied a visa to Laurence R. Birns of the Council on Hemispheric Affairs. On October 28, Birns divulged that he planned to travel to Cuba to look into human rights violations there. On November 4, he called me again to report the visa had been denied.

The Council on Hemispheric Affairs, a militant critic of administration policy, had not been conspicuously attentive to human rights in Cuba. Cuba rarely denied visas to leading figures or persons inclined to view it favorably. The denial to two U.S. congressmen who had wanted to look into narcotics trafficking in 1983 had been unusual. The denial to Birns suggested Cuba now felt the same sensitivity about human rights.

An Americas Watch news conference in New York discussed Cuban incarceration of five human rights activists and the expulsion of two foreign correspondents for reporting it. Havana, it was asserted, was holding nearly one hundred members of the Cuban Committee on Human Rights in prison.

Fara Ray described the prison death of Aramis Taboada, and Giselda Hidalgo Dolgicer told of the fourteen-month solitary confinement of her brother Ariel. Aryeh Neier commented that Cuba's crackdown on the Committee might be due to its "increasing visibility" in the international arena.[24]

The White House agreed to include Cuba in "human rights day" in December. Traditionally this had been the preserve of those concerned with the Soviet Union. Armando Valladares was featured with Yuri Orlov on December 10 and spoke on Cuban practices at a ceremony attended by President Reagan.

Human rights action against Cuba was taken for the first time in the United Nations in November. Ambassador Vernon Walters assailed arbitrary arrests and lack of freedom on the island. A resolution on Cuban human rights violations was introduced in the third committee of the UN General Assembly. Much of this was due to the work of the Cuban–American National Foundation. Cuba responded bitterly, but henceforth the spotlight would never go out on Cuban treatment of domestic dissent.

RADIO INTERFERENCE—FROM MOSCOW

A troublesome new form of radio interference cropped up late in 1986, ironically as part of the U.S.–Soviet rapprochement. Radio Moscow, broadcasting from Cuba, was causing new interference in the United States.

U.S. Information Agency Director Charles Wick, whose VOA broadcasts to the Soviet Union were still jammed, had been exploring with Soviet counterparts an idea whereby the jamming would stop and Radio Moscow could broadcast from Cuba to the United States. However, such Soviet broadcasting from Cuba in the past had resulted in harmful interference with AM broadcasting in the United States, a fact of which Wick may have been unaware. Cuba, still skittish about transmitting its own broadcasts to the United States, could easily hide behind Moscow on the issue. Meanwhile, the new form of interference provoked internal controversy in Washington, with Wick indignantly denying that he had contributed to the new problem.

CASTRO HITS THE ROOF

On December 9, claiming that a U.S. reconnaissance aircraft had again flown over Cuba the previous day, Havana escalated the war of nerves. Millions of Cubans had been taking part in military exercises aimed at a hypothetical U.S. invasion.[25] All that day and into the night thousands of

Cubans demonstrated in front of the U.S. Interests Section in the old embassy by the Caribbean.

On December 10, the demonstrations continued, making normal work in the interests section impossible. I called in René Mujíca, acting chief of the Cuban Interests Section, to express concern about the government-sponsored disruption. Nevertheless, the demonstrations continued on December 11.26 I called in Mujíca again at 4:30 P.M. and warned pointedly that we would study carefully these disruptions to see if they showed Cuba no longer wanted an official U.S. government office in Havana. Mujíca assured me that Cuba did. He meant, of course, that Cuba wanted to retain its own office in Washington. By 8:30 P.M. that evening, Mike Joyce, our acting principal officer in Havana, called to report that the crowd was finally receding outside the interests section.

But the Cubans had decided only to switch to a new form of harassment more prolonged and burdensome than noisy demonstrations. December 13 brought really bad news. Our principal officer in Havana was summoned by Vice Minister Alarcón and told that the U.S. Interests Section would be permitted no more cargo or pouch charter flights and that visas for visitors to the embassy would be harder to obtain.

The ban on cargo and charter flights was serious. Since its creation in 1977 the U.S. Interests Section had depended on these flights to carry on its normal range of activities and to supply its staff with goods unobtainable in Cuba. The cargo flights had been required for the upgrade of the interests section, including its communications, which had taken place after the signing of the Migration Agreement when the section faced a greatly expanded workload.

Use of the Cuban official airline, Cubana de Aviación, to supply the interests section was not a realistic option. In addition to security considerations, it would put a substantial dent in the embargo and open Miami to the Cuban carrier. Psychologically, it would be an admission of defeat.

The Cuban Interests Section in Washington had neither the same needs nor the same vulnerabilities. The Department of State responded by informing the Cubans that their couriers could no longer serve the interests section in Washington and the Cuban Mission to the United Nations in New York on the same run, a slap on the wrist by comparison with the Cuban measure.

Why had Castro decided to harass the U.S. Interests Section? Clearly he did not welcome the emphasis being placed on human rights violations. The economic crisis in Cuba was growing steadily and would become a good deal worse in 1987. The U.S. embargo had some, if minor, influence on this development. Cuba had complained about surveillance overflights before, with little impact. The Cubans might have wished to escalate the level of their protest.

The following January, when principal officer Curtis Kamman was leaving definitively, Ricardo Alarcón hinted at what might have been the chief cause of Castro's action. The U.S. Interests Section had long suffered bad communications with the Department of State. The break in communications at the time of the intervention in Grenada had only been the worst example of a recurring problem. During the 1985–86 technical upgrade of the interests section, communications capacity had been significantly enhanced, as the Cubans could see by looking at various antennae on the roof of the building.

Perhaps Fidel Castro did not like the new appearance of the roof. In January, a Cuban architect would officially complain about it on "aesthetic" grounds, although the Cubans were not known for their architectural punctilio. Perhaps they felt that our interests section would henceforth be a more effective "listening post" for the U.S. government. In any case, Fidel Castro hit the roof as 1986 came to an end. U.S.–Cuban relations had gone from bad to worse. But the nadir had not nearly been reached.

NOTES

1. *NYT*, March 10, 1986, I, 1:1. Correspondent William Schmidt reported that prisoners in Atlanta had been locked down for twenty-three hours per day since their major 1984 riot.

2. Gonzalez and Ronfeldt, *Castro, Cuba and the World*, p. 71. One of those dismissed from the Politburo was Ramiro Valdés, heretofore one of Fidel Castro's closest associates.

3. Ibid., p. xii and pp. 82ff. The authors note Castro read a "litany of ills that plague Cuba's mismanaged and malfunctioning economy" but remained fundamentally opposed to decentralization and other liberalizing reforms.

4. Translated by *Foreign Broadcast Information Service VI* (Latin America), December 4, 1986, pp. Q2–3. *Havana Television Service*, December 1, 1986.

5. *NYT*, April 21, 1986, I, 11:3.

6. Ibid., May 20, 1986, I, 5:1.

7. Denial of visas to Cuban officials brought the Department of State into conflict with such personalities as former President Carter, who wanted to bring the Cuban Minister of Health to a conference he was hosting in Atlanta, and on several occasions with the Latin American Studies Association, which was inviting Cuban counterparts. The conflict with the Bureau of Consular Affairs was over a letter which Secretary Shultz had written to the International Pen Club favoring a more liberal visa policy in general. But the Secretary of State did not mean to apply it to the Cubans under current circumstances.

8. *Miami Herald*, June 10, 1986, 16:1.

9. *NYT*, July 3, 1986, I, 1:5.

10. After departure of the U.S. delegation from Mexico City, the Cubans sent two bottles of rum to the U.S. Embassy for Kozak and me. Since we had already left, the Counselor of Embassy for Administrative Affairs took charge of the rum. It went with his personal effects when he was transferred unexpectedly to Pakistan. It was a fitting end to the Mexico City talks. Like the U.S. government, Kozak and I came up dry in Mexico.

11. *NYT*, July 18, 1986, I, 27:2.

12. *United States Code, Congressional and Administrative News*, 99th Congress, 2nd Sess., 1986 (St. Paul: West Publishing Co., 1987), Vol. 6, pp. A116–117.

13. General del Pino told Radio Marti in 1987: "Aircraft would come in from Panama with relatives and they would turn over $10,000 to the CIMEX corporation to buy the release of persons from Cuba." *General del Pino Speaks*, p. 45.

14. *NYT*, Aug. 11, 1986, I, 1:2.

15. One prisoner died in Cuba on his way to freedom.

16. *NYT*, Sept. 16, 1986, I, 1:3, 22:3, 22:4; Sept. 17, 1986, II, 10:1.

17. *Washington Post*, Sept. 16, 1986, 3a.

18. *NYT*, Sept. 25, 1986, I, 7:1.

19. Ibid., Aug. 31, 1986, I, 9:2.

20. Ibid., I, 7:1 and 5:1.

21. Emilio Rivero Caro, brother of a former Cuban Communist Party member who had just been arrested in Havana, told me he felt that only maximum publicity could be helpful now that arrests were being made in Cuba.

22. Conde Hernández arrived October 18. *NYT*, Oct. 29, 1986, I, 3:4.

23. Kenneth N. Skoug, Jr., *A Spotlight on Cuba* (Washington, DC: U.S. Department of State, Bureau of Public Affairs, Current Policy No. 881, October 1986).

24. *NYT*, Nov. 13, I, 19:1.

25. Ibid., Dec. 9, 1986, I, 4:6. One Cuban asked a member of the interests section: "They always say you are going to invade Cuba. When are you finally coming?"

26. Ibid., Dec. 12, 1986, I, 16:6. *The Times* reported 100,000 Cubans outside the interests section.

8

1987 (I)—The Squeeze

"Communism will require a Communist conscience, or there will be no communism, only societies of beasts like those we see in the United States," Fidel Castro declared in October 1986 to the Congress of the Union of Cuban Journalists.[1] It could never be equated with anything so crude, vulgar, and absurd as a "society of abundance." Two months later he told the Cuban National Assembly that "discouragement and defeatism" were the only things for which the minds and hearts of revolutionaries should have no room.[2]

As 1987 began, a socio-economic crisis was brewing in Cuba. Castro was resolved not to take the path of Soviet leader Gorbachev. His rectification and *perestroika,* a Soviet expert on Cuba later wrote, "progressed in diametrically opposite directions. The undeclared purpose of Castro's campaign was to forestall or ... eradicate any reformist ideas in Cuba prompted by the radical political and economic reforms in the USSR and Eastern Europe that could weaken Castro's grip on power."[3]

East Bloc trading partners were disinclined to increase their subsidy. Nor could Cuba count on Western Europe or Japan, which, although they might sympathize, were unready to put good money after bad, especially as Castro inveighed against the "unpayable foreign debt."

Castro's rectification campaign had little positive economic effect. On January 31, 1987, discussing construction problems, he admitted: "We are in a crisis, a growing crisis."[4] He did not fear for his own future, however.

The crisis to which he referred was the failure to create a new socialist man in Cuba.

Some in Washington blamed Cuba's distress on the United States and charged, "Whatever Castro may have been three decades ago, we've helped make him what he is today."[5] But Castro had forged his own path and had no doubts of his own rectitude and the rightness of his historical approach. Cuba's distress did not soften his stand toward the United States. Castro had decided he could live with Radio Marti and leave the Migration Agreement in suspension. Cuba focused on the activities of the U.S. Interests Section.

SQUEEZING THE YANKEE—TIGHTENING UP ON USINT

Cuba had found a lever. Alarcón's threat of December 14, 1986, was not an idle one. Cuba authorized no more air charters to carry the diplomatic pouch between Havana and Washington via Miami or to transport bulk cargo to the U.S. Interests Section (USINT), forcing it to devote more time to its subsistence.

The Department of State responded on January 9 by requiring the Cuban Interests Section in Washington to maintain all contacts with the executive branch of the U.S. government through the Coordinator for Cuban Affairs. To have been more effective, this would have had to include Congress, but State believed that some members of Congress would have objected to such action, thereby rendering the measure self-defeating.

Since Cuba denied that the United States had a right to supply flights, which had been used since the interests section was established in 1977, State researched the origin of the commitment. Bill Luers, president of the Metropolitan Art Museum in New York, had signed the agreement establishing the interests section when he was Acting Assistant Secretary of State for Inter-American Affairs in 1977. Luers now confirmed that he had specifically asked at that time for supply (support) flights along the model used to facilitate U.S. Embassy Moscow. However, no written document covering the flights had been signed by both parties.

On January 16 I read to Felipe Alvarez, acting head of the Cuban Interests Section, the Department's of State's report on the May 30, 1977 conversation on charter flights between Luers and Cuban Vice Foreign Minister Pelegrín Torras de la Luz. It bore out what Luers had told me, but it was an internal U.S. document. Alvarez could offer no rebuttal, but when Ramón Sánchez-Parodi returned from Cuba, he immediately contradicted the U.S. interpretation of the oral assurances made by Torras to Luers.

Diplomatic notes and modest countermeasures were not sufficient to cause the Cubans to relent. The only potentially effective countermeasure—hinting that the interests section might have to close—had to be used with subtlety, lest it be seen as a bluff.

Cuba set considerable store by its own interests section. Its main function had always been contact with Congress, the press, and sympathetic Americans. With the staff of the Cuban Mission to the United Nations confined since late 1982 to a radius of twenty-five miles from New York, Havana relied more heavily than before on the interests section. Sánchez-Parodi, with ten years on site, was an asset of singular value to his government. Cuba did not want to see this institution closed. Therefore, it had to gauge how much squeezing of the U.S. Interests Section Washington would tolerate. As with Mujíca the previous December, I told Alvarez in January that we were obliged to wonder if Cuba wished to see the two interests sections closed. However, we needed something concrete to get their attention.

Curtis Kamman, principal officer in the U.S. Interests Section, was leaving Havana early in his assignment—at his own request—to take a job in Washington, but the Cubans did not know this. Word of his transfer was out by January 21. It was important that Cuba be left to speculate on its meaning. As we hoped, the U.S. press, well aware of the Cuban squeeze on the interests section, put its own interpretation on the transfer and on the fact that State had named no one to replace Kamman. Some journalists linked his departure to Cuban pressure.[6]

On January 29, Fidel Castro summoned Kamman to assure him that Cuba did not want the U.S. Interests Section to close. He explained that his concern was inspired by my comments to Cuban representatives in Washington and by the way the U.S. government had handled Kamman's departure. Castro ascribed the restrictions on charter flights to new communications equipment we had put into the interests section. He knew charters had carried the equipment. We had gained Castro's attention. Yet this far from resolved the issue. The ban on flights continued.

In reality there was no disposition in Washington to close the U.S. Interests Section. The two sections were points of direct diplomatic contact. Contrary to many inaccurate notions, some held even in high places,[7] the United States and Cuba did not do business through third parties or intermediaries. This happened only when Cuba sought to use private citizens or other U.S. government officials as conduits to get around the Department of State. Business with the Cuban government was conducted directly, even though the de facto ties were not formal diplomatic relations.

There was also little (and belated) understanding in some quarters in State of the need to use the threat of closing the sections as a lever. This made coordination of resistance to the Cuban squeeze more cumbersome. Purely by chance, there was another tenuous—and delicate—lever to use against Cuba's ban on charter flights to the U.S. Interests Section. Cuba insisted on flying its large athletic team to the Pan American Games in Indianapolis by nonstop charters. They refused to stop for a U.S. Customs clearance in Fort Lauderdale, Florida. If they could not fly nonstop, they made clear to their would-be hosts in Indiana and on the U.S. Pan American Games Organizing Committee (PAX-I), that there would be no Cuban representation at the games.

This threat by Havana was certain to get attention. Cuba was the only real competition for the U.S. team. Without the Cubans, the games would be a U.S. romp. Without the prospect of international competition, few tickets would be sold, and television rights to the games would be diminished. Cuba therefore had the ears of PAX-I and official Indianapolis, which had a strong pecuniary interest in Cuban participation. Cuba also had an unexpected but forceful advocate near the top of the Department of State.

Even the specter of a Fidel Castro visit to Indianapolis did not bother Ed Derwinski, Counselor of the Department. It would be good for business, in his mind. On January 2, Derwinski called on Elliott Abrams to discuss the Cuban quest for nonstop charter flights between Havana and Indianapolis. He persuaded Abrams to agree that the PAX-I could assure the Cubans in principle on a charter flight but that conditions would have to be spelled out later. Although the formula left some room for creativity, Derwinski was determined that the Cuban charters must be permitted to fly.

On February 11, I had a vigorous exchange with Sánchez-Parodi while handing him a diplomatic note about the continuing Cuban ban on charters. He contended that Cuba had not ruled them out if we wanted to "discuss" the subject. Sánchez-Parodi explained that he had no need for access to the tarmac for pouch transfer, as did our interests section, because there were no direct flights from Latin America to Dulles Airport. The offer to "discuss" the ban meant that the United States could bargain anew for what it had been doing since 1977.

Cuba ignored the U.S. diplomatic note. Shipments intended for the interests section piled up in a U.S. government-leased warehouse in Miami. Although diplomatic couriers could transport small pouches by hand, large pouches were delayed. Cargo could not be moved at all.

On March 30, while presenting Sánchez-Parodi another note on the issue, I inquired why, if the Cubans were prepared to discuss the matter as they had said, they had not replied to our note of seven weeks earlier. Sánchez-Parodi claimed to see an ultimatum in the U.S. note and said the two sides were talking past each other.

Havana's April 3 response to the two U.S. notes offered no remedy. Ominously, it asserted that the interests section had engaged in unspecified intelligence activities. The Cubans reiterated that there was no basis for support flights. Only a passage expressing willingness to discuss the "reasonable" requirements of the U.S. Interests Section seemed potentially responsive.

Coincidentally, State's personnel system exacerbated the problem by "announcing" the Kamman vacancy on April 8 to all potential applicants for the position.[8] While this action was technically internal to the Foreign Service, word of the new opening might go beyond its ranks and alert Cuba to the fact that there was no U.S. intention to close the interests section despite the harassment. Amid these complications, ARA strove to keep an element of doubt about both the Indianapolis charters and the future of USINT.

Elliott Abrams and I called on Indiana Senators Richard Lugar and Dan Quayle on April 6 and 8, respectively. Both suggested a visit to Indianapolis to talk over the matter with appropriate authorities there. Ticket sales were going slowly. Quayle noted there was still talk in the PAX-I group of inviting Fidel Castro to attend and that a large delegation was preparing to visit Havana, where it might do precisely that. Abrams induced the PAX-I group to reduce its delegation to thirteen persons and to confirm it would not invite Castro. To bind the deal, a Department of State press release revealed Pax-I had stated it would not invite Castro to the games.

By April 9 the pouch situation in Havana had worsened. Cuba refused to allow shipment of large unclassified pouch bags, insisting they be sent as cargo through "normal" importation procedures. By April 13, there were sixteen pouches on hold in Miami.

On April 14, Abrams and I visited Indianapolis, where he addressed a none too friendly group about to leave for Cuba. The travelers, especially those cut from the delegation, knew who had spoiled their intended fun. Two days later they were told in Havana that Cuba would not participate if denied charter flights.

It was a foregone conclusion that the Cubans would get their charter flights to Indianapolis, where their presence was almost desperately welcome. It was equally clear that the Department of State would put a new principal officer into Havana, thus demonstrating that it was not planning to close the post. Some hope remained, however, that the Cubans could not yet be sure of either point and that progress could be made while uncertainty persisted. We had to make the element of doubt work on our behalf.

USINT, although it dealt directly with the Cuban Foreign Ministry, was subsumed to the Swiss Embassy in Havana. It was to the Swiss that the United States now turned about the pouch issue. Swiss Ambassador to Washington Claus Jacobi was briefed on the problem and provided with copies of prior diplomatic notes. The Swiss responded at once. Peter Hollenweger, Swiss Ambassador in Havana and a solid friend of the United States, sought an appointment with the Cuban Foreign Ministry to discuss the issue.

On April 17, 1987, one hour before Hollenweger was to be received, Acting Foreign Minister José Viera called in Mike Joyce, our acting principal officer in Havana, to reiterate that Cuba was prepared to discuss charter support flights. He offered no give on any flight already requested. Ambassador Hollenweger was then told by Viera that access to the tarmac in Havana could be permitted on a reciprocal basis. While Sánchez-Parodi had made clear that his section needed no such access in Washington, it was possible the Cubans were offering this as a way out of the impasse. The Department instructed USINT to draw up an aide memoire, which was then carefully vetted in Washington, to leave with the Foreign Ministry.

Meanwhile José Sorzano, assistant for Latin America in the National Security Council staff and a Cuban-American, presented his view that the only satisfactory result would be restoration of the *status quo ante* December 14. He argued that the Cubans did not want the U.S. Interests Section to close and would give in if the U.S. government were firm enough. Although I agreed with his reasoning, the decisions to allow Cuba charter flights to Indianapolis and to name a new principal officer in Havana meant that the United States was not going to seem that firm in the crunch. Still, appearances might count.

On April 29, I went to Havana to discuss the charter flight problem.[9] I was accompanied by Joan Donoghue of the Legal Office and Gene Scassa and Steve Nolan of the ARA executive office. As ARA's senior administrative officer, Scassa might be presumed to be looking at procedures for closing the post. Once in Havana we found the Cubans had been noncommittal in their meeting with Joyce on charters and tarmac access.

May 4 was a key day in the visit, when Vice Minister Alarcón, José Antonio Arbesu and Luis García Peraza of the Foreign Ministry lunched at the U.S. residence with Mike Joyce and our delegation. We sat at the same table where I had cautioned Alarcón and Arbesu in 1985 not to overreact once Radio Marti came on the air, but the room looked very different in

1987. Joyce, who was still living in his own separate quarters, had left that elegant edifice empty except for bare essentials. There was not a single picture on the wall and nothing to tip off the Cuban guests that the personnel system of the Department of State was even then selecting a new representative to occupy it in the near future.

I assured Alarcón we sought no "pretext" for closing the interests section but could not be indifferent to their denial of what was necessary to operate the post. In view of the facts, even this was going out on a limb. I also urged the Cubans to put an end to the suspension of the Migration Agreement, but got no response. Alarcón said only that there would be action on some refugee cases, which I presumed to mean the prisoners Castro had offered to Jacques Cousteau but who had been denied permission to leave in January. Alarcón did not respond to my statement that the United States was prepared to discuss improvements in relations as neighbors if the Cubans wanted.

On May 5, however, García invited me to call on Alarcón in the Foreign Ministry. Joyce, Donoghue, and Scassa also attended a session that lasted two hours and ended inconclusively. Alarcón proposed talks in Washington or in Havana to resolve problems of "the two interests sections." I said we wished first to resolve the tarmac and charter problems of the U.S. Interests Section. Alarcón responded that Cuba was willing to delink the two issues formally but held out for talks on problems affecting the Cuban Interests Section too. Finally he inquired, "What's next?" It was agreed that Cuba would first respond to Mike Joyce's aide memoire.

The presence of Alarcón, a senior Cuban official, in Washington would have been a gain for Cuba over an issue which, like the Mariel crisis, Havana had created. Had he been willing to discuss ending suspension of the Migration Agreement, it might have been worth it, but he had been unprepared to do so. I was therefore ready to return to Havana for further talks, if necessary.

On May 8, there was distressing news in the Department of State: a new principal officer for Havana had just been named. That same day, without identifying the individual, I tried to turn the event to some benefit—or as a minimum to cut our losses—by informing Sánchez-Parodi that the Department had decided to name a new principal officer for our interests section because of the positive results of my meeting with Ricardo Alarcón. Sánchez-Parodi had little to say. If he had received from Havana news about that conversation, he showed no sign of it. Certainly nothing I had said in Havana would have been very reassuring to the Cuban Interests Section, the grievances of which I had not been willing to link to the charters and tarmac access issue.

I put a better interpretation on the conversation with Alarcón than the facts warranted because it might conduce to a favorable end to the impasse if the Cubans, after the Swiss démarche, were looking for a graceful way out. Had I interpreted the results as disappointing, the news about a new principal officer would have produced scornful amusement in Havana. In any case, the news would have been out soon.

Differences now emerged with NSC staff aide Sorzano, who shared our will to make no concessions but seemed to suspect that I was bent on making some. At a "blue sky" session on May 11 at a rural Virginia retreat, Sorzano detected a conflict between my allegedly conciliatory conversation with the Cubans and a tougher line against Cuba that a policy review group had approved a few weeks earlier. The policy review group decision had opposed closing the U.S. Interests Section and called for unspecified "sanctions" which would supposedly force Cuba to back off. It sounded macho, but there were no new sanctions available other than those we were already trying to apply. No one had suggested a single specific measure which would help our beleaguered diplomatic post, deprived of pouch deliveries and supplies. Three days later Sorzano and George Vest, director general of the Foreign Service, were both criticizing me—the first for not being tough enough on Cuba and the other for "revealing" to Cuba that we were sending a new principal officer to Havana.

While this was transpiring, Don Shannon of the *Los Angeles Times*, having just spoken with Sánchez-Parodi, called to try to induce me to confirm that Kamman's transfer came about strictly because he was offered a new job and was not a sign of political concern. This was, of course, the truth, but it was not for me to confirm it. I expressed no comment. A diplomat has no obligation to proffer information that would undercut his country's position.

As a result of the fracas, responding to an angry NSC directive, State agreed to inform the Cubans that no new principal officer would *go* to Havana until the impasse was resolved and that there was still no decision on their charter flights to Indianapolis. This correction was less than met the eye. Our "sanction" was to inform Cuba that we would deny ourselves a potentially key man in Havana, not to hint that we were considering closing the post. To keep the post open, but leaderless, would be self-defeating. If the Cubans had wished, they could have accepted our self-inflicted wound and kept on squeezing.

But we had nevertheless achieved some positive mov small. Once our views were transmitted by Mike Joyc Antonio Arbesu complained of U.S. "pressure." But on Ju finally authorized two charter support flights. Our earlier hi the sections, linked to the decision not to send a new principal oⅠⅠⅠⅭⅭⅠ ɑ time—and the help of our Swiss friends—had seemingly worked. Although Cuba had not yet agreed to a regular program of flights, it was a start in the right direction. From then on, our tack could be different, building on the favorable trend.

On June 29 a cargo charter flight was permitted into Havana. Seven hours were spent in loading the aircraft in Miami and unloading it at José Martí Airport in Cuba. Cuban aircraft subsequently were permitted to fly Cuba's athletes to Indianapolis where, by all accounts, the large Cuban delegation provided staunch competition for the United States and achieved considerable publicity, most of it favorable (except for beating up some hecklers).

The squeeze on USINT charter flights and tarmac access was ending, but the Cubans would within a week find a new issue with which to assail the section. When it came to galling fire, they were never out of ammunition.

DEFENDING THE EMBARGO

The most serious challenge to the Cuba Embargo in the Reagan administration had been the Regan v. Wald decision upholding the authority of the U.S. government pursuant to the Trading with the Enemy Act to limit financial transactions covering travel to and in Cuba. In 1987, the same challenge arose in the form of draft legislation introduced in the House of Representatives by Barney Frank and Howard L. Berman to eliminate existing financial controls.

Although we had some knowledge of the Berman-Frank effort in January, I was surprised to learn late on March 23 of a move by Berman, whose Section 362 of the Export Enhancement Act would deny the president authority to regulate financial transactions with respect to Cuba. The bill had been vetted by several bureaus of State—including those for Economics and Business, Congressional Relations, and Counter-Terrorism—but the Inter-American Bureau had not been consulted. Economics and Business had posed no objection, although this was the very issue we had taken to the Supreme Court in Reagan's first term. Congressional Relations had not done its job as coordinator for the Department with respect to Congress. Representative Berman understandably thought he had State's acquiescence.

After a key phone call from Jim Michel to his contacts there, I went to Capitol Hill on March 24 for an ad hoc meeting with Berman and Morton Halperin in an alcove of the House Committee on Foreign Affairs committee room. I told them that it would have a seriously adverse effect on our policy toward Cuba for the same reasons as we had spelled out before the Supreme Court in Regan v. Wald. Moreover, Cuba's suspension of the Migration Agreement and denial of charter flights to our interests section in Havana made the proposal even less appropriate than it had been three years earlier.

Representative Berman offered some cosmetic adjustments which would not, however, have altered the effect of his proposal. He wanted to kill the restrictions. Representative Larry Smith of Florida joined the discussion. After learning of the proposal's impact on the Cuba Embargo, he voiced opposition.

I was asked to stand ready to testify before the committee, but Representative Gilman, drawing in part on points I presented, introduced his own amendment, which largely nullified Berman's proposal. Only an anodyne provision about exchange of information survived. Gilman's amendment was adopted. As we shook hands, Representative Berman remarked: "You can smile. You won."

The following day Elliott Abrams sent a handwritten message: "Dear Ken, you simply saved the day yesterday on Cuba—for the millionth time. Thanks for quick thinking *and* acting. Great work. Elliott." I was pleased to have his comments since I occasionally heard views of another nature.

It was also necessary to discourage well-meaning private initiatives aimed at making U.S. policy more conciliatory to Cuba. A persistent effort to influence U.S.–Cuban relations was made by Robert Matteson, a senior gentleman from St. Paul with government service in his background, who wished to conduct "photo diplomacy" on the model of the "ping-pong diplomacy" associated with the change in U.S.–Chinese relations in the Nixon administration. A collection of nineteenth-century photographs of Cuba by Matteson's grandfather earned him a visit there and fired his interest in U.S.–Cuban relations. Matteson drew on personal contacts with Deputy Secretary Whitehead, Under Secretary Armacost, and former Chief Justice Burger to keep his proposal afloat. However, "photo diplomacy" did not prosper.

A similar proposal, which surfaced in January 1987, was to stage a "Cuba Festival" in the Twin Cities. The University of Minnesota scheduled a lecture series on Cuba, including one by Ramón Sánchez-Parodi. There would be a Cuban jazz band. A Cuban baseball team was invited, and thought was given to pitting it against the Minnesota Twins. (I was a Twins fan, but the "New York Yankee rule" applied: we could not allow a professional sports team to do business with Cuba. The Cubans settled for the University of Minnesota Golden Gophers instead.) The events were to coincide. This "festival" was unmistakably intended to make a political statement. Although the Cuban baseball team was authorized to come to the Twin Cities, where it demolished the Gophers, the Department of State made clear it would not authorize a range of visas for a "Cuba Festival."

I took part in the lecture series at the University of Minnesota on May 27, 1987, during our efforts to get pouch and cargo flights to the U.S. Interests Section in Havana. My comments reflected the strain in bilateral relations, focusing on Cuba's socioeconomic crisis, its human rights violations, and its disinclination to negotiate seriously with the United States on nonideological, bilateral issues which we should have been able to solve as neighbors.[10]

Another challenge was from the Latin American Studies Association. On January 23, 1987, Professor Cole Blazier of the University of Pittsburgh, newly elected president of LASA, told me of his intention to lobby against the President's Proclamation of October 4, 1985, restricting Cuban official travel. I tried to convince Professor Blazier, as I did others promoting academic exchanges with Cuba, that resolution of the migration issue should precede such agreements. I asked that he and other American academicians make this point strongly to Cuban counterparts in order to build support in Cuba for an end to the suspension of the Migration Agreement.

There was value in academic exchanges, even though the Cubans would be selected by their government and under its control. Exchanges might build points of contact for the day when conditions in Cuba would be more open. They might even advance that day. This had to be weighed, however, against the costs of facilitating Cuba when it was refusing to carry out the terms of an agreement on migration it had freely signed with the United States.

THE LAUTENBERG BILL—ABANDON ALL HOPE

The most dangerous threat to the U.S. government's migration policy was that Congress would oblige the administration to issue preference immigrant visas to Cubans and to take all former political prisoners without a quid pro quo. This would have eliminated the last chance to make Cuba take back the Excludables.

In 1987, such a proposal was introduced by Senator Frank Lautenberg of New Jersey, the state with the second highest number of Cuban-Americans in the United States.[11] A Lautenberg staffer had called in December 1986 to inquire about the status of former political prisoners in Cuba. It was explained that the U.S. Interests Section lacked sufficient staff, absent Cuban implementation of the terms of the Migration Agreement, to process thirty thousand ex-prisoners and families or the twenty thousand persons who would be eligible for processing as preference immigrants annually. The staffer brushed these considerations aside, arguing that State should simply ask the Cubans to accept additional U.S. personnel in Havana to handle these tasks.

Although Representative Rodino had urged resumption of immigrant processing and Representative Bill Richardson was working separately for a political prisoner program that he said would help State with INS, the Lautenberg Bill was pressed in 1987 with a partisan zeal not associated with other congressional initiatives. In the meantime State's own Refugee Bureau had a new head, Jonathan Moore, who challenged current policy and came to urge a large refugee program for Cuba. Although ARA and the Legal Office worked to oppose the Lautenberg Bill in Congress, other views may have been conveyed to congressional contacts by the Refugee Bureau and the Bureau of Human Rights and Humanitarian Affairs, which also urged a large refugee program without regard to Mariel.

With Cuba showing no sign of yielding, our policy risked undercutting both from Congress and internally. The factor that lent special strength to forces in Congress and State demanding a new migration policy was support by the influential Cuban–American lobby. Unlike challengers to the embargo and restrictions on official Cuban travel, Cuban-Americans had great influence with the Reagan administration.

On April 28, on the Washington–Miami leg of my flight to Cuba to try to break the charters-tarmac access impasse, CANF's Washington representative Frank Calzon took the empty seat beside me. During our conversation Calzon quietly took credit for the Lautenberg Bill. Calzon was one of the most energetic and effective lobbyists in Washington. He had been a major proponent of Radio Marti and was an ally in defeating Representative Berman's bid to end licensing requirements for tourist travel to Cuba. But he could be a fierce opponent. Ironically, Calzon was to be separated from CANF at a meeting he attended that very day in Miami, but he and CANF continued to lobby for the Lautenberg Bill.

Some congressmen and staffers supported State's efforts to force Cuba to restore the Migration Agreement and to block or delay the Lautenberg

Bill. They pressed for a sense of Congress resolution calling on Cuba to restore the agreement. In view of the power of the Cuban–American lobby, especially in Florida and New Jersey, however, it was an uphill fight to stop the Lautenberg Bill. Efforts to hold Senators Graham and Chiles in line were unsuccessful. This suggests that by late 1987 the pressure of the Cuban–American lobby to reopen migration from Cuba unconditionally outweighed the counterpressure to expel the Mariel criminals, at least in those two states. After the summer congressional recess, Lautenberg's proposal went forward into the Appropriation Bill. Enactment seemed only a matter of time.

HUMAN RIGHTS AND WRONGS

World attention was first called to the plight of political prisoners and dissidents in Cuba in 1987. The spotlight of 1986 was now trained on Cuba in the UN Human Rights Commission in Geneva. In this undertaking the U.S. government enjoyed but lukewarm support from West European members and none from Latin American members of the Human Rights Commission.

The Reagan administration selected Bob Wallach (e. bob wallach, as he wrote it) to be the U.S. representative on the Human Rights Commission. He invited the now-celebrated ex-*Plantado* Armando Valladares to be a member of his delegation. This was audacious since Valladares spoke very little English.

Meanwhile, an incident in Dublin illustrated a prevalent European attitude towards human rights in Cuba. Cubana, the official Cuban carrier, flew to Prague via Dublin. On January 22, 1987, a young Cuban named Pedro Pablo Sosa requested asylum from Irish officials during the Dublin stopover. The Irish informed the U.S. Embassy and warned that unless it could immediately promise that the United States would accept Sosa, he would be sent on to Prague with the Cubana aircraft. The Irish refused to consider accepting Sosa even for an interim period unless such commitment was forthcoming. The embassy contacted the Consular Bureau of the Department of State, but permission to accept a would-be asylee required more time than the two hours the Irish allowed.

My office learned of this only after the action had been concluded—Sosa had been sent on to Prague and from there back to Havana. On January 31, Tomás Regalado subsequently reported that Sosa had been seen by his mother and was facing trial. Having embarrassed Cuba by his attempt to escape, his future was not bright.

On February 3, Irish Ambassador McKernan was called in by the Assistant Secretary of State for Europe, Roz Ridgeway, to discuss the Sosa case. I stressed the humanitarian considerations of the incident. McKernan had no apologies to make and insisted Ireland would do the same in future cases. Although he did not say so, Cubana landing rights were lucrative, and Dublin did not wish Cuban asylum cases to put the business at risk.

In Havana, Ricardo Bofill voluntarily left the French Embassy. His wife, trying to call him in Havana, found his phone disconnected. She hoped the U.S. delegation in Geneva would be able to use information about human rights violations that he had provided in his letters, which supplemented others smuggled out of Cuban prisons and communicated to U.S. representatives in Geneva. Bofill remained under great pressure from Cuban plainclothesmen.

In Geneva, the Europeans came around to support our position, after considerable stroking; enough other delegations did the same to make the issue close. Valladares and others with personal awareness of Cuban conditions argued the case persuasively to those open to argument. High-level démarches, including messages from the Secretary of State, were made in capitals of countries thought to be wavering.

The Cubans narrowly escaped censure in Geneva. On March 11, an Indian procedural resolution killing the U.S. motion was adopted by one vote, with Venezuela, Colombia, Argentina, and Peru voting in favor. The West Europeans, including Ireland, stood opposed.

The Latin Americans resisted our appeals. For them it was mainly a matter of solidarity with another Latin American country. This allegiance of race and culture that once had borne the name of *Hispanidad* enabled Latin American leaders to overlook inconvenient facts. The proclivity of Latin American foreign ministers to stand well to the left of their own governments and to make decisions in concert at international meetings may have proved decisive.

Cuba's victory was Pyrrhic. The debate in Geneva opened the Cuban system to world scrutiny. The spotlight on human rights violations in Cuba would not be extinguished. The United States would bring it up again, and the day would come when Cuba no longer had the votes to escape condemnation for its treatment of those "outside the revolution."

In his May 24, 1987 interview with a reporter for the French Communist newspaper *l'Humanité*, Fidel Castro condemned Valladares as "neither an invalid nor a poet" but conceded that "this campaign has hurt us." He assailed Ricardo Bofill as "a renegade encouraging a micro-fraction for years" whom Cuba "of course" had denied permission to leave.[12] Castro sought to counteract unfavorable world attention to human rights matters in Cuba by continuing a cautious dialogue with the Catholic Church, including U.S. churchmen, about political prisoners. His cultivation of the U.S. Catholic hierarchy seemed linked both to his quest for improved relations with the church and to his search for allies in the United States against U.S. policy.[13]

On June 3, Mike Joyce called from Havana to report that Cuba had offered 231 prisoners, as well as ex-prisoners and family members, to the U.S. Catholic Conference. The Cuban list contained the names of many persons who had been on no known roster of political prisoners. And it was expanded by Cuba.

On June 5, Father DiMarzio, who had just returned from Cuba where he represented the Catholic Conference, explained the Cuban proposal to an interagency group meeting chaired by Jonathan Moore. The meeting welcomed the news that Castro was willing to liberate more prisoners, but expressed caution about the insertion of 144 new names into the list. There were no guarantees that all of these persons would be found eligible for admission to the United States.

Subsequently the Cubans either clarified or adjusted their position on the prisoners, asserting that the *Plantados* on the list they had given Father DiMarzio could be taken only *after* all the other 348 persons whom they had selected. Again, the Cuban measure was take it or leave it, combining an apparent gesture on human rights with an effort to control processing of former political prisoners. It left the U.S. government with the dilemma of accepting everyone the Cubans wished to expel or of jeopardizing the freedom of everyone else on the list.

On August 20, a novel proposal was presented to Acting Secretary of State John Whitehead by Adrian DeWind, who was in line to become chairman of Americas Watch. DeWind spent thirty minutes with Whitehead and me, followed by another hour in my office, developing the idea of a "joint commission" between the United States and Cuba and of joint prison visits to jails in each country.

I found this proposal unpersuasive. The composition of the "joint commission" was one issue. Clearly the Cuban side would be selected by the Cuban government, which was the entity the Department of State was trying to bring under world scrutiny. Its representatives would participate in the joint visits and could intimidate persons in Cuba, who would be well aware that after the prison inspectors had come and gone they would still be at the mercy of the same system that had prevailed for nearly thirty years.

Another issue was the commission's mandate. The prime concern in Cuba was that persons were routinely incarcerated for the commission of acts which would either not be punishable at all in open society or which would be punished by much less severe sentences. The use of cruel and unusual punishment on prisoners would of course be a legitimate subject in either country, but the freedom of a prisoner to complain about it to visiting inspectors of his own nationality would be infinitely greater in the United States than in Cuba. Moreover, U.S. prisons could be inspected at any time by duly constituted outside authority in a system governed by the rule of law.

Cuban prisons, until that time, had been inspected by no outside authority. However, because of heavy international pressure generated at the outset largely by U.S. official representatives, there would for the first time be a chance for independent scrutiny. A U.S.–Cuban joint commission and joint inspections might merely have enabled Cuba to appear open while in reality limiting the damage that a window to the world could cause.

I drafted a letter to DeWind along those lines for Whitehead's signature. The draft had the vigorous support of Richard Schifter, the Assistant Secretary of State for Humanitarian Affairs. Whitehead signed the letter.

THE WATCH ON RHINE

The three-cornered relationship between Cuba, the United States, and Western Europe could be delicate. Europeans looked upon Cuba as a U.S. problem. Few shared American concerns about the security of the Western Hemisphere or the symbiotic Soviet–Cuban geopolitical approach. For Cuba, in dire economic straits and under criticism for human rights violations, Western Europe was a potential source of economic assistance and political understanding. Havana wished to have Europeans see events in the Americas in a more sympathetic light. It diligently cultivated Spain and France. In spring of 1987 the Cubans seized an opportunity to win friends in the most important West European state—the Federal Republic of Germany.

The Foreign Ministry in Bonn appeared interested in some kind of interchange with Cuba. How far it might lead was open. On June 26 and 27, the Friedrich Naumann Foundation presented a conference in Koenigswinter, across the Rhine from Bad Godesberg, on Cuba and Western Europe. The Naumann Foundation was linked to the Free Democratic Party whose leader, Hans-Dietrich Genscher, was foreign minister. The meeting offered a way for West German officials and intellectuals to get to know Cuba better.

Cuba sent to Koenigswinter two of its most skillful advocates, Vice Foreign Minister Ricardo Alarcón and Carlos Martínez Salsamendi, an adviser to Carlos Rafael Rodríguez. The West European participants were predominantly German with a sprinkling from the Netherlands and other countries. Government officials and academicians were prominent in attendance.

The Naumann Foundation invited me to join former Representative Michael Barnes at the conference. (Barnes missed the plane and the first day of the session.) I found myself virtually programmed to undercut Cuban efforts to portray themselves as victims of the United States.

Presumably hosts and Cubans alike hoped to avoid controversy at the conference, but it arose almost inevitably. A Dutch parliamentarian bluntly criticized Cuba for human rights violations. This led to a sharp Cuban riposte. I was called on to explain why the United States had introduced a resolution on this subject at the recent U.S. Human Rights Commission meeting in Geneva. Ricardo Alarcón then made a harsh rejoinder, *ad hominem*, questioning my presence as an outsider at the conference, although I had been invited. Radio Rebelde in Havana broadcast his personal attack the same day (June 26).

Michael Barnes arrived thereafter. Although as chairman of the Latin American Subcommittee of the House Foreign Affairs Committee he had been highly critical of the administration's Central American policy, he supported democracy in the region. Furthermore, American politicians seldom go abroad to criticize their own country. It was important that my rebuttal enjoy his support.

On June 27, after a chummy lunch with his German hosts, Alarcón sharply assailed the United States. The U.S. response was deliberately understated. Barnes endorsed my urging of Europeans to work for democracy and human rights in all of Latin America. Later I presented additional remarks in response to numerous audience questions about U.S. policy, setting out American principles under both Carter and Reagan and supporting democracy for Central America, including Nicaragua. I carefully rebutted Alarcón's points one by one.

Alarcón posed four rhetorical questions for me more politely than on the previous day. My suspicion that he did not really want answers was confirmed when the Cuban chairwoman announced time had expired before I could respond. With Barnes' support the meeting was extended, and I answered Alarcón.

As a former deputy director of the Office of German Affairs, I spoke German and gave press and radio interviews reflecting U.S. views on Cuba while in Koenigswinter. I felt as the conference ended that Cuba probably had not succeeded in augmenting its standing in Germany. I had not improved my relations with Ricardo Alarcón, however, and our parting was cool. We would next meet under very different circumstances in another foreign country.

THE GREAT SPY CAPER—DIRTY PICTURES ON CUBAN TV

During our February 1985 meeting, President Castro alluded enigmatically to unacceptable behavior by our interests section in Havana. The Cuban diplomatic note of April 3, 1987 referred to "intelligence activities" conducted by the section. In July, Cuba clarified this mystery.

July 6 began well. In the morning Sánchez-Parodi called on me, most unusually at his own request, on a minor matter. That resolved, he wanted to talk. We addressed the matter of what Fidel Castro had meant in talking with Father DiMarzio of the Catholic Conference. DiMarzio had belatedly mentioned that Castro said something about wanting to discuss the Mariel issue.[14] Sánchez-Parodi could not elaborate, but he seemed receptive to my idea of a small, very confidential session to discuss restoration of the Migration Agreement. He offered to respond as quickly as possible.

This news kept me euphoric for several hours. I hoped a confidential meeting among Alarcón, Arbesu, Kozak, and me might save the day. Then Mike Joyce reported from Havana having been summoned to Alarcón, who complained of espionage by the U.S. Interests Section and warned that Cuban television would expose these activities that same night and thereafter. Sánchez-Parodi had surely known this. The effect was all the more stunning for his having let me infer we might be close to a solution to the migration issue.

When it came to delivering punishment, the Cubans were almost invariably at least as good as their word. Cuban television began to show nightly films of persons identified as staff members of, or temporary official visitors to, our interests section in Havana. These persons were revealed in compromising positions, placing or servicing intelligence drops for Cuban agents. The supposed Cuban agents were identified and told their stories. They had only pretended to carry out missions on behalf of interests section personnel. They had been doing so almost as long as the section had existed—nearly ten years.

When they put this exposé on television, the Cubans were aware that a key intelligence operative, Major Florentino Aspillaga, who knew many of the details of Cuban counterintelligence work, had just defected to the United States.[15] They had to assume that their secret had been disclosed.

It was now clear to what Fidel Castro was alluding in his comments to me in February 1985 about USINT and also obvious why he did not elaborate. The administration responded cautiously to Cuba's unfolding campaign. Although the Cuban Interests Section in Washington was loaded with intelligence officers, there was little point in trying to compete in exposés.

Cuba was careful not to expel even those members of our interests section currently in Havana who had been named and photographed in the exposé, but they could no longer perform useful service and were shortly withdrawn. In retaliation, the Department of State ordered the expulsion of two members of the Cuban Interests Section.

The Cubans showed their films to American and other Western visitors, but there was little impact in the United States. Americans were watching the Ollie North hearings. Havana went for overkill, showing or listing scores of American officials who had been in Cuba in the past ten years. Although not named as a spy, I saw a picture of myself on the steps of the interests section. Cuban television explained that Fidel Castro had given me a stern lecture about these activities. This was accompanied by a separate picture of Castro gesturing angrily. However, the angry Castro on the Cuban television screen was not the polite individual who had invited me for a chat in Santiago in 1985.

Cuban television explained that the role of their double agents was to provide disinformation to U.S. intelligence. This was true and helped persuade the U.S. government that Cuba would engage in massive disruptive broadcasting if we put Radio Marti on the air. (Yet it was quite feasible for Cuba to have done so in May 1985. In this case, the intelligence would have been correct.) A U.S. intelligence official passed along a taunt from a Cuban counterpart: "You underestimated us. We overestimated you."

On July 20, Joe Treaster of *The New York Times*, who had seen the Cuban television series, asked what it meant. I put the series in the context of the pressure Cuba had been exerting on USINT since the mass demonstrations of December 1986. I traced the root problem to Cuba's internal crisis and the rectification campaign that was persuading even insiders to flee the country.

Treaster's account of the spy caper appeared on July 26. He reported the Cuban government was charging that many American diplomats in Havana had been spying and plotting to assassinate Fidel Castro. A U.S. diplomatic note that the Cubans had made public protested these charges and denied any plans to harm Castro. "Cuba has given no conclusive evidence of spying by Americans or of attempts to kill Mr. Castro," Treaster wrote. But it had accused 151 American diplomats of some kinds of spying. American officials in Havana, he said, had been unwilling to discuss the espionage charges beyond those in the diplomatic note, which they conceded was authentic. Treaster pointed out that the United States in "its strikingly blunt diplomatic note" had asserted that "all officials and employees" of the Cuban diplomatic mission in Washington, "without exception," were members of the Cuban intelligence service.[16]

A NOTABLE DEFECTION

High-level defections from Cuba were relatively rare, but on May 28, a defection dealt Havana a shattering psychological blow. Brigadier General Rafael del Pino Díaz flew a Cessna aircraft to the Boca Chica Naval Air Station at Key West with his wife and three children. A second hero of the Bay of Pigs had arrived in Florida, following Colonel Montero Duque by just less than a year. However, Rafael del Pino had fought for Fidel Castro's side that day in 1961 and had shot down two aircraft.

Del Pino was a senior Ministry of Defense official and had been a living icon. The Cuban government at first maintained silence, but the Cuban press lost no time in branding him a psychiatric case.[17] Subsequently Havana demanded return of the Cessna, which had earlier been taken out of the United States by Cuba after its formal seizure by the U.S. government.[18]

Del Pino was a sensation in the United States, particularly in Miami, where it was forgiven, though not forgotten, that he fought on the wrong side at the Bay of Pigs. The press was eager to interview him. After three months, General del Pino met the press on August 26 in the Department of State. The location was a compromise designed to satisfy the many requests for an interview while meeting security requirements.

General del Pino held forth for two hours in a conference room in the Bureau of Inter-American Affairs. Although an interpreter was present and the ground rules called for questions to be presented in English and translated, some Hispanic journalists present began posing questions in Spanish. Non-Spanish speakers could not follow the questioning, and an element of control was lost.

Responding to one question, General del Pino let slip the verb *justiciar*. It nearly passed unnoticed. However, Mexican journalist Alfonso Chardy of the *Miami Herald* heard it and asked del Pino directly if he had meant to use it. *Justiciar* can mean *execute*. Chardy was asking directly if del Pino had intended to say that he had wanted to kill Fidel Castro. With the question so posed, del Pino took the macho way out and confirmed it.

Chardy reported that, according to del Pino, a small number of dissatisfied Cuban military officers had secretly organized an informal opposition group to undermine Fidel Castro. "The defector said that he had even considered on occasion assassinating the Cuban leader himself," Chardy wrote, adding that del Pino never followed through on his ideas. "If I had had the opportunity to kill Castro, I would have done it. . . . I just thought about it."[19]

This remark made in the Department of State led to two harshly worded Cuban protest notes in early September. The Department of State responded to both notes in strong language. On the second occasion, the acting chief of Cuban Interests Section, Manuel Davis, asserted that Cuba had evidence of a plot to kill Castro and that the Department of State could not escape responsibility for having provided a forum for General del Pino to make his alleged threat. Davis did not have to say that the offhand remark well fit Cuba's unsupported accusation that personnel assigned to the U.S. Interests Section in Havana had conspired to assassinate Cuba's head of state.

MORE RADIO INTERFERENCE FROM MOSCOW

Radio Moscow broadcasting from Cuba continued to interfere with domestic reception. USIA Director Wick said he had endorsed such broadcasting only if it did not interfere with U.S. stations, but it invariably did.

The United States formally protested interference caused by Cuban broadcasting of Radio Moscow on weekends. The Federal Communications Commission, which monitored the interference, was receiving complaints from several Florida stations. Despite the protest note, interference continued. The Cubans appeared emboldened by the Soviet connection, and the Soviets apparently based their action on their version of a previous discussion with Wick.

On July 10, Representative Mica of Florida suggested that a deal had been made to acquiesce in the broadcasting. Neither State, USIA, nor the FCC were of a mind to acquiesce in the broadcasting, but stopping it was not so easy.[20]

On July 23 I handed to Bienvenido Abierno, a Cuban Interests Section official—ironically, one being expelled for espionage—a diplomatic note on more radio interference detected on July 20 and 21. Without even reading the note, Abierno grumbled that he would forward it to Havana.

Cuba saw no reason to stop. On August 5, Arbesu told our new acting principal officer in Havana that the radio issue must be solved before there could be progress on migration. The solution, he said, must allow Cuba to broadcast to the entire United States. Thus Cuba's position seemed unchanged since Mexico City. The United States had nothing to offer and no effective way to stop the interference. The Cubans, arguing that the United States had offered to let Radio Moscow broadcast from their territory, kept it up.

On September 10, I handed Manuel Davis a note protesting Cuban radio interference detected on September 4. In response he asserted that the interference was related to Radio Marti programming and that Cuba would assert its own interests. He left the impression that Cuba would interfere with U.S. radio broadcasting at will.

THE U.S. POLICY CONSENSUS CRUMBLES

On the morning of June 12, Leo Cherne of the International Rescue Committee, accompanied by another IRC official and Frank Calzon, paid a call on Elliott Abrams. Abrams chatted briefly but was called out to see Secretary Shultz, leaving me to address Cherne's concern that the U.S. government was not processing all former political prisoners in Cuba.

I explained that, with limited resources in Havana, we were processing first those persons who had served longest. Even if we were to process all prisoners, priorities would be necessary, because we could not interview all at once. I noted that Havana could then establish its priorities and insist, as in the latest proposal to the Catholic Conference, that prisoners be taken by the United States in an order dictated by Cuba. I explained that our objective was to persuade Cuba to restore the Migration Agreement, which provided for a substantial refugee program and for essential supplementary employees in the U.S. Interests Section.

Cherne listened but did not say much. Evidently he rejected the explanation. His objective was to convince Elliott Abrams of the moral necessity of opening up the refugee program in Havana to all who wished to apply. Apparently Cherne did subsequently speak directly to Abrams and succeeded in persuading him. Perhaps he provided the last nudge for a move Abrams was already considering. Abrams, though troubled that few former political prisoners were being processed, had supported the policy. As long as he did, it would stand.

On June 24, he called a meeting to discuss refugee policy with Dick Schifter and the acting chief of the Refugee Bureau, Bob Funseth. There was no argument among them. Abrams accepted readily their thesis that ex-prisoners who had served shorter terms must be processed. He had gone off the reservation before the meeting. My arguments had no effect; having been assigned as Ambassador to Guatemala, Jim Michel was no longer around to help.

Funseth understood the new line also to comprise Cubans who had gone to third countries—whatever the time in prison they had served and whatever funds may have gone in the process to the Cubans, the Panamanians, or other third parties. It was to be open sesame.

Abrams justified his switch on the former prisoners as necessary to head off the Lautenberg Bill. However, the proposal would do so only in the sense of providing for ex-political prisoners by executive action what the senator wanted to mandate by law. Lautenberg also would have obliged the executive branch to resume processing preference immigrant visas.

In July, Abrams concurred on a response to Senator Lautenberg, drafted by Schifter, endorsing refugee processing at once for everyone who had been a political prisoner in Cuba. When I asked him why he was changing his mind, Abrams stated simply that the present policy had not worked.

By early August, on the basis of the proposed policy change, the Refugee Bureau produced a draft memorandum opening processing to all former political prisoners in Havana. Prospects for preserving the post–May 20, 1985 policy on Cuban migration now looked almost nonexistent.

Yet I felt it worth exploring whether Cuba might be interested in a confidential dialogue. On the morning of July 6, before Cuba began denouncing spies, Ramón Sánchez-Parodi had seemed responsive to the idea of a small, highly confidential session to resuscitate the Migration Agreement. I called him in on August 5 to hand him some diplomatic notes but also to see if he had news about the meeting. Sánchez-Parodi had no news.

I inquired about the proposal Castro supposedly made to Monsignor DiMarzio and the hope for an early reply to the idea of a chat. Sánchez-Parodi, recalling that he had been in Cuba, said he thought there was supposed to have been a Cuban response. I asked if he knew what the response was supposed to have been. Sánchez-Parodi did not know. But maybe the events of the past month, he suggested, had some effect—negative of course. When I asked Sánchez-Parodi if he would find out what was going on, he said he would try but couldn't promise because he was going on vacation in a few days. And go on vacation he did.

Meanwhile a memorandum went to Secretary Shultz signed by three assistant secretaries of state including Elliott Abrams, proposing a new, open-ended Cuban refugee program. A draft letter from George Shultz to

Attorney General Meese, informing him of this change, was attached for the Secretary of State's signature. Justice might not welcome such a change. But with the Lautenberg Bill, of which the Cubans were well aware, advancing in the Senate and with the old consensus in State shattered, it appeared that Cuba's patience would outlast that of the U.S. government.

THE SECRETARY OF STATE DECIDES

When the memorandum recommending a policy change in refugee processing went to the Secretary of State, there was no formal indication of a dissenting view in State. The three supporting bureaus had not requested a concurrence from the legal adviser. But the Secretary of State presumably was aware that another opinion existed. He would not agree easily to such a quantum change in direction. In particular, after his meeting with Valladares he was an advocate of liberating Cuban political prisoners. But he also recognized the distinction between persons currently serving long, onerous terms in Cuban prisons and the thirty thousand or more outcasts who had been prisoners but who were now at least outside jail.

George Shultz was not persuaded by the memorandum in front of him. He requested a legal opinion. This presented a final opportunity to argue the case for current policy. It fell to Deputy Legal Adviser Michael Kozak to present it. Kozak submitted his views in two parts—one concerning the legal ramifications of a change in policy, and the second from the standpoint of the chief negotiator of the Migration Agreement. Since my own chain of command to the Secretary of State ran through Abrams, I was estopped from endorsing Kozak's memorandum, with which I fully agreed.

It was essential that the Secretary of State understand what would be lost in terms of Cuba policy if he signed the letter presented for his signature. Kozak spelled out clearly what was at stake. The United States would not be able to restore the Migration Agreement if it presented to Cuba, unilaterally, the main benefits which Havana would otherwise enjoy only if it ended its suspension of the agreement.

The hard decision was for George Shultz. He read the defense of current policy and the implications of the proposal which had been put before him. He accepted Kozak's reasoning and rejected the proposal. Currently valid policy still stood.

Meanwhile, the Lautenberg Bill was moving forward in Congress. But what if the Cubans had had enough?

NOTES

1. Havana Television Service, October 27, 1986. Translated by *Foreign Broadcast Information Service*, VI (Latin America), October 30,1986, p. Q11. Castro said problems had arisen "because of our inability to be sufficiently revolutionary. . . . Anybody who makes a mistake deserves to be punished. . . .We must adopt measures against criminals, counterrevolutionaries and parasites."

2. Radio Reloj, Havana, December 26, 1986. Translated by *Foreign Broadcast Information Service*, VI (Latin America), January 2, 1987, p. Q8.

3. Pavlov, *Soviet–Cuban Alliance*, pp. 114ff. For Castro, Ambassador Pavlov comments scornfully, there was nothing wrong with one-quarter of the Cuban GNP being produced in the Soviet Union, where the population's living standards were lower than those in Cuba.

4. Havana Television, January 31, 1987. Translated by *Foreign Broadcast Information Service*, VI (Latin America), February 3, 1987, p. Q6.

5. *Washington Post*, April 30, 1987, p. 19. In an article captioned "Still Snubbing Castro," reporter Michael Kinsley quoted without challenge my assertion that Cuba was a tight dictatorship, with a declining standard of living, which encouraged revolution in Latin America, but he attributed the blame to the United States.

6. *NYT*, May 2, 1987, I, 1:6. *The Times* noted principal officer Kamman's "recall" had followed the large-scale Cuban demonstrations.

7. On March 21, 1988, I was dumbfounded to hear John Whitehead, Deputy Secretary of State, tell a visiting clergyman that the United States dealt with Cuba through third countries like the USSR. In truth virtually all communications went through the two interests sections. If the second-ranking official in the Department of State was unwitting, I wondered what others with a more limited access to the facts might think.

8. There were at once a number of candidates for the vacancy, one of whom called me on an insecure line from South America to say he was the "ideal" candidate, "heavy" on management experience. The officer was indeed heavy but was far from ideal.

9. I took the occasion presented by the Havana visit to raise with the Papal Nuncio, Monsignor Giulio Einaudi, human rights matters such as the situation of Ricardo Bofill, the young Cuban whom the Irish had denied asylum, and problems of the Catholic Church in Cuba.

10. Kenneth N. Skoug, Jr., *Cuba's Growing Crisis* (Washington, DC: U.S. Department of State, Bureau of Public Affairs, Current Policy No. 976, July 1987). Reprinted in *The World and I* (December 1987), pp. 139–147.

11. Renee Gernand, *The Cuban-Americans* (New York: Chelsea House, 1988), p. 15. She states that by 1980, presumably before the Mariel Boatlift, Hudson County, NJ, alone had 47,000 Cubans.

12. *L'Humanité,* May 25, 1987, pp. 16–17.

13. Professor Dominguez states that the Roman Catholic Church had long lobbied for an open door toward Cuban migration. Dominguez, "Cooperating with the Enemy?" pp. 86–87.

14. We never learned what Castro told DiMarzio about the Mariel Agreement. This may have been another case of Cuba's inexorable proclivity for passing messages through nonprofessional channels. On another occasion, a U.S. congressman who had seen Castro in Cuba was cross-examined by a Cuban diplomat back in Washington as to whether he had passed on Castro's message. The congressman, well briefed before he left, had heard nothing that he thought was new, but the Cubans apparently felt there was a "message." It would have been simpler to pass it in existing channels of communication.

15. *NYT.*, Aug. 10, 1987, I, 3:6. *The Times* did not connect Aspillaga to the Cuban television exposé.

16. Ibid., July 26, 1987. Treaster cited Radio Marti staffers as the source of its report on the defection of Aspillaga.

17. In response General del Pino told Radio Marti, "Why, if I have mental problems, was I sent on April 20 to the Soviet Union to coordinate with their military the annual draft of our pilots?" *General del Pino Speaks*, p. 1.

18. Although the return of a defector's aircraft was standard practice, General del Pino had defected in a Cessna that earlier had been seized by the U.S. government as property of a Cuban-controlled company. The Cubans had flown it out of the United States before physical possession could be taken.

19. *Miami Herald*, Aug. 27, 1987, 1:3.

20. USIA Director Wick wrote to Secretary Shultz to complain about State's inability to terminate the Cuban broadcast interference.

9

1987 (II)—Resolving Mariel, Definitively

The Lautenberg Bill passed into the Appropriations Bill for the Departments of Commerce, Justice, and State on September 23. While Cuban representatives in Washington did not discuss this draft legislation with the Department of State, it is reasonable to assume that they were acutely aware of the bill's progress in Congress.

What was Havana thinking? We did not know, of course, and signals remained mixed. On the positive side, Cuba agreed on September 3 to authorize a number of charter and cargo supply flights to the U.S. Interests Section. The anti-spy campaign was running out of steam. A new principal officer would soon arrive in a less beleaguered post.

Cuba was under pressure. The U.S. economic embargo on Cuba, as their diplomats had conceded, was tighter than ever. The Cuban economic-social crisis continued unabated as Castro stood by his rectification process and his work brigades. He was about to make what he would call his "happiest" trip to Moscow to press Gorbachev (successfully) for more aid, but he could not ignore favorable trends in U.S.–Soviet relations that ran counter to his own approach.

Pressure aside, Havana could consider whether there might be positive value in conciliation. It could live, however uneasily, with Radio Marti. If the impasse on the Migration Agreement could be broken, tension would be reduced. Still the Cubans played hardball. After learning Carlos Martínez Salsamendi, whom I had met in the disputatious session in Koenigswinter, had sent me regards, I responded through the interests section in Havana with a "personal message" on the value of direct intergovernmental contact. I said we were puzzled at receiving no response to my July 6 suggestion to Sánchez-Parodi for a confidential talk. Salsamendi was close to Carlos Rafael Rodríguez, thought to be a sober realist.

On September 16, Salsamendi's response arrived. He wanted access for Sánchez-Parodi to the "policy level" in the U.S. government, surrender of the U.S. base at Guantánamo, Cuba brought into the Angola talks, and so on. He said nothing about a confidential chat on migration.

Perhaps Havana was making a last effort to find an alternative means of dealing with the U.S. government than the one which ran through the Department of State. In early September, they sought to open a new channel via Madrid to the Justice Department. Justice wished to pursue this. State was convinced that this was another Cuban ploy to get around established channels of communications. It insisted that the link be through ARA or the U.S. Interests Section in Havana.[1]

On September 25, Craig Raynsford of INS called to remind me that the patience of Commissioner Alan Nelson had its limits. We should be returning Excludables to Cuba, Raynsford explained. I said State was doing everything feasible.

INDIAN SUMMER—CUBA AGREES TO A
CONFIDENTIAL CHAT

On September 28, the new principal officer in the U.S. Interests Section in Havana, John J. Taylor, reported a talk with Vice Foreign Minister Ricardo Alarcón in which the Cuban official who had lambasted me in Koenigswinter a few months earlier mentioned a number of matters he would be prepared to discuss with Michael Kozak "and anyone Kozak wants to bring along" to Havana. Alarcón's list read like Salsamendi's: Angola, Sánchez-Parodi's access problems in Washington, the return of General del Pino's Cessna aircraft, and so on. He was also willing to discuss radio interference and Radio Martí.

This was the first concrete evidence that the Cubans were prepared for a confidential talk, but the agenda and venue were unacceptable. We were not interested in Alarcón's grocery list on everything but meat. Moreover, it would be better to talk at a site where there would be little publicity.

Our reply through the interests section in Havana was that any talks must be in New York or on neutral ground. The agenda must be the same as in

Mexico. We wanted to disabuse Alarcón—again—of any thought he might still entertain that we would pay a bounty to regain a bargain once struck.

Before Cuba responded, State reminded two important players, CANF and INS, how determined it was to resolve the Mariel impasse. The Cuban–American National Foundation had proposed a luncheon to discuss its plan for a privately financed refugee program with State and INS. State was ready to discuss the idea, but it also wanted to explain U.S. foreign policy. The lunch, hosted by Joan Clark, Assistant Secretary for Consular Affairs, took place on October 5 at the Watergate Restaurant in Washington. In attendance for CANF were Jorge Mas Canosa, Francisco Hernández of the CANF "Exodus" Committee, and José Antonio Font, its new Washington representative. Deputy Commissioner Mark Everson and Craig Raynsford represented INS. For State, in addition to the hostess, it was Ambassador Newlin of Consular Affairs, Mike Kozak, and I.

Hernández explained CANF's concept of a privately financed refugee program for Cubans stranded in third countries. The foundation would handle the arrangements, in conjunction with INS. Under the plan, INS would process Cubans in third countries who had left Cuba *before* the President's Proclamation of August 22, 1986, but who were either ineligible as preference immigrants or would have to wait many years for their numbers to become current under U.S. immigration law. The plan was humanitarian and did not conflict with U.S. foreign policy objectives. The U.S. government representatives endorsed it in principle.

In turn, Kozak and I explained U.S. policy toward Cuba, emphasizing that restoration of the Migration Agreement would provide important benefits to Cuban-Americans as well as the only feasible way of returning the Excludables to Cuba. The CANF representatives expressed support for this objective. They volunteered to drop their advocacy of the Lautenberg Bill, although Hernández explained it was too late to cancel a large demonstration of Cuban-Americans for the bill planned for Congress on October 8. CANF agreed to help push the draft joint resolution in Congress for restoration of the Migration Agreement.

CANF sent a letter to State and INS confirming its understanding of U.S. government receptivity to the privately funded refugee program. (An agreement was worked out formally between CANF and INS and signed in 1988.) The CANF letter also confirmed the organization's support for U.S. Government efforts to restore the Migration Agreement. State thus had a pledge of cooperation on migration policy from the most important Cuban–American group. As for INS, it had direct fresh evidence of State's emphasis on doing what Commissioner Nelson said he wanted to do—return the Excludables to Cuba.

On October 4, a *New York Times* article by Joe Treaster hinted at a breakthrough. Captioned "U.S. Ties with Cuba in Warming Trend," the article asserted, "The icy relationship between the United States and Cuba has warmed slightly over the last few months, with both countries softening their positions and indicating a willingness for at least some compromise in hopes of reinstating a key immigration agreement." Treaster reported that I had met with senior Cuban officials in Havana in May and that a few weeks later "both sides made concessions on certain uses of chartered flights between the United States and Cuba." The United States put a new principal officer in its interests section in Havana. In August and September Cuba released thirty political prisoners and allowed them to come to the United States. "None of these developments is directly related to negotiations to restore the immigration agreement," Treaster acknowledged, but quoted me as saying, "I can't underscore enough the importance of reinstating that agreement."

A Cuban diplomat in Washington, according to Treaster, said, "We're interested in resuming the immigration agreement." However, the Cuban added the customary caveat that differences over Radio Marti had to be resolved first. Cuban officials acknowledged to Treaster that the suspension of the Migration Agreement had been an "angry reaction." "We are now more flexible in the way we see Radio Marti," the unidentified Cubans told Treaster. They added that the campaign against U.S. diplomats in the U.S. Interests Section in Havana was intended mainly to counter the impression of defections in Cuba itself.[2]

I was less optimistic than Treaster made it appear. Still, it was possible that the Cubans were telling him something they would not tell State directly. Treaster's article induced a Justice official to visit me October 6. I told him that I detected positive movement but made no forecasts. INS seemingly was still telling Justice that prospects to recover the Migration Agreement were poor.

On October 21, following further discussions between Alarcón and our interests section in Havana, the Department proposed a meeting in New York, Montreal, or Nassau to discuss restoration of the Mariel Agreement and radio matters, the same agenda as at Mexico City the previous year. On October 24, the interests section reported Alarcón had accepted the date of November 4 and selected Montreal as a site. He planned to bring Arbesu and Sánchez-Parodi. Thus, there finally had been achieved a long-sought tactical objective: a confidential meeting with Alarcón to discuss resumption of the Migration Agreement before the U.S. position could be undercut by a bill in Congress or by changed attitudes in the Department of State.

Consideration was given to including INS in the U.S. delegation, although there was no need for any substantive INS input. While we knew that INS officials might resent being excluded, our objective was precisely the one they had been urging throughout the entire Reagan administration. We had just assured INS at a high level that we were giving the issue the highest priority. There was, moreover, a risk that INS Commissioner Nelson, who had been unsatisfied with the 1984 agreement, might seek changes State deemed unattainable, such as a Cuban guarantee of no more Mariels. He might insist on a cabinet meeting, as he had before, to rehash the matter. This would have meant more delay and informing a wider circle of persons about the confidential chat.

Secrecy was deemed of overriding concern, and INS was not informed. The best hope of success would be to get Cuba to end the suspension of the agreement as it stood, without changing a word of it. We had no intention of opening up the substance or seeking emendations to a bargain that had been in the U.S. national interest when struck. We felt that the chemistry in the room would be most conducive to successful negotiations if limited strictly to the minimum number of players essential to resolve the impasse.

On October 26, a message was passed to Alarcón accepting the November 4 session in Montreal. The same day I left for London with Elliott Abrams for a third round of U.S.–Soviet consultations on the Caribbean Basin. The London bilaterals were held in a friendlier atmosphere than the previous sessions. The new Soviet delegation chief, Vice Foreign Minister Yuri I. Pavlov, was more in tune with the style of Mikhail Gorbachev than had been Vladimir Kazimirov, sent in the interim as ambassador to Angola. Atmospherics aside, however, there were no substantive results in London.

Pavlov, who states in error in his 1994 book that the London session took place in 1988, has Elliott Abrams recognizing that Cuba was not on the agenda of the "Soviet–American talks on the Central American conflict" but arguing that it would be difficult to discuss the situation in the region without touching on Cuba's involvement as a principal supporter of the Sandinistas and the FMLN. Pavlov states that he agreed to discuss this and Soviet–Cuban relations but on the condition that U.S. policy toward Cuba would be discussed as well. He urged that the U.S. relax the embargo on Cuba. Since Abrams' reply was negative, Pavlov states that the U.S. objective was to "induce changes in the Castro regime or strangle it economically, not lighten Moscow's burden of keeping it afloat."

When Abrams, according to Pavlov, stated that Moscow should use Cuba's economic dependence to pressure Castro into more responsible international behavior in keeping with Gorbachev's new political thinking, Pavlov says he replied—"not quite sincere(ly)"—that it was not Moscow's practice to attach political strings to its economic aid. He concedes that the USSR was actually doing all it could within the limits of its dwindling export resources to "keep Fidel Castro happy."[3]

In fact, the U.S.–Soviet talks never had an agreed agenda. At each session, the United States raised Cuba as a serious impediment to regional stability and to our bilateral relationship. It was the Soviets, especially Kazimirov, who argued that the talks were limited to Central America and struggled vainly to keep Cuba out. It is true that in 1987, and 1988, the U.S. side had no interest in alleviating the Soviet burden in Cuba. This not a concern of Washington. The United States delegation hoped (faintly) that the Soviets might come to see the high cost to them of maintaining an aggressive but nearly bankrupt ally.

In London, Abrams raised Cuban radio transmission of Radio Moscow programming with Pavlov, arguing that this was an impediment to improved U.S.–Soviet relations. Pavlov did not reply at the table but in a private session with Abrams said the Soviets would look into it. They did not wish it to become an issue between us, he added. Following this conversation, nevertheless, there was no observable change in Radio Moscow broadcasting from Cuba. Although nothing tangible resulted from this diplomatic round, its timing was fortuitous. We knew the Cubans would be concerned about London. These concerns gave us a small Soviet card to play in Montreal.

A GIANT STEP IN A SMALL ROOM—LETTING OTHERS HAVE YOUR WAY

We had insisted on an agenda limited to migration and radio interference in Montreal. That was the purpose of the session, and success in that was a *sine qua non* for discussing anything else. On the other hand, informality permitted discussion of other matters if we succeeded in the main objective. Chet Crocker, Assistant Secretary of State for African Affairs, wanted to bring Cuba into his conversations about Angola. Thus on November 2, the day before the U.S. team left for Montreal, Abrams and I met Crocker to discuss the Cuba–Angola angle. Crocker said Cuba should make a substantive contribution in order to be dealt into the game. He suggested I ask

Arbesu, who was involved in Angola on the Cuban side, why Cuba now wanted to participate in the talks.

On November 3, Kozak and I went to Montreal. Why had the Cubans decided to join us there? We hoped it was because Havana had decided that a change in policy would be in its interest. In part, our sanctions must have hurt. At least equally important, they may have realized that their reaction to the start of Radio Marti was costing them more in lost benefits than the radio itself. Moreover, Cuba knew that U.S.–Soviet relations were improving, even if Moscow was still stirring the Central American pot. Finally, we were the team with which Cuba had already reached an agreement, and we were still standing by our word on that accord.

We did not intend to paint Havana in the corner. The sanctions on travel due to suspension of the Migration Agreement were discrete from the embargo. The latter was addressed to Cuba's adversarial role in world affairs. Sanctions addressed to the suspension could be undone if the condition were removed which had given rise to them.

Our meeting began on what could have been a sour note. The Cubans' trip had been less prosaic than ours. They related having been placed under detention by INS in New York after their Iberia flight landed there rather than Montreal due to *force majeure*. They had been formally "expelled" from the United States and their names entered into the INS lookout book for illegal entry. They might have been in high dudgeon about this treatment but had decided to see the humorous aspect. This was auspicious. Alarcón did not bring up our last meeting along the Rhine. Neither did I. That water had already reached the North Sea.

Alarcón explained that he and Arbesu comprised Cuba's delegation. Sánchez-Parodi had come separately but would not attend working sessions. This was confirmation that the agenda was the one we wanted.

The meeting took place in Kozak's room. It was swift and decisive. Alarcón suggested we discuss radio matters and migration first, putting off the subjects Cuba would like to raise. We finessed this point. If we did not reach agreement on the first matters, there would be no discussion of the others. In fact, Alarcón continued, we could perhaps just discuss radio matters while restoring the Migration Agreement. This was also acceptable.

Alarcón, however, went on quickly to say that we would not be able to agree on a radio frequency in the United States for Cuba, which continued to insist on equal access to the U.S. public. This remained a matter of principle. This statement seemed to show little change in what Cuba had proposed in Mexico City. If restoration of the Migration Agreement still depended on satisfying Cuba's principles on radio broadcasting, we had come to rainy Montreal in vain.

After Alarcón's remarks, we sat for a while in silence. Then I said that it seemed strange that creative minds could not brainstorm a formula to break the impasse which each of us knew had bedeviled bilateral relations to the advantage of neither side since May 20, 1985. This remark elicited from the Cuban representatives the message they had come to tell us. Alarcón, with a faint smile, explained that he had given the *official* Cuban position. However, he added, he had a *personal* idea which did not yet enjoy the endorsement of the leadership of the Cuban government. His personal idea, he said, was simply to announce restoration of the Migration Agreement while agreeing to continue to discuss radio matters.

With this sentence from Alarcón we knew we had won.

This was in a few words the solution to the long struggle over the Migration Agreement. If diplomacy had been given the chance to avoid the shock of May 20, 1985, and if Cuba had reacted differently, the course of the bilateral relationship in the Reagan administration might have been modestly different.

Kozak and I were careful to conceal our elation. We responded that Alarcón's idea sounded like a good one. It was something we could recommend to our own government. Alarcón stressed that his idea would have to be approved by Fidel Castro, then in Moscow for what turned out to be one of the last celebrations of the Great October Revolution. We expressed confidence that Alarcón's powers of persuasion would have the same effect on Cuba's president as they had on us.

At the lunch break, Kozak expeditiously came up with language, which we then provided to the Cubans. On the morning of November 5, Alarcón came to our makeshift conference room, having simplified and improved Kozak's draft. His rewrite included only one unacceptable phrase about the "abnormal" situation in radio broadcasting "since 1985." We could not, of course, agree that the "abnormality" began in 1985. This sentence was expunged.

Alarcón was proposing a reinstatement of the Migration Agreement and a commitment to discuss radio questions later. Neither side devoted much time in Montreal to radio matters. We had precious little to offer (then or later). The Cubans, unwilling to bargain for a little, preferred to stand on principle and accept nothing in practice. That was obviously all right with us.

We suggested announcing the good news as soon as Havana notified Washington that Alarcón's "private" proposal had been endorsed by the Cuban government. But Alarcón perceived the need for a formal session and proposed we meet in Mexico City, a more convenient site for Cuba. Alarcón, however, seemed uncertain when the formal session might be held. Here was a potential risk. A long hiatus might beget harmful leaks. The prized bargain we almost had in our hands could slip between our fingers, especially if those who opposed an agreement or others who might want to levy new demands, were to learn the news. In reality, the facts leaked out after the Cubans briefed a Western diplomat in Havana. His report to his capital was circulated to third governments, including the United States.

We did not want to risk delay. Now was the time to play the Russian card. I had mentioned casually the Abrams–Pavlov meeting in London, of which I said I assumed Cuba was already fully informed. I did not say what we and the Russians had discussed, and the Cubans, following custom, did not betray any curiosity. We knew, however, that the notion we and the Russians were discussing Cuba would not be a matter of indifference to them.

I called attention to the upcoming December visit of Gorbachev to Washington. Kozak and I mused that it would be only too typical if the press concluded that Cuba had changed its mind on the Migration Agreement as a result of the U.S.–Soviet summit. Some would see this as confirmation that Cuba was a Soviet satellite.

This was a message which the Cubans quietly accepted. We gained the impression that they would recommend concluding the bargain well before the Soviet leader arrived in the United States. We had taken a giant step in a small room.

Having done so, we then discussed matters of interest to Cuba such as General del Pino's aircraft,[4] Cuban participation in the Angolan talks, and the activities of and limitations on the Cuban Interests Section. No decisions were taken on any of those subjects. I presented our views on Angola as Chet Crocker had asked: Progress was being made in the talks as presently constituted. What did Cuba believe it could contribute to them? Alarcón stated Cuba was willing to discuss withdrawal of Cuban troops if given a place at the table. While this assertion could mean much or little, it clearly would be welcome to Crocker.

At the conclusion of the second day there was a good-humored round of drinks. The three Cubans, including Sánchez-Parodi, gave no impression that they thought they had surrendered. Everyone seemed relieved that we had rolled a heavy stone out of our path. But when Kozak and I boarded our aircraft the following morning for Washington, we felt close to a significant achievement for the United States. Kozak commented that negotiating skill had not been needed. Our work had been done in advance.

ONE SHINING MOMENT—THE FAIR BARGAIN REGAINED

In Washington, on November 6, we notified Secretary Shultz, whose judgment had made the outcome possible, that our sanctions had been essential to this favorable result. We had paid the price of being considered unresponsive to humanitarian considerations, but now we could have the means to handle both immigration and refugee processing expeditiously and rationally under U.S. law.

On November 12, Alarcón called Kozak in a positive mood. It looked like a green light in Havana. We were anxious to advance lest any development occur to offset attainment of the objective.

Meanwhile an issue arose that potentially could have had a very adverse impact. Venezuela was releasing Orlando Bosch from prison. Bosch, a Cuban émigré physician, had engaged in terrorist activities in the United States and left the country in violation of parole. Havana held him responsible for the sabotage of a Cuban airliner in 1976 with loss of all on board. As a result Cuba had denounced the U.S.–Cuba anti-hijacking agreement of 1973.

Bosch, with some suspected collaborators, had been in jail in Venezuela for a number of years without having been brought to trial. A move by Venezuela to release him for lack of evidence in 1980 had brought a Cuban threat to do something very unpleasant to Venezuela. Shortly thereafter a Venezuelan aircraft was hijacked to Cuba. Whether for this or other reasons, the Herrera Campins government in Caracas held Bosch in jail indefinitely. But Bosch, as a man who dealt violently with Cuban targets, was a hero to many Cuban-Americans.[5]

On November 12, Jorge Mas called me from Miami to say Bosch was free to return to the United States, where he was, however, wanted on charge of parole violation. I told Mas that Bosch would have to apply for a U.S. visa at our embassy in Caracas. I explained that in view of his record he had no assurance of receiving one and would have to expect prison in the United States if he returned. Mas accepted this. He hoped to get Bosch to renounce terrorism and that account would be taken of his time in jail in Venezuela (nearly 10 years). Bosch's early arrival in the United States could complicate restoration of the Migration Agreement. Cuba had already denounced one bilateral agreement with the United States because of him.

On November 16, the U.S. government received a third government's report on Cuban reaction to the Montreal meeting. Since this report might be widely circulated within the U.S. bureaucracy and elsewhere, there was a danger of a leak. When Kozak apprised him by phone of the news, Alarcón promptly agreed to advance the date of the formal meeting to November 19.

On November 16, I informed José Sorzano of the National Security Council staff of the talks in Montreal. Sorzano seemed less than enchanted with the news and probed our agreed statement for hidden concessions to the Cubans. At a November 17 strategy session with Elliott Abrams, I raised for consideration the idea of taking an INS official in the delegation. Abrams and Kozak thought not, on the same grounds that had limited our team in Montreal. It was so decided. Once we were sure of Cuban agreement, State would immediately inform Justice and INS, members of Congress, and others with a legitimate interest in advance of the actual announcement, with the proviso that the announcement could be delayed if there was any objection.

Negotiations in Mexico City were conducted on November 19 at the official residence of U.S. Ambassador Pilliod. The Cubans accepted without change the language which Kozak drafted and Alarcón refined in Montreal. The only note of Cuban criticism was that we had been slow to begin implementation of the agreement in early 1985. They hoped we would move faster this time.

The Cubans arrived late to a session which began around twilight. To pass the time while we awaited them, our interpreter, Neil Seidenmann, played soft music on the residence piano. He was holding forth when Alarcón led his delegation into the residence. Seeing a fire in the hearth and listening to the tinkling piano, Alarcón sniffed, "I feel like dropping concessions all around." However, the Cuban concession had already been dropped in chilly Montreal without benefit of fire or music.

It was agreed that, unless objection was perceived in either capital, the announcement of the reinstatement in force of the Migration Agreement would be made in Washington and Havana the following day at noon Eastern Standard Time. I passed on the news that evening to Abrams by telephone.

On November 20, we met at the residence of the Cuban Ambassador. Before the announcement of restoration of the agreement could be made in either capital, however, Arbesu informed us that Miami TV Channel 4 had broken the news at 10:00 A.M., probably based on information provided to the Florida congressional delegation or to Cuban-Americans. It seemed not to matter.

Upon our notification the previous afternoon that the Migration Agreement was being restored to force, the Department of State had been informing interested parties of the fact. The Deputy Attorney General and the Commissioner of the Immigration and Naturalization Service were rightfully among the first to be informed. Neither perceived any problem with an announcement at noon on November 20. No one requested that the announcement be delayed.

Although principals in Justice did not inform the Bureau of Prisons, which was in charge of the detained Mariel Excludables, the Department of State at Kozak's request directly notified Michael Quinlan, Director of the Bureau, who voiced appreciation. First reports from Miami were that most Cuban-Americans there were "jubilant" at the prospect of having friends and relatives join them in the United States, whereas non-Hispanic whites and blacks were described as upset by the news.[6] The jubilation among Cuban-Americans was well warranted. But their mood was to change overnight.

The fair bargain had been regained, at long last, without concessions. Henceforth, there would be the Mariel Agreement and Radio Marti, too. The Cuban people could still hear the truth about their country and the world. Men and women who had suffered for their convictions would be coming to the United States. Felons who had abused their welcome in the United States and who had cost the American taxpayer millions of dollars annually would be going back to Cuba, in accordance with U.S. law and with Cuban consent. It was a result which ought to satisfy Congress and the American public, including the Cuban-Americans.

Or so we thought.

THE PRISON RIOTS—THE TUMULT
AND THE SHOUTING

On the morning of Sunday, November 22, came news that Cuban prisoners quartered in a minimum security facility, the Oakdale (Louisiana) Federal Alien Detention Center, had taken over and largely destroyed the installation and were holding a number of hostages, with the intent of avoiding being returned to Cuba. Oakdale was a facility operated jointly by INS and the Bureau of Prisons, both under the Department of Justice.[7] Opened in April 1986 as a minimum-security detention center for illegal aliens and candidates for political asylum, it became in November 1986 a long-term holding facility for Cubans.

That evening Jorge Mas called me to offer to do whatever possible to help at Oakdale. He said he knew the development would be of no service to the Cuban–American community.

On the following day, however, the situation took a turn for the worse when, more than seventy-two hours after the announcement of the restoration of the Migration Agreement, Excludables took over the maximum security Atlanta federal penitentiary, seizing hostages and burning the prison. The objective of the insurrection was clear. It had been known at least since 1983 that no Mariel criminal would willingly return to Cuba. The Excludables sent home in 1985 had gone quietly, if involuntarily. There had been no riots and no demonstrations by the Cuban–American community.

In 1986 no special precautions had been taken with the prisoners during the unsuccessful Mexico City round. The point was moot since the agreement had not been restored. Yet the record of disturbances in federal, state, and local facilities where the Mariel Excludables were detained after 1980 demonstrated a history of violence. Their reputation for being dangerous rested on a solid foundation, even if not everyone detained was a threat to society.[8]

Several thousand persons with a history of violence and access to weapons had been long detained. They had been hoping for release in the United States rather than return to Cuba and had been encouraged by the protracted suspension of the Migration Agreement. Some may have been encouraged to believe that their release was almost at hand. News of restoration of the agreement, with the implication that many might return after all to Cuba, was a shock and led to new prison violence.

Attorney General Meese stated that Justice had been given sufficient time to have taken action to prevent the prison outbreaks. No one had requested a short delay in order to deal with this contingency. In hindsight, it was clear that the prisoners ought to have been better secured at both installations, but it was not so evident how this could have been done in a short period of time. Given the volatility of the prisoners, an attempt to tighten security at Oakdale—where unarmed guards were in fact doubled before the takeover began—might only have touched off what the government hoped to avoid. And thirty-six hours notice proved insufficient to prevent the Atlanta takeover.

Cuban–American leaders such as Agustin A. Roman, auxiliary bishop of Miami, Armando Valladares, Jorge Mas Canosa, and Roberto Martin Pérez provided helpful mediation in resolving the prison takeovers peacefully.[9] There was widespread sympathy in the Cuban–American community for the rioters, whose actions were taken as evidence of the harsh nature of Cuban society and a condemnation of the U.S. government for agreeing to return them there.

Thus, the objective pursued so ardently throughout both terms of the Reagan administration, with the full support of Congressional and public opinion in the United States, was turned on its head—at least for many Cuban-Americans—by the violent reaction of persons who were in detention precisely because they were violent and who had trashed such institutions repeatedly in the past.

The bizarre situation produced the predictable range of suggestions for dealing with the Excludables. Senator John B. Breaux of Louisiana called for their transfer to some third country.[10] General Vernon Walters, then U.S. representative at the United Nations, suggested that Mexico be asked to accept them.[11] But these persons were welcome nowhere, last of all in Mexico.

Mayor Xavier Suarez of Miami and columnist George Will argued against returning the rioting prisoners to Cuba. They appeared to believe that the U.S. Government was obliged to abide by the wishes of the rioters once they had demonstrated a preference for life in the United States over return to Cuba. But their volition on this score had never been in doubt. Some Cuban-Americans, such as Dade County manager Sergio Pereira, the World Federation of Cuban Former Political Prisoners, and José Duarte Oropesa, commander of the Miami-based American Legion Howard F. Anderson Post No. 1 (Havana exile), expressed more positive views.[12] The Cuban–American National Foundation, having committed itself at the October 5 lunch to endorsing the U.S. government's quest to restore implementation of the Migration Agreement, judiciously refrained from joining in criticism arising in some sectors of the Cuban–American community.

For more than twenty years, scrupulously honest insight into and balanced interpretation of Cuba had come from Cuban exiles in the United States, Spain, and elsewhere. Some of these scholars, finding the Miami milieu too emotionally charged for coldly objective analysis, had performed a second "migration" to universities or organizations elsewhere in the United States, such as Harvard, Georgetown, Adelphi, Pittsburgh, Cincinnati, and the Rand Corporation. The contribution by Cuban exiles to an understanding of the Cuban reality was profound. Inevitably, however, the ostensible Cuban-American mood in 1988 seemed to reflect less the objectivity of these scholars than the suddenly pessimistic outlook of ordinarily well-informed persons who now took counsel in their fears.

Many Cuban-Americans were not only caustically critical of the agreement but outspokenly suspicious about the thrust of the administration. On December 11, *The Wall Street Journal* printed as "Notable and Quotable" a statement in the November issue of *News Cuba*, published by the Huber Matos organization, Cuba Independiente y Democrática. The quoted passage, which could have been written before or after the restoration of the Migration Agreement, stated, "The time is especially propitious for Fidel Castro to reactivate the immigration agreement because the gravity of the situation inside Cuba has no known precedents." It mentioned the growing penal population in Cuba, desertions from the armed forces, "10,000 (*sic*) fallen in Angola," and continued "The dictator should have good reason to be worried and to be completely in agreement with Kenneth N. Skoug, Jr. of the Office of Cuban Affairs of the Department of State, commenting on the immigration agreement: 'I can't underscore enough the importance of reinstating that agreement.' "[13]

The inference could be drawn from this sentence that a favor had been done to Fidel Castro by restoring an agreement whereby Cubans could enter the United States who would otherwise have had to remain in Cuba as opponents of the regime. The hardline element of the Cuban–American lobby seemed to want it both ways: The United States should not keep Cubans from coming to this country, but it should not help Castro by removing his enemies.

While it would be have been illogical to expect Cuban-Americans to welcome the repatriation of some of their countrymen, the Migration Agreement provided the means for large-scale immigration from Cuba to the United States and a special program for outcasts who might not qualify for immigrant visas. It seems likely that American public opinion would have questioned a large new influx of Cubans, as provided in the Lautenberg Bill, if the Cuban government were continuing to reject the return of the Excludables.

In an effort to assuage Cuban–American concerns, Acting Secretary of State Whitehead and Associate Attorney General Arnold Burns received on December 18 a group of seven Cuban-Americans under the nominal leadership of Auxiliary Bishop Román, who had helped quell the disturbances. The leading spokesman for the group was Eduardo Peñalver, an attorney who argued that no one should be returned to Cuba, whatever the cause. Burns explained that the U.S. government would return to Cuba the persons on the list of Excludables unless the review process planned by Justice showed in individual cases why it should not. The émigrés left, unsatisfied.

At the end of the year, one month after restoration of the Migration Agreement, Senator Lautenberg achieved adoption of his legislation as part of a continuing appropriation for the fiscal year 1988 as Title VII "Cuban Political Prisoners and Immigrants."[14] With unintended irony, Section 702 (a) began: "In light of the announcement of the Government of Cuba on

November 20, 1987, that it would reimplement immediately the agreement of December 14, 1984, establishing normal migration procedures between the United States and Cuba. . . ." This preamble, of course, rendered the remainder of the bill superfluous.

The act (Public Law 100–202) provided that State and INS would process refugee applications from "any Cuban national who was imprisoned for political reasons by the Government of Cuba on or after January 1, 1959, without regard to the duration of such imprisonment except as may be necessary to reassure the orderly process of available applicants." Also, notwithstanding Section 212 (f) and Section 243 (g) of the Immigration and Nationality Act, State must process "immigrant visa applications by nationals of Cuba located in third countries on the same basis as immigrant visa applications by nationals of other countries."

A casual reader might suppose Cuba's "announcement" on November 20, 1987, was unrelated to various pressures applied by the U.S. government since May 20, 1985 to force such action, or to a statement the same day by the U.S. government. Lautenberg's strictures, in the absence of "the Cuban announcement," would have removed the U.S. sanctions which helped cause it. By making the operative sections of the law contingent on Cuba having reimplemented its performance of the Migration Agreement, Congress appeared to make Cuban fulfillment of the agreement a condition for the act itself.

The act, by leaving a proviso for "orderly processing," also tacitly recognized that it would not be possible to process thirty thousand potential refugee applications at the same time and that some rational criteria would have to be established to ensure that justice was done—for example, that those who had waited for years could be processed expeditiously. Moreover, since the number of refugee admissions each year was worked out in consultation with Congress, it was unlikely that more than three or four thousand Cuban refugees would be permitted to enter the United States in any given year, whatever the strictures about their eligibility for processing in Cuba.

Had anyone, in fact, paid serious attention to the new piece of legislation, it could only have raised false expectations. The only action required by the act was processing of immigrant visa applications submitted by Cubans in *third countries*. It did not even require processing in Cuba. Under the Migration Agreement Cubans could be processed as immigrants in Cuba or in third countries alike. Yet it was fortunate this benediction was read after the congregation had left the church. Had it been read earlier, there would have been the devil to pay.

The United States had struck a bargain according to which:

—The criminals from the Mariel Boatlift of 1980 would be returned to Cuba in a lawful manner.

—Migration to the United States for Cubans in Cuba or in third countries would be normal.

—A special program would bring to the United States former political prisoners and their families in Cuba.

—The U.S. Interests Section in Havana could be enhanced in number in order to deal with the additional workload.

—Radio Marti could continue to broadcast to the people of Cuba.

—The United States and Cuba would discuss, without commitment, possibilities for Cuban broadcasting to the United States which would not interfere with U.S. stations.

Restoration of the Migration Agreement did not mean that the Reagan administration had gone soft on Cuba. It would go after Cuba again on human rights and other issues in 1988. But migration had been removed, at least for a time, as a serious issue between the two countries.

NOTES

1. Justice continued to plug for this channel into 1988.
2. *NYT*, October 4, 1987, I, 22:1.
3. Pavlov, *Soviet–Cuban Alliance*, pp. 205–207.
4. Alarcón asserted that del Pino's Cessna had been transferred to a Cuban company by American Airways Charter just *before* Treasury's blocking order against the latter. Operations of American Airways Charter, which flew between Miami and Havana, had been terminated in April 1982 when it was determined to be Cuban-controlled. *NYT*, April 10, 1982, 5:1 and April 17, 1982, 3:1.
5. Gernand states that in 1983 "citizens" in Miami proclaimed March 25 Orlando Bosch Day in honor of his planting a fatal bomb on a Cuban Airlines flight which killed 73 persons. *The Cuban-Americans*, p. 87.
6. *NYT*, Nov. 21, 1987, I, 1:1.
7. Dixon and Galan, *The Immigration and Naturalization Service*, p. 80.
8. After the riots ended, thousands of homemade machetes were found in the Atlanta penitentiary. *NYT*, Dec. 11, 1987, I, 28:3.
9. *NYT*, Nov. 27, 1987, II, 12:4, and Nov. 30, 1987, I, 1:1.
10. Ibid., Nov. 25, 1987, II, 6:1; Nov. 28, 1987, I, 1:4.

11. Ibid., Nov. 29, I, 54:3. Walters argued that it would be more difficult to criticize Cuba for human rights transgressions before the UN Human Rights Commission in 1988. NYT, Nov. 30, 1987, IV, 17:4. It had no such effect.

12. Duarte criticized Bishop Román for providing moral sanction for zealots. *Miami Herald*, Jan. 8, 1988, 15:3.

13. *Wall Street Journal*, Dec. 11, 1987, 24:4.

14. *United States Code, Congressional and Administrative News*, 100th Congress, 1st Sess., 1987 (St. Paul: West Publishing Co., 1988). Public Law 100–202 (H.J. Res. 395), December 22, 1987. Continuing Appropriations, Fiscal Year 1988, Title VII, Cuban Political Prisoners and Immigrants, Vol. 1, p. 101, stat. 1329–39 and 1329–40.

10

1988—*Ménage à Trois*

Migration had been "normalized," but 1988 would bear faint resemblance to 1985. Although relations improved, Fidel Castro offered no olive branch as he coped with Cuba's socioeconomic crisis, a deteriorating situation in Central America, and cooling relations with Moscow. Cuba armed and trained Noriega's forces in Panama and facilitated the northward flow of narcotics.

Washington pressed Cuba on human rights with unprecedented intensity. Although it was brokering an international agreement that included Cuban withdrawal from Angola, a process in which Cuba was permitted to participate, there were no new bilateral negotiations. Not having gone soft on Cuba, the administration could not afford even to look soft.

The third party in the relationship, the Cuban–American *comunidad,* watched developments with disenchantment. Some in Miami fanned suspicion that if the U.S. government had not already offered Cuba secret concessions, it was preparing to do so. In an election year, the administration, including George Bush, knew Florida had more electoral votes than Cuba.

THE MIGRATION AGREEMENT AND ITS CRITICS

The Migration Agreement was suspended no longer, but little movement of persons took place. Even in future years far fewer Cubans, either immigrants or refugees, would migrate than the negotiating partners had anticipated.[1]

The bargain for ending peacefully the prison disruptions obliged the Department of Justice to provide additional review procedures for persons it intended to "exclude." Some Cuban-Americans tried to exact commitments that no one would be returned, whatever the crime. There were reports on March 6 that Vice President Bush had promised Cuban exiles in Miami he would "deport" no Cubans in a Bush administration, but privately his office gave assurance that this did not rule out "exclusion," the term Justice used for Mariel criminals.[2]

It took many months before the first criminals returned to Cuba, and the number would lag far behind the total to which Havana agreed in December 1984. By the end of 1988 INS had reviewed 4,400 cases of persons potentially excludable, resulting in the release into U.S. society of nearly 2,500 detainees whose exclusion Justice had decided not to seek.[3]

Cuba showed no haste about moving former political prisoners to the United States, perhaps in part because Cuba was again in the dock at the annual spring meeting of the U.N. Human Rights Commission in Geneva. This time it faced a U.S. delegation headed by Armando Valladares. The numerically largest element of migration, processing of preference immigrants, also started slowly. As of March 31, no preference immigrants had left Cuba, and only about 4,600 immigrants traveled by September 30.[4]

Since both sides recognized the consequences of not holding an early review session on implementation of the Migration Agreement in 1985, they decided at Mexico City in November 1987 to hold the first review early in 1988. A U.S. team composed of Kozak, Raynsford, and me—with support from State's Visa Office, ARA/CCA, and the Legal Office—flew to Mexico City on January 11 to meet a Cuban delegation headed by Alarcón.

The talks were positive in tone but minimal in results. The Cubans backed away from an assertion that they could refuse an Excludable found to have AIDS, a theoretical issue since neither side was aware of anyone on the list suffering from this disease. They refused, however, to permit direct flights for transporting immigrants to the United States, apparently because they could earn more dollars by requiring them to traverse third countries.

While chatting informally, Alarcón and Arbesu forecast (correctly) that Cuba would boycott the Seoul Olympic Games despite the Soviet Union's decision to participate. It was a matter of "principle," they noted. Support of North Korea was a serious matter for Fidel Castro, who had recently visited Pyongyang to arrange weapons deliveries, some of which were destined for Panama. The Panama arms deal was another illustration that agreement on migration would not cause Fidel Castro to alter what he called "internationalism."

The review session did not expedite implementation of the agreement. Problems continued, such as a one hundred dollar charge applied by Cuba for medical examination of emigrants. In the U.S. view, they should have been payable in Cuban pesos by persons who would have to foresake virtually all of their assets anyway upon leaving Cuba. But Cuba wanted dollars.

On February 4, the Kastenmeier subcommittee of the House Judiciary Committee held hearings on the Oakdale and Atlanta prison takeovers. Mike Quinlan, head of the Bureau of Prisons, was present but was not asked to testify. His bureau had been told in late 1987 by an INS official that State could not end Cuba's suspension of the Migration Agreement. Associate Attorney General Burns stated that more advance notice from State would have permitted Justice to do a better job. Asked how it might have prevented the prison takeovers, he said Justice had teams that could have used persuasion on the inmates to control their reaction. The State official at the hearings, Kozak, did not attempt to rebut Justice. State did not believe a few days advance notice would have secured the prisons, if they were not already secure. More advance notice to Justice would have helped State avoid sharing the onus, but this was a bureaucratic consideration.

In view of Cuban–American fears and misrepresentations about the Migration Agreement, and conflicting concerns of other Americans that hordes of Cubans might now enter the United States,[5] I sought to clarify the situation in an address at the University of Virginia Law School in Charlottesville on March 9. The speech recalled the infeasiblity of detaining the Mariel criminals indefinitely and noted that a second option, their release into American society, had resulted in a high incidence of crime. The third alternative was to repatriate them, as provided by U.S. law. This we had pursued. The United States negotiated a fair solution in 1984 and later orchestrated a campaign to oblige Cuba to end its subsequent suspension of the agreement. After November 1987, the Mariel Excludables could be returned to Cuba and Cubans would henceforth be able to come to the United States—as immigrants or special refugees—under U.S. law. Also the U.S. government would process intending immigrants and refugees with a modest increase in staff at the U.S. Interests Section in Havana.

We would pursue better observance of human rights in Cuba but did not believe the returning Excludables would be punished by Cuba on political grounds, I said. Evidence was that, according to Cuban authorities, three-quarters of the 201 persons returned to Cuba in 1985 had been released. If the Migration Agreement could survive the vicissitudes of U.S.–Cuban relations and the temptation to link its implementation to other foreign policy objectives, it would remove migration from the agenda of contentious issues with Cuba and perhaps help resolve practical problems with important social and humanitarian benefits for hundreds of thousands of persons.[6]

However, the "vicissitudes" proved this conclusion too optimistic after 1993.

ALARMS AND EXCURSIONS

In early January, a prominent Cuban-American in the administration called me to complain of wild rumors in Miami, which he traced to remarks by a Department of State spokeswoman. However, it developed that the statements were being made by Cuban-Americans who had attended the December meeting with Acting Secretary Whitehead and Associate Attorney General Burns. Some were warning that the U.S. government was ready to transfer to Cuba any Cuban-American who violated U.S. law.

A statement attributed to INS Commissioner Alan Nelson at a February academic conference engendered additional alarm in Florida. The *Miami Herald* quoted Nelson as saying that "any Cuban who commits a crime, whether he is a resident or citizen of the U.S., and if the law so sees fit, can be deported." Nelson reportedly said, "There would be no purpose in sending 2,500 refugees now and not be able to deport anyone else in the future for committing crimes."[7] It seems doubtful that Nelson would have described these individuals as "refugees." He was only explaining that under U.S. immigration law, the government had always possessed the option of deporting immigrants, but the article contributed to fears in Miami that all were now suddenly at risk because of the Migration Agreement.

Other examples of Cuban–American unhappiness and concern were reported. Leaders of the Cuban community in Union City, NJ opposed the agreement.[8] A "Coalition to Support Cuban Detainees" was organized to try to prevent deportation of a handful of Cuban women to avoid separation from children they might have borne in the United States.[9] Bishop Román in Miami was quoted as saying the Department of Justice had not lived up to the spirit of the agreement for full and fair review of the case of each detainee intended for return to Cuba.[10] Yet Justice was releasing five times as many Cubans from detention as were freed in a comparable period before the prison riots.[11]

On February 16, Deputy Secretary Whitehead met with Richard Capen and Roberto Suarez of the *Miami Herald*. Suarez, editor of the Spanish edition of the *Herald*, had recently speculated in print about possible secret deals or sellouts that U.S. negotiators might have entered into with their Cuban counterparts for who-knows-what objectives. Whitehead was diffident in his reproval, saying mildly that baseless speculation would needlessly alarm people in Miami.

Such efforts to assuage suspicious Cuban-Americans were largely unsuccessful. The agreement to resume implementation of an accord that had been signed without lamentation in December 1984 was a hard-fought triumph of Washington over Havana. Yet many Miami Cubans acted the part of the loser. The improvement in bilateral relations with Cuba after the nadir of 1987 was inevitable and desirable in the wake of restoration of the Migration Agreement. This was not a conspiracy to jeopardize any other U.S. interest, but it was hard for some to see the distinction.

On May 1, two lengthy articles by Alfonso Chardy in the *Miami Herald* spoke of a new warmth in the bilateral relationship. Chardy's spin fed the fears of his worried Cuban–American readership.

One Chardy article was published under a banner headline: "Havana, Washington Edging Closer."[12] He asserted that the United States and Cuba were quietly laying the groundwork for a more stable relationship that could result in the renewal of diplomatic ties. He spun together complaints of Cuban exiles with hints that Washington was ready to move to a closer relationship with Cuba.

Chardy cited an April 6 letter from thirty Cuban exile organizations informing President Reagan that a "wide cross section of the Cuban–American community wishes to express to you our disappointment and concern over the direction of U.S. policy toward Cuba." Pragmatists were in ascendancy over ideologues, Chardy asserted. He stated that both U.S. and Cuban officials cited the November 20, 1987 restoration of the Migration Agreement as the "turning point in bilateral relations," an agreement he said U.S. officials believed would have been impossible had Castro been in a strong position vis-à-vis the Soviet Union.

Chardy attributed the thaw in part to John J. Taylor, the newly arrived principal officer in the U.S. Interests Section, whom he said had pleasantly surprised a group of administration critics from the Institute for Policy Studies by discussing favorably the restoration of diplomatic relations. Chardy cited a Cuban official as calling Taylor "the best American envoy to Cuba since Wayne Smith." Another favorable straw in the wind for Cuba, Chardy wrote, was designation of Michael Kozak, whom Havana highly regarded, as principal deputy to Elliott Abrams. Yet another sign of progress, Chardy wrote, was Cuban expectation that "the conservative director of the

State Department's Office of Cuban Affairs (referring to me) would soon be reassigned."

Chardy stated that the staunch defender of Cuban–American positions on the NSC staff, José Sorzano, had lost influence as "sensitive foreign policy initiatives generally (have) passed from the NSC back to the State Department." He hinted that the United States was considering granting a Cuban request made in Mexico City for a clear channel for broadcasting to the United States. "Were Washington to grant such a frequency, Cuban radio could be heard clearly through large portions of the U.S. on regular AM band, especially at night," he wrote. The United States had rejected this in 1986, Chardy stated (actually it rejected a request for *four* such channels in 1986), but Washington agreed to reopen the radio frequency issue in order to get Cuba to restore the migration agreement. Finally, Chardy asserted that Treasury had dropped a proposal to tighten restrictions on travel to Cuba.

It was not true that the Department of State was considering offering Cuba a clear channel for broadcasting to the United States, although the Cubans were still seeking one or more. Nor had there been any proposal to tighten travel restrictions which Treasury had dropped. But Chardy's readers could not know that. His article seemed to stoke their fears.

A second article on the so-called rapprochement was published under a headline quoting a Cuban Interests Section official (probably Sánchez-Parodi): "Reagan 'talked tough but acted softly.' "[13] In it, Chardy cited a February 29 letter from fifteen exiles to Vernon Walters, expressing disappointment over recent developments with respect to Cuba. Cuban-Americans had "hoped that Cuba would be a free country by the time President Reagan left office," the exiles complained. The thrust of Chardy's article was to show (correctly) that President Reagan's actual policy was from the outset much more restrained than the 1980 threat by candidate Reagan to blockade Cuba.

According to Chardy, "the thaw began in May (1987) when the State Department's director of Cuban affairs, Kenneth Skoug, secretly traveled to Havana and met with Castro." This was a sentence sure to inflame his Miami readership. I had not traveled "secretly" to Cuba in 1987 or any other time. I did not meet Castro in 1987, although I stood ready to see him if he had again invited me. I was identified in one Chardy article as the harbinger of détente, whereas in the other I was a "conservative" whose coming transfer would supposedly promote détente still more.

Chardy spun relentless administration critic Wayne Smith into both stories. In one article, Smith gave a characteristic view: "This administration has been nothing more than smoke and mirrors." In the other, Smith saluted the administration: "I applaud the Reagan Administration. There's a degree of greater pragmatism with respect to Cuba." For Chardy's clientele, Smith's "applause" was probably more alarming than his customary contumely.

Chardy's articles heightened suspicion in Miami that the Department of State was preparing to coddle Havana, if it had not already done so. Misperceptions in Miami were so general that I was only mildly surprised to hear on May 11 from Armando Valladares, who had been the official U.S. representative at the UN Human Rights Commission session in Geneva, that he had taken part in a march by various Cuban–American groups in Miami to protest U.S. policy toward Cuba.

Miami was particularly upset by the U.S. tour of the Tropicana Revue of Havana, a colorful nightclub troupe dating to pre-Castro days. It was still a tourist attraction, although in Cuba it also served the agit-prop mechanism. The Tropicana included anti-Western numbers in its repertoire as standard fare in Havana under Castro[14] but presumably was discreet enough to drop them while touring the United States.

The *Miami Herald*, under a banner headline of "Cuban troupe granted visas for shows in U.S.," carried an April 30 story that the Department of State had given the Tropicana Revue a visa after having "adamantly" opposed one earlier in the year. This was not true: The Tropicana would have been refused visas in 1987, but the President's proclamation on Cuban official travel had been more liberally interpreted since restoration of the Migration Agreement. The article quoted Paul Trautman, Manhattan-based promoter, as expecting to invest "at least $300,000" in the enterprise.[15] However, the Tropicana tour turned out to be anything but a success for all concerned. It continued well beyond the time authorized, aided by some of the same administrative snafus that had plagued State-INS efforts to expel Havana Mayor Fernández Mell six years earlier. Ultimately the troupe narrowly missed being stranded in Miami, out of funds.

On May 13, I told the Florida Economics Club in Tallahassee what we were doing and not doing with Cuba. While this was primarily a north Florida businessmen's forum, publication of the text by the Department of State would enable its use more generally. Whereas the talk to Virginia law students had been intended to show the value of the Migration Agreement, the Florida remarks were designed with Cuban-Americans in mind and to put the agreement into the broader context: Relations had improved but were strictly limited by differences of principle with Fidel Castro.

The speech reviewed the Migration Agreement and radio talks with Cuba in February 1988 and mentioned talks with Cuban officials about their withdrawal from Angola. We had agreed to admit some cultural delegations, I said, and envisioned some cooperation to preclude a Chernobyl-type nuclear accident around Cienfuegos, Cuba, where the Soviets and Cubans were building the first of two planned nuclear reactors at Juragua. Although relations were thus "warmer" than one year before, basic policy toward Cuba was unchanged. We pressed Havana on human rights. We broadcast the truth on Radio Marti. Contentious relations seemed foreordained to persist. For example, Cuba sought to exacerbate problems between the United States and Panama and tried to persuade Third World countries to reject foreign debt as "illegal, immoral, and unpayable."

We would discuss bilateral issues such as migration, radio interference, and safety of life at sea, but to speak of a warming trend was unwarranted, I said. Fidel Castro still coveted the role of firm and unyielding adversary, a role incompatible with any fundamental improvement in U.S.–Cuban relations.[16]

Fears of a basic change in U.S. policy toward Cuba in the last year of the Reagan administration were vastly overblown. State contemplated no such change, nor would one have been approved by the administration.[17]

It was regrettable to say things which, although accurate, under other circumstances would have been left unsaid. The nervous reaction in Miami to even a slight rebound in U.S.–Cuban relations required it. The Cuban-Americans had become a formidable interest group, whose fears, however irrational, had to be taken into account. Some even forecast that Cuban–American disquiet would cost the Republicans Florida's electoral votes in November 1988, but this did not happen.

RADIO BROADCASTING AND INTERFERENCE TALKS

Alarcón's "private idea" had been to restore the Migration Agreement at once and continue talking about radios. Now that the agreement was no longer suspended, we were obliged to discuss how Cuba might broadcast to the United States without interfering with the domestic AM frequency band. State kept in mind that some Cuban-Americans would be on the lookout for any concessions in such talks as a "payoff" for restoration of the Migration Agreement.

Kozak and I met in Mexico City on February 8 with Alarcón and Arbesu. The key member of our support team was Bill Jahn of State's Communications Bureau, who had attended the 1986 Mexico City talks and who regularly met Cuban counterparts while representing the United States in International Telecommunications Union meetings.

Alarcón was assisted by Cuban communications expert Carlos Martínez Albuerne, who returned to his 1986 proposal to cover the entire United States on the medium waveband. The Cubans did not want to relent on their "principles," which in this case were to broadcast to as large a portion of the United States as Washington could reach in Cuba. Their proposition, however, was as non-negotiable in 1988 as it had been two years before.

Since Alarcón was suffering from a severe headache, formal conversations were brief. This permitted a discussion on the margin with Arbesu, who as deputy chief of the America Department of the Communist Party was particularly well informed about developments in the Western Hemisphere. Arbesu probed how much provocation the United States would tolerate from General Noriega in Panama. Cuba was supplying weapons to Panama on Panamanian airplanes and covertly giving sabotage and intelligence training.[18] It might have been indirectly implicated in various shooting incidents against U.S. forces there. On the other hand, Cuba had a vested interest in maintaining a neutralist, anti-American regime there until 2000, the year when under terms of the U.S.–Panama Treaty, control of the Canal would be taken out of American hands. Thus Havana did not want Noriega to provoke U.S. intervention.

Arbesu suggested that Noriega, by demanding the departure of the U.S. Southern Military Command (Southcom) from Panama, seemed to have put himself in a dangerous position. I sought to leave him with the impression that our patience with the provocations had clear limits and that Noriega, and Cuba, should keep that in mind. There was little more that could be said. I was aware of no plan at the time for using force against Noriega.

On February 10, Carlos Martínez lectured about past and present discrimination against Cuban broadcasting by the United States. Kozak and Jahn detailed years of radio interference by Cuba. This led Alarcón to complain of what he called inflammatory private broadcasting by Cuban-Americans, who were even advocating the assassination of Fidel Castro. These broadcasts were beamed to Cuba eighty hours per week, according to Alarcón. If this continued, he warned, the Cubans might give the United States a dose of interference. Kozak asked Alarcón to "withdraw his threat." Alarcón denied he had made one.

The essence of the problem was Alarcón's need to get something in the radio broadcasting area because of his concession in Montreal. The U.S. side would have liked to be helpful had it been possible to do so without interference with broadcasting on the AM band in the United States.

However, Cuba's minimum terms could not be met. It was finally agreed to study the matter further and perhaps exchange technical information about mutual incompatibilities.

In this last of four meetings with Cuba in Mexico City, little was achieved in substance other than to help the Cubans cover their retreat on the Migration Agreement. We had been as good as our word—but no better. Nevertheless, a new three-cornered issue was emerging. One possibility which had been explored in the past was that Cuba might broadcast on the so-called "expanded AM band," which many newer radios in the United States could receive. Cuba's agreed share of the expanded band in the region would be one additional frequency.

State's Communications Bureau supported a regional solution which would give Cuba the frequency at 1610 kHz. Jahn and his associates had discussed this possibility with a U.S. expert they sent to Geneva in early January. When the information got to Radio Marti, some of its staff may have misinterpreted this action for a U.S. government agreement to give a clear channel on the regular AM band to Cuba, a notion Chardy later aired in his "warming trends" articles.

The Cubans, however, had not shown much interest in a frequency on the expanded band. Many of the older radios in use in Cuba could not receive it. They wanted the full panoply of broadcasting which they had sought in the 1986 Mexico City talks. Even the limited proposal of 1610 kHz, however, presented a conflict because Radio Marti wished to be awarded this frequency on the expanded band as a potential backup in the event Cuba began to jam its regular broadcasting on 1180 kHz. A backup frequency might not help much against prospective Cuban jamming, however, since jamming would presumably also be addressed to the backup as well.

During the fourth U.S.–Soviet meeting on the Caribbean Basin, held in Rome in mid-April, Elliott Abrams sought without success to draw from Yuri Pavlov some commitment against radio interference. The Soviets saw nothing to gain from relaxing this annoyance, however, which was something they could provide Havana at a time when Soviet–Cuban relations were becoming less smooth.

In June, with TV-Marti on the horizon, radio interference emanating from Cuba was strongly felt again on 1040 and 1160 kHz. Worried about the radio interference following a meeting with a visiting Cuban communications specialist, National Association of Broadcasters President Fritts wrote to express his opposition to TV-Marti.

ANOTHER KIND OF "HERO"—ORLANDO BOSCH
RETURNS TO MIAMI

The Reagan administration was tough throughout on anti-Castro terrorism in the United States, most of it attributed to the organization OMEGA-7. In 1982, it arrested four persons for the March 1980 bombing of the automobile of Cuban UN representative Raul Roa Kouri.[19] In 1983, federal agents arrested Eduardo Arocena, believed to be the leader of OMEGA-7, and found submachine guns and automatic pistols with silencers in his apartment.[20] Arocena was formally charged with attempted murder and several bombings in Manhattan and Miami.[21] He was subsequently convicted and sentenced to prison. Fidel Castro acknowledged this record in public comments early in 1985.

A new challenge now presented itself: the unlawful reentry of Orlando Bosch, who had left the United States illegally after committing terrorist acts for which he was a hero to many Cuban-Americans. Bosch visited the U.S. Embassy in Caracas to discuss prospects for a U.S. visa. He was a fugitive from U.S. justice for having violated parole by leaving the United States. That is where the matter appeared to rest.

The government of Venezuela, however, wanted Bosch to leave that country, where he had spent many years in jail without being convicted of any offense.[22] His continued presence inhibited reestablishment of diplomatic relations with Cuba, which had withdrawn its ambassador in 1980 over an aborted Venezuelan move to release Bosch. This was a monkey Caracas wanted off its back—even if it settled on ours.

Late in the afternoon of February 16, the Department of State learned from INS that Orlando Bosch was about to become a U.S. problem again. An aircraft of the Venezuelan carrier Viasa was minutes from landing at Miami with Bosch on board. Venezuelan Disip (security) officials had escorted Bosch to the plane and boarded him at Maiquetia Airport, near Caracas, although he had no U.S. visa.

It appeared that INS had some prior knowledge, although State had none.[23] Had State known in time, it could have instructed Embassy Caracas to inform Venezuelan authorities prior to takeoff or during flight that the aircraft would not be permitted to land in Miami with Bosch on board. He was listed under a false name (Saul Cordero) on a plane carrying only four passengers. To allow Bosch simply to walk away would ignore his past transgressions and imply indifference toward his future conduct. To detain him would displease his admirers and add to the furor in Cuban–American quarters. Urgent telephonic coordination among State, INS, and Justice ensured that Bosch was taken into custody when he arrived on U.S. soil.

The *Miami Herald* reported that it was a "quiet return to Miami" for Bosch, a pediatrician "who has been revered as a patriot among many Cuban exiles but regarded as a fugitive terrorist by federal officials." Many Cuban-Americans welcomed news of his return. Former Miami Mayor Maurice Ferre, of Puerto Rican descent, said, "He (Bosch) was responsible for taking a bazooka shot at some Polish ship. I don't classify that as terrorism unless you want to say that the Boston Tea Party was terrorism.... There are not that many people that have that kind of courage." Banker Bernardo Benes recalled that there were people like Bosch who became prime minister in Israel. Jorge Mas Canosa said, "I think he is a patriot. I consider him a friend. I don't necessarily agree with everything that he has done in his life." Broadcaster Salvador Lew commented that Bosch had "every right to integrate himself into free society." He was sure Bosch did not advocate violence.[24] Bosch denied any role in the bombing of the Cubana airliner, admitting only that he had violated "certain laws of the U.S." and asserting that he would now abide by them.[25]

On February 17, Jorge Mas called, offering assistance by getting Bosch to promise that he would engage in no more terrorist activities in the United States. Mas said he did not want to see relations between the *comunidad* and the Department of State, and particularly my office, become any worse.

State, INS, and Justice cooperated to forestall a premature release, but at no time was any consideration given to returning Bosch to Cuba since it was obvious he could not obtain a fair trial there. Nor did the Cubans request such action or volunteer any advice. With Bosch no longer in Venezuela, Cuba could seek to normalize diplomatic relations with Caracas. Ostensibly, at least, the Cubans seemed satisfied to have Bosch back in the United States.

INS detained Bosch on grounds of: violation of parole and illegal entry into the United States, a charge on which INS could hold him only as long as there was a reasonable chance he could be returned to Venezuela or another country. Deputy INS Commissioner Mark Everson stated the U.S. government's position on the matter, "We think the parole commission should return him to prison for completion of his term. We will move to deport him once that is completed."[26]

Bosch's continued detention was another cause for unhappiness among Cuban-Americans. In late June when President Reagan visited Miami, they raised the detention of Bosch with him. The president's request to State for a memorandum on the subject led Elliott Abrams to urge his release on humanitarian grounds. In view of the background of this case, however, it was decided that the U.S. government should first make a vigorous diplomatic effort to send Bosch back to Venezuela.

Subsequent efforts to return Bosch to Venezuela or a third country (not Cuba) were unsuccessful. Neither President Jaime Lusinchi nor his successor, Carlos Andres Pérez, was willing to see Bosch return to Venezuela. Pérez conceded that Venezuelan authorities (under Lusinchi) had committed a wrong in putting him on a Venezuelan government-owned aircraft to Miami. Pérez had various suggestions of third countries that might be willing to accept Bosch. He even volunteered to raise the matter with Spanish Premier Felipe González. How hard he tried is open to question. No one was willing to take Bosch.

As officer in charge of our embassy in Caracas when we asked Pérez to take back Bosch, I understood how the Venezuelans felt. They did not need one more problem. The whole episode stemmed from the fact that the system in Havana, where no opposition was tolerated, bred persons like Bosch, who were prepared to respond to tyranny with their own brand of private violence. But the U.S. government could not condone private violence. Bosch was subsequently released into U.S. society in the Bush Administration.[27]

HUMAN RIGHTS—CUBA IN THE DOCK

The year 1988 witnessed a surprising choice as head of the U.S. delegation to the U.N. Human Rights Commission (UNHRC) in Geneva: Armando Valladares, who had but recently become an American citizen and whose knowledge of the English language was rudimentary. In view of his intense feelings and his very recent U.S. citizenship, some felt his selection was an error. It appeared that the administration had made its choice with an eye to the discontent in Miami.

However, Valladares knew as much as anyone about Cuban prisons, and he was determined to press charges against the Castro government with renewed vigor. Valladares was as committed to fight the regime in Havana as those who used violence, but he was far more effective using the written or spoken word. Never in his wildest dreams could Fidel Castro have foreseen that the prisoner he released five years earlier to French President Mitterand would draw world attention to abuses in Cuba as the spokesman for the U.S. government.

The narrow defeat in Geneva in 1987 had led to recriminations within State as to who bore responsibility for the failure to adopt the U.S. resolution, focusing attention on the plight of political prisoners and dissidents in Cuba. In truth, it was because most Latin American representatives supported Cuba. The same would occur in 1988.

Arguments began well before the session. Valladares was critical of restoration of the Migration Agreement. On November 23, 1987, the same day as the rioters took over the Atlanta penitentiary, he told Elliott Abrams that return of the Excludables to Cuba would allow Castro to use them before the UNHRC in Geneva. That Cuba had not used any of the 201 Excludables already returned for this purpose in 1987 seems to have escaped Valladares' attention.

The human rights battle soon raged internally in State with a vehemence that would hardly be exceeded in Geneva. From New York, Ambassador to the United Nations Vernon Walters voiced the view that it would be more difficult to condemn Cuba because we had restored an agreement on migration.

Richard Schifter, Assistant Secretary for Humanitarian Affairs, argued for an approach which by not singling out Cuba might win a majority. His arithmetic showed that without Latin American support, we could not win a direct vote on Cuba. It turned out that he was right on the numbers. But a resolution that was not Cuba-specific would have had less impact.

The strong effort by Valladares and his delegation in Geneva was supported by presentations in capitals of states whose votes would be critical. As in 1987, Secretary Shultz actively sought votes for a resolution calling on the UNHRC to investigate the situation in Cuba. This time the West Europeans and other friendly states on the UNHRC gave willing support, but the stand of Argentina, Colombia, Mexico, and Peru for Cuba (Venezuela abstained) prevented the resolution on Cuba from being adopted. Nevertheless, Valladares pronounced himself elated with the outcome. In response to a Cuban proposal, the UNHRC adopted a Colombian resolution to send a five-member investigating team to Cuba. "This was not a spontaneous and voluntary offer by Cuba," Valladares pointed out.[28]

Thus, the restoration of the Migration Agreement and the violent prison seizures by Cuban exile prisoners had no negative effect on the results in Geneva, which were better than those of 1987 from the U.S. point of view. Only with the demise of communism in Eastern Europe would there be a majority in the UNHRC for a resolution condemning Cuba. That lay in the future. In 1988, however, public attention newly focused on the subject benefited Cubans whose plight might otherwise have been further neglected.

In the United Nations, sympathy for Cuba and antipathy to the United States still were in vogue. Later in the spring the UN Economic and Social

Council elected Cuba and Panama to the UN Human Rights Commission while defeating the candidacy of democratic Costa Rica.

State promoted human rights in Cuba by publicizing Havana's crackdown on the little group around Ricardo Bofill. Whereas Bofill, perhaps because of his frail French connection, managed to stay out of prison, his colleagues drew the wrath of Cuban authorities. Havana blamed the U.S. Interests Section for allegedly "tutoring" Bofill, who had no more need for it than did Armando Valladares.

One possible effect of the outside pressure was an offer by Castro to John Cardinal O'Connor of New York in April to release several hundred political prisoners remaining in Cuban jails.[29]

Cuba in 1988 welcomed groups which might come away with a positive view of human rights on the island, but this new strategy sometimes backfired when visitors detected evidence of persecution. Alice Heflin and Michael Posner of the New York Bar Association told Richard Schifter and me on March 3 that while in a punishment building in Combinado del Este prison in Havana, they heard of beatings. A Seattle academician, Sharon Georgianna, who participated in a World Affairs Council tour of Cuba, insisted on attending Protestant services at a church in Havana and there learned of strong-arm tactics against the church.

On June 3, Enrique Hernández, a dissident who had arrived in Miami that morning from Havana, called to report a hunger strike and the beating of *Plantados* protesting a "whitewash" of their cells in Combinado del Este prison. The whitewash was designed to make the cells look better to outside visitors. Hernández and Edmigio López, a recently released human rights activist, were put in touch with *The New York Times* so it could hear their stories firsthand.

The *Times* account focused on the hunger strike and beatings rather than a list of political prisoners that the Cuban government was circulating. Forty-four prisoners, all of whom had been in prison over twenty years, had refused meals in protest against being moved to new rooms to mislead human rights experts from the International Committee of the Red Cross and the United Nations, the *Times* reported.[30]

On the following day, the *Times* reported that Castro, in a letter to John Cardinal O'Connor, said he was ready to release all but forty-four of his political prisoners. He said he would release 385 of the 429 who still remained in Cuban jails. The *Times*, with reference to the forty-four prisoners who had engaged in the hunger strike, noted that there was no explanation as to why Castro was holding back just that number of prisoners.[31]

Fidel Castro offered the same political prisoners to various groups, exploiting them as bait for discrete targets of influence. For example, on June 2 Representative John Bryant of Texas, who had gone to Cuba with "The Human Rights Project," told me of a list of fifty prisoners whom Castro was willing to release to that group. When a copy of the list was obtained, it was found that forty-two of the fifty names were already on a list promised to the U.S. Catholic Conference. Although there was no shortage of political prisoners in Cuba, some did double or triple duty on the "gratuities" list. In all of the prisoner release cases, Cuba insisted that those listed be taken immediately by the United States. While this was no doubt consistent with the volition of most prisoners, they were given no choice of remaining in Cuba.

In mid-1988 the Cuban government permitted Elizardo Sánchez Santacruz, a dissident, to visit the United States and return to Cuba.[32] On July 8, Sánchez was received in ARA/CCA for a conversation that was polite but relatively uninformative. Sánchez appeared to be under some sort of suasion from the Cuban Interests Section, just as had been the three Cuban bishops who visited the Department of State in 1985. This may have been part of the bargain for his unusual opportunity to travel in the United States. Moreover, Sánchez had broken with Bofill, with whom he had hitherto been closely associated. He was viewed as less extreme than Bofill by the Cuban government, which may have assumed that Bofill could be undercut by letting this more nuanced critic travel.

Later Argentine journalist Jacobo Timerman called on Sánchez Santacruz in Havana. Noting that Sánchez was President of the Cuban Commission on Human Rights *and National Reconciliation* (italics supplied), Timerman described him as a man with a dream of peaceful reform that did not annul "socialism," was achieved from above, and was "led by Fidel Castro."[33] Timerman said he "refrained from telling this . . . lucid, penetrating humanist that his dream can materialize only after Fidel Castro."[34]

WARMING, BUT NOT WARM

U.S.–Cuban relations improved as a consequence of renewed implementation of the Migration Agreement. While no new negotiations were undertaken, State scaled down the special sanctions applied since 1985.

There was little change on strategic issues. Cuban influence was being weakened by events over which the United States had little direct control. Economic decline and social unrest at home were complemented by trends in Central America and southern Africa that made Havana less relevant.

On the far horizon was the sea change in U.S.–Soviet relations that would weaken the Soviet–Cuban symbiosis and eventually turn Cuba into a nuisance rather than a threat to the United States. In 1988, Fidel Castro viewed this trend with concern. Even though neither he nor anyone else could then foresee the dramatic changes of 1989 and 1990, he sensed enough to speculate that Cuba might be the last enemy of the United States.

In Central America, Havana hung tough, hoping to see the Sandinistas consolidate their regime while the U.S. Congress denied aid to the resistance, but Cuba's power to influence events was reduced by the Soviet Union's loss of zeal and by developments in the region. There were not enough revolutionaries imbued with Fidel Castro's spirit as the decade drew toward a close.

On the issue of U.S.–Cuban contacts—which had been severely restricted by the Reagan administration, especially after Cuban suspension of the Migration Agreement—some strictures were relaxed but others were held constant. Despite Cuban–American fears, and partly because of them, relaxation did not extend far. It applied mainly to Cuban official visitors. The President's Proclamation of October 4, 1985 remained in force, but the Department of State implemented it to allow Cubans more access to the United States.

One area where cooperation was seen to be in U.S. interest was nuclear safety. The Department of State approved requests by Ramón Sánchez-Parodi to call on the U.S. Nuclear Regulatory Commission and to visit a nuclear facility in the United States. The positive decision was influenced by the fact that the Cubans, with Soviet assistance, were building a nuclear reactor at Juragua, near Cienfuegos on the south coast of Cuba. With Chernobyl fresh in mind, the prospect of a nuclear accident so close to the United States warranted cooperation in nuclear safety matters.[35] While the denouement of this exchange transpired after I ceased to be coordinator of Cuban Affairs, Havana did not fulfill its commitment to let an NRC team visit Juragua.

The embargo, which was directed against Cuba's continued adversarial role in world affairs, was not relaxed. Listing of Cuban front organizations by Treasury continued, and a vessel owned by one such front that tried to load cargo in Savannah was required to unload and was fined $250,000.

Although visa issuance for Cuban officials was liberalized in 1988, this did not extend to measures which would create an impression of normal bilateral relations. A proposal for a Cuban team of "prison inspectors" to come to the United States pursuant to the recommendation of Adrian DeWind was rejected as inappropriate on the same grounds as in 1987.

Visas for senior Cuban officials were issued dependent on the nature of the visit. Ricardo Alarcón was denied a visa to attend a meeting in Georgia to which he had been invited by a private group, the National Security Archive. However, he was authorized to meet in New York, along with senior Cuban Communist Party official Carlos Aldana, with representatives of the African Bureau of the Department of State concerning Cuban troop withdrawal from Angola.

Once in New York, Alarcón developed a wish to come to Washington to see Kozak. Apparently he had another agenda in mind. The Cuban Interests Section organized an Alarcón lecture and a reception in his honor. It also informed the press that Alarcón and Arbesu would be meeting Kozak and me in Washington, a meeting which had neither been requested nor scheduled. We declined to sanction Alarcón's travel from New York to Washington and reminded the Cuban Interests Section that the limited progress made since November would be jeopardized if Cuba pressed too hard to exploit it.

State and the Drug Enforcement Administration (DEA) faced a difficult decision with respect to reported Cuban narcotics trafficking. Even as information accumulated about Cuban involvement in the flow of drugs from Colombia to the United States, Havana made known its interest in discussing cooperation against narcotics trafficking. Such discussions, if undertaken, might have undercut charges of complicity without changing Cuba's behavior. If the reports were true—as they later turned out to be—top Cuban authorities could hardly have been ignorant of the activity.

On February 26, a Miami grand jury returned sealed indictments against seventeen persons who reportedly used Cuba as a waystation to smuggle cocaine from Colombia to south Florida.[36] Moreover, the February 4, 1988 indictment of Manuel Noriega and fifteen others had named Fidel Castro as playing a role in settling Noriega's dispute with the Medellin Cartel. Castro indignantly denied the charge, asserting he could provide evidence about actual drug trafficking.

In mid-May, tapes from the Miami processing of a narcotics trafficker appeared to show that he used Cuban territory to bring drugs from Colombia to the United States. The question was whether it would be possible to use Cuban Air Force facilities for such a purpose without the knowledge of top Cuban officials.

Two weeks later Rabbi Arthur Schneier of New York, who had recently been in Cuba on humanitarian business, called me to relate that he had met there with Vice President Carlos Rafael Rodríguez. Rodríguez had mentioned that the United States and Cuba could do something together on drugs.

Representatives of State and DEA on June 10 considered whether to respond to such Cuban signals of willingness to discuss narcotics bilaterally. Evidence that drugs were passing unimpeded through Cuba with official knowledge of the fact argued against negotiations, which would have been difficult to justify. No negotiations were proposed or held.

During the Bush administration, Havana admitted the involvement of senior officials in narcotics trafficking. General Arnaldo Ochoa Sánchez, an authentic war hero, paid with his life for alleged participation in this trade. Subsequent evidence from the trials of General Noriega and Colombian drug dealer Carlos Lehder also demonstrated that the Cuban narcotics connection was real.

The decision of mid–1988 that Cuba was not an appropriate negotiating partner for the United States for controlling the flow of drugs was thus confirmed by subsequent data. These would not have been good faith negotiations. More likely, such talks would have allowed the inference that Cuba was seeking to cooperate against the drug trade at the very time it was secretly furthering it.

TV MARTI CASTS ITS SHADOW

After the long struggle in Congress over enactment of the Radio Broadcasting to Cuba Act of 1983 and the delay in startup, Radio Marti had provided objective information about events in Cuba to the Cuban public. Under the direction of Ernesto Betancourt and Humberto Medrano, it developed credibility and a substantial Cuban audience.

Just as Radio Marti had been fathered intellectually by the Cuban–American National Foundation, which also had great influence on its personnel selection and day-to-day operation, so too did CANF promote the idea of a television service to Cuba to be called "Tele-Marti" or TV-Marti. The idea was popular in south Florida, as indicated by a 1986 quotation from Senator Chiles, who said, "I see great advantage in backing the words of Radio Marti with the pictures of TV-Marti." Chiles said he had been informed by USIA Director Charles Wick that USIA was trying to find out how much a TV service for Cuba would cost and whether the project was technically feasible.[37]

The possibility of television broadcasting to Cuba had long been considered within the U.S. government, in part as a possible electronic countermeasure if Fidel Castro had made good his threat to disrupt radio communication in the United States. Previous studies of television broadcasting to Cuba indicated, however, a serious flaw: The cost would be high in relation to any probable benefit because the signal could easily be jammed. Hence, unless new data could be developed to demonstrate the contrary, it would probably not be an effective instrument.

Proponents of TV-Marti nevertheless pushed hard in early 1988 for U.S. government television for Cuba. The issue was on the political horizon by June 13, when a meeting was scheduled in the Old Executive Office Building to witness the signing of the agreement between INS and CANF for a private refugee program for Cubans in third countries.

Before the session, I advised Elliott Abrams to show caution about any commitment to TV-Marti if the subject should arise. The data so far were not encouraging about its prospects for getting through. When the issue came up, Abrams showed restraint. He volunteered that the subject had not arisen in our radio talks with Cuba, which was true, and guaranteed it would not come up in the future. The audience cheered this spontaneous commitment that TV-Marti, like Radio Marti, would be non-negotiable. But Abrams gave no assurance that the U.S. government would endorse TV-Marti unless studies proved that it was feasible and cost effective. Shortly thereafter Vice President Bush entered the room and, to widespread jubilation, flatly endorsed TV-Marti.

The day was not over before I had a terse message from Abrams, providing instructions on how to deal with the TV-Marti issue at an upcoming interagency meeting scheduled for June 17 in the White House: "No excuses; full speed ahead." At the meeting, Abrams endorsed TV-Marti, pointing to the enthusiastic support the idea had received from Vice President Bush, but others mentioned problems, especially the fact it would be easy for Cuba to jam at low cost.

On June 22, the White House sent out a "tasker" seeking agency views on TV-Marti. My reaction was that it was unwise to spend millions of dollars for an instrument that could be easily jammed by Cuba. I suggested to Mike Armacost that TV-Marti receive careful interagency study. Pressure for TV-Marti in an election year, however, prevailed. In August, the U.S. Senate approved $7.5 million for the initial ninety days of broadcasting by the future station.[38] It was a dubious idea, but its time had come.

When TV-Marti went on the air in the Bush administration, the Cubans responded by jamming it and Radio Marti as well.[39]

NOTES

1. From November 1987 to September 30, 1988, 2,650 former prisoners and their families came from Cuba to the United States as refugees. Dominguez, "Cooperating with the Enemy?", p. 83.

2. In view of the Bush statement in Miami I called Phil Brady of his office, reminding him that there had been no more vigorous supporter of returning the Mariel criminals to Cuba than the Vice President. Brady assured me on March 7 that Bush had referred strictly to deportation and not to exclusion. This meant that persons on the list of Mariel Excludables could go back to Cuba in a Bush administration, but that no Cuban would be deported.

3. Dixon and Galan, *The Immigration and Naturalization Service*, p. 90. Obviously many of the 4,400, although in detention, were not on the list of persons whom Cuba agreed in 1984 to accept.

4. Dominguez, "Cooperating with the Enemy?", p. 83. The number of preference immigrants in fiscal years 1989 and 1990 was only about three thousand. The *maximum* number of preference immigrants who might come from Cuba (or any other state) to the United States in a single fiscal year was twenty thousand. There were presumably far more than three thousand Cubans who were qualified to enter the United States as preference immigrants in those years.

5. *NYT*, Jan. 12, 1988, I, 18:4. An opinion poll showed that non-Hispanics had negative views about a new Cuban influx.

6. Kenneth N. Skoug, Jr., *The U.S.–Cuba Migration Agreement: Resolving Mariel* (Washington, DC: U.S. Department of State, Bureau of Public Affairs, March 1988).

7. *Miami Herald*, Feb. 26, 1988, 1:1.

8. *NYT*, Jan. 3, 1988, XI, 1:3 (New Jersey edition).

9. Ibid., Jan. 5, 1988, II, 5:5.

10. Ibid., Jan. 26, I, 23:1.

11. Ibid., Feb. 1, 1988, I, 18:5.

12. *Miami Herald*, May 1, 1988, 1:1.

13. Ibid., 22:5.

14. I saw the Tropicana Revue while visiting Cuba. On May 3, 1987, I witnessed a scrawny white "Tarzan" and a blonde "Jane" being humbled by four tall blacks pounding large wooden stakes. This racist presentation was obviously designed to show how "colonialism" and "neocolonialism" were doomed to be crushed by Cuba's version of the Third World's revenge.

15. *Miami Herald*, April 30, 1988, 1:1.

16. Kenneth N. Skoug, Jr., *Cuba, Our "Last Adversary?"* (Washington, DC: U.S. Department of State, Bureau of Public Affairs, Current Policy No. 1085, July 1988). Shortly before, Castro had declared his readiness to be the "last adversary of the United States," if necessary.

17. Researchers Gonzalez and Ronfeldt of the Rand Corporation reached the conclusion that Castro had failed to succeed with the Reagan administration in

using tactics which had put previous U.S. administrations on the defensive. Gonzalez and Ronfeldt, *Castro, Cuba and the World*, p. 94.

18. Oppenheimer, *Castro's Final Hour*, pp. 174–175. Panamanian Air Force flight logs showed the first shipment of Cuban arms had been made on December 7, 1987, a few days after restoration of the Migration Agreement and following a Castro visit to Moscow and Pyongyang. More than eighty thousand weapons were sent to Noriega's forces over the next two years. In recounting Cuban support to Noriega in the final two years of his regime, Oppenheimer notes Castro told Noriega's emissary in September 1987 that he could not send troops. "That would invite an immediate U.S. intervention. We have to maintain a low profile. That would be best for us, and for you too." Castro sent military advisers, mortars, rocket-propelled grenades, antipersonnel, and antitank mines, machine guns, and so on, but he drew the line on a Panamanian request for fifty SA-7 surface-to-air-missiles, pp. 177ff.

19. *NYT*, Oct. 3, 1982, 42:4.

20. Ibid., July 23, 1983, I, 1:3.

21. Ibid., Dec. 29, 1983, II, 7:1.

22. A Venezuelan military court had acquitted Bosch, Hernando Ricardo, Freddie Lugo, and Luis Posada for lack of evidence. *NYT*, Sept. 27, 1980, 3:1. Cuba recalled its diplomatic representation from Caracas the following day. A witness to the December hijacking heard one of the gunmen say it was to "protest the case of a Cuban plane." *NYT*, Dec. 6, 1980, 3:3.

23. *Miami Herald*, Feb. 26, 1988, 1:1. According to the press account, Bosch's attorney said he had heard on February 15 that Bosch might be returning that week and had asked county manager Sergio Pereira to call INS officials and inform them that Bosch could be coming with the help of the Venezuelan government.

24. Ibid., Feb. 17, 1988, 1:1.

25. Ibid.

26. Ibid., Feb. 26, 1988, 1:1.

27. Oppenheimer, *Castro's Final Hour*, pp. 325–326. Far from altering his views or retiring from the scene, Bosch thereafter defended the 1976 airplane bombing as a "legitimate war action," and he participated actively in fund-raising efforts in Miami to finance an armed rebellion in Cuba.

28. *NYT*, March 11, 1988, I, 11:1. The favorable outcome in Geneva apparently owed much to the work of the Seneghalese chairman of the UNHRC, who made sure of the bonafides of the group that subsequently visited Cuba.

29. Ibid., April 22, 1988, I, 3:1.

30. Ibid., June 4, 1988, I, 5:1.

31. Ibid., June 5, 1988, I, 4:1.

32. In May, probably due to the debate in the UNHRC in March, Sánchez Santacruz and Bofill had been allowed access to foreign reporters as Castro relaxed his grip. *NYT*, May 11, 1988, I, 4:3.

33. Jacobo Timerman, *Cuba: A Journey* (New York: Alfred A. Knopf, 1990), p. 125. Timerman's trip to Cuba was in summer 1987. He met Elizardo Sánchez Santacruz on August 28, 1987. After describing Sánchez as an idealist, Timerman observed that Sánchez in 1989 was once more in jail.

34. Ibid., p. 107.

35. Ironically, Fidel Castro in December 1984 had scoffed at the possibility of a nuclear accident in Cuba, claiming such problems were limited to capitalist countries, whereas "we rely on Soviet technology where all the responsibility the socialist state can muster goes into technological progress with safety." Gonzalez and Ronfeldt, *Castro, Cuba and the World*, pp. 83–84, citing *NYT*, May 1, 1986, p. 8.

36. *Miami Herald*, Feb. 26, 1988, 8:1.

37. Ibid., June 11, 1986, 7:1.

38. *NYT*, Aug. 7, 1988, I, 16:3.

39. Oppenheimer, *Castro's Final Hour*, p. 333n. The author asserted that he never ran into a single Cuban who had seen or heard TV-Marti.

Epilogue

At the end of the Reagan administration, Fidel Castro remained in power, defiantly prepared to be the last adversary of the United States. Cuba had not become a free country, as some Cuban-Americans reminded President Reagan in 1988. Soon no one in Latin American history would have ruled so long.

Cuba had not been "turned" from its allegiance to the Soviet Union, as President Reagan and NSC Director Bud McFarlane may have hoped. Although Fidel Castro had been willing in 1985 to discuss certain bilateral issues, he had never been prepared to change his principles or his politics, including the Soviet alliance and support for revolution and anti-U.S. nationalists like Noriega.

The Reagan administration never tried to overthrow Castro. It never went to the source. Violence between U.S. forces and armed Cubans on Grenada occurred because of communications problems and because Cubans were ordered to defend their position with their lives. Nor had the administration sought to "turn" Castro from his deeply held principles. It offered no blandishments, nor would these have worked. Castro wanted respect for what he saw as his historical achievements in Cuba and the region. His idea of "internationalism" was incompatible with American views of regional security.

However, the administration could point to three significant achievements with respect to Cuba in the Reagan/Shultz years:

First, thanks to its global strategy—and to the judicious restraint of Gorbachev—it wrested the initiative in the Western Hemisphere from Cuba and its allies, who in the last years of the Carter administration had seemed to have the wind at their back. When Reagan left office, Cuba was a less influential force in regional politics, well on its way to becoming a nuisance and an anachronism rather than a threat to U.S. security. Although Castro was an invited guest at the February 2, 1989 inauguration of President Carlos Andres Perez of Venezuela, he looked out of place in his military uniform among the luminaries attending a democratic process in Caracas that could not have occurred in Havana. He was in the group but not a potential leader.

Second, it left Cuba a less attractive model for emulation by third countries.[1] Cuba's economic and social crisis was brought on by Castro's own policies, which entrapped Cuba in dependency on countries which were themselves economic failures. Tight enforcement of the U.S. embargo made it harder for Cuba to mitigate its distress. Castro's "rectification" campaign helped him to elude responsibility for the crisis but did not address the underlying problem. The debate in the UN forum on human rights violations in Cuba was an embarrassment, not a threat, to the Cuban government, but international attention to this issue did nothing to recommend Cuba as a model for others.

Third, it advanced, albeit modestly, the cause of freedom in Cuba by making it more difficult for Castro to manipulate his countrymen. Radio Marti supplied valuable information about Cuba to the population. This obliged Cuba's information media to deal with issues that might have gone unmentioned or been presented in more distorted form.

There was no new dawn in Cuba, not the faintest reflection of the dramatic changes about to transform Eastern Europe and ultimately the Soviet Union. Fidel Castro shouldered out the dawn with his forceful personality and his refusal to alter his fundamental outlook on man and society. No outside manipulation, no matter how cunning, could have prevented this—other than the use of military force.

Throughout the entire Reagan administration, Washington was gripped by the tar baby of the Mariel Boatlift. Ironically, it was the U.S. constitutional order which made it virtually impossible to resolve this issue without engaging in negotiations with Cuba. This gave Havana a valuable lever. Cuba played hard to get and endeavored to link migration negotiations to other issues.

While the Reagan administration, unlike its predecessor, was unwilling to discuss other matters at the same time as migration, the need to resolve

Mariel was a restraint on a more assertive policy toward Cuba. The criminals he sent in 1980 were the single most effective card Castro had to play against Reagan.

Negotiating a Mariel solution at no cost to U.S. interests was not simple. Cuba did not want the criminals back. At a minimum it wished to select those whom it would accept. The United States insisted that Havana accept all the names it presented to Cuba in 1984. Agreement was achieved because both sides could maintain their principles. Having studied the vexing migration issue, Professor Jorge Dominguez wrote: "Both in 1984 and in 1987 diplomacy and diplomats mattered. Both times there was thorough staff background work to brief the negotiators. Both times the level of professionalism at the talks was very high. Both times the negotiators were skillful."[2] The administration, however, was reluctant to celebrate its success. It preferred to maintain a tougher image on Cuba, both because it was concerned by Cuban conduct in world affairs and because of domestic politics.

The single unfortunate decision with respect to Cuba made by President Reagan was to authorize Radio Marti's start without any diplomatic preparation. The tendency in Washington to be macho in May 1985 found a responding chord in Havana, and both sides suffered the consequences. After reaching an agreement with Cuba, Reagan was under pressure from Cuban-Americans to commence surrogate broadcasting. Their views were understandable, but it was unnecessary to forgo a short delay which would have provided a final chance to discuss Radio Marti with Cuba before the die was cast.

Some administration officials, but not those close to the Cuban reality, may have believed that Castro's public relations campaign of spring 1985 was a sign of weakness, an indication that the United States had "leverage" to exploit with the Cuban leader. This was a serious error of judgment. Castro's response meant that after May 20, 1985, the United States could address the Cuban public directly—a big plus—but it also meant that the laboriously achieved solution to the Mariel Boatlift was undone. Cuba asserted that Washington could not have Radio Marti and return the Mariel Excludables. They continued to cost U.S. taxpayers millions of dollars annually and ravaged the very institutions where they were detained.

Most of the second Reagan term was spent in overcoming this Cuban challenge so that, ultimately, the United States did have both. But the prison takeovers, and the decision of too many Cuban-Americans to condemn their own government, diminished the achievement. The number of persons who would eventually return to Cuba was reduced, and the process was long delayed.

The Reagan presidency illustrated more sharply than heretofore the three-cornered relationship among Washington, Havana, and Cuban Miami. The political weight of the Cuban-Americans in Florida—and to a much lesser extent, New Jersey—grew with their numbers, and their influence on policy was enhanced by the organization of a powerful lobby, the Cuban–American National Foundation. With CANF in the lead, Cuban Miami made its hardline views against Havana deeply felt in Washington. Yet Miami's own weakness—the concern of the émigrés for family reunification and the Cuban diaspora—gave Havana a potent weapon to use against Washington.

The main strategy used by the United States to regain the Migration Agreement after 1985 was to restrain Cuban migration northward. This worked (again) but antagonized Cuban-Americans, who used their new political muscle with Congress to try to force a policy change.

As the issue played itself out, the main bilateral objective of the Reagan administration with respect to Cuba—exclusion of the Mariel criminals—was no longer shared by the most powerful interest group concerned with Cuban policy. Although no group in the United States gained more than Cuban-Americans from normal migration and a special program for former political prisoners and families, the *comunidad* lost sight of this. On migration issues, Miami stood closer to Havana than to Washington; each focused on maximum movement northward.

Was repatriation of the Mariel Excludables worth the vast amount of energy and political capital expended? Less than twenty percent of the persons on the list of names accepted by Cuba had been returned by 1991.[3] This focus on the Excludables was unavoidable in the first Reagan term, when public insistence on a solution was nearly universal. Once Cuba set aside implementation of the agreement, the political imperative of not allowing the other contracting party to an agreement has its benefits while renouncing its obligations was added to the original need to return the Excludables. Defeat on this issue after 1985 would not have concerned Cuban Miami but would have been unsatisfactory to other Americans.

In one area the administration needlessly alienated Cuban-Americans and violated its own principles. It should have moved more swiftly to bring long-term Cuban political prisoners still in detention, and their families, to the United States whenever Castro offered conditionally to release them. The mistaken notion that delayed processing of these prisoners was a means for forcing Cuba to accept the Mariel criminals blotted the administration's escutcheon and was one reason why Cuban-Americans in 1988 were prone to condemn Washington and to imagine that its diplomatic representatives were making evil bargains with Cuba.

On the plus side, the administration eventually called world attention to violations of human rights in Cuba. Cuba had been accustomed to sit in judgment of other states. Havana was uncomfortable facing outside scrutiny. While U.S.–led efforts to put a spotlight on Cuban human rights violations did not end them—such a result was beyond the means of outsiders using no weapons except the human voice and the printed page—the issue would hereafter not go away.

The remaining question that needs to be addressed is whether the United States missed an opportunity to reach a genuine understanding with Fidel Castro. Frank McNeil thought there was such an opportunity after Grenada. Chester Crocker wondered if Castro was ready for an Angolan settlement in 1985. In both 1984 and 1985, there were feelers through third parties, and in the wake of the Migration Agreement, Castro was clearly prepared to discuss an agenda of low-key bilateral issues.

Analysis of what Castro was saying, however, leaves no doubt that for him the alliance with Moscow and the "internationalist" imperative of supporting revolution in the Third World were not negotiable. Yet without such a change in Cuba's fundamental approach, there was no chance of a real improvement in U.S.–Cuban relations during the Reagan administration. The two sides would merely have talked past each other.

Had the crisis not erupted over Radio Marti, it might have been possible to make progress on bilateral issues of low strategic or ideological content. This would have been in the interest of each, but it would not have altered the basic adversarial relationship. Even a *modus vivendi* on the smaller agenda would not have been a guaranteed success. It must be recalled that Castro's "media blitz" was primarily aimed at keeping Radio Marti off the air.

Chet Crocker, whose description of the Angolan conflict is abstracted from the U.S.–Cuba bilateral relationship, argues that it might have been wise to let Cuba join the negotiations with the Popular Movement for the Liberation of Angola in early 1985.[4] Although Crocker does not mention it, this was when Castro's public relations campaign was in full swing. But the adverse criteria, especially the Gorbachev foreign policy, which caused Castro to agree to withdrawal in 1988 were much less evident in 1985.

After the collapse of European communism, it came into vogue to count the days of Castro and to anticipate impatiently the post-Castro era in Cuba. Despite the failure of the system he introduced, his will to power and his capacity to rule were not weakened. Neither economic disaster nor moral suasion could move him from bedrock. The Fidel Castro whom I met in

1985 seemed healthy and more determined than ever to guide his country's destiny for as long as possible.

In a speech in 1987 at the University of Minnesota, I referred to a new slogan in Cuba—"With Fidel into the 21st Century"—and stated the following about Castro's personal prospects: "There is no good reason to doubt that the new century will see him at the helm in Havana, but there is also no reason to believe that the next 12 years will achieve for Cuba what the first 29 have not."[5]

To have brought Castro down was beyond the power of diplomacy and economic sanctions. This was as true of the Reagan–Shultz era as it was of prior administrations. It was, however, possible to deprive him of the means to achieve his objectives. After 1981 Castro was frustrated and his fortunes declined.

Inevitably, Cuba will rejoin the comity of American republics—even if it be in the twenty-first century. Then the historic ties between the United States and Cuba, strengthened by the bond of blood between Cubans living on either side of the Florida Straits, should help Cuba to regain more quickly than many now imagine a place of leadership in the hemisphere.

Despite all the trouble with Cuba in the Castro era, it is likely that the future will see the United States and a prosperous Cuba living together as close neighbors, excellent trading partners, and even good friends. That was also the vision of Phil Bonsal, the last American ambassador in Havana, but with the caveat that it would happen after Fidel Castro had ceased to rule Cuba.

While Castro holds power, genuine rapprochement between the United States and Cuba is difficult to contemplate. While the trouble with Cuba persists, American expectations should be realistically limited. Cuba is no longer a danger to the United States, but it will not be turned around.

After the Castro era, rapprochement is all but inevitable.

CODA

I was replaced as Coordinator for Cuba on August 8, 1988 and assigned as a special charge d'affaires in Managua. I was not granted a visa to enter Nicaragua, however, because the Department of State would not permit Nicaraguan Ambassador to the United States Tunnerman, who had been expelled as persona non grata, to return to Washington in his other capacity as head of Nicaragua's mission to the Organization of American States.

Instead I was assigned in October 1988 to the American Embassy in Venezuela as deputy chief of mission. I became charge d'affaires, a.i. (acting chief of mission) in Caracas in July 1989 and served in that capacity until my retirement from the Foreign Service in September 1990.

NOTES

1. Carlos Alberto Montaner, *Castro en la Era de Gorbachev* (Madrid: Instituto de Cuestiones Internacionales, 1990), pp. 39–40. Montaner asserts that the greatest success of U.S. foreign policy was eroding Castro's image.

2. Dominguez, "Cooperating with the Enemy?" p. 66.

3. Only 501 of the 2,746 persons on the list accepted by Cuba had been returned by January 1991. However, returns continued.

4. Crocker, *High Noon in Southern Africa: Making Peace in a Rough Neighborhood* (New York: W. W. Norton & Co., Inc., 1993), p. 224. Crocker, however, points out that Cuban troop strength in Angola had been growing from some twenty thousand to twenty-five thousand in the early 1980s to thirty thousand by 1984 (p. 208). Castro's plan then would have been to leave the final drawdown of Cuban troops to a joint decision between Havana and the Angolan MPLA (p. 211).

5. Skoug, *Cuba's Growing Crisis*, p. 3.

Selected Bibliography

PUBLIC DOCUMENTS

Castro, Fidel. *Ier Forum Nacional de Energia: Discurso, 4 de diciembre de 1984.* Havana: Editora Política, 1984.

————. *Congresos de Pediatria, Cuba-84. Discurso ll de noviembre de 1984.* Havana: Editora Política, 1984.

————. *El Pensamiento de Fidel Castro: Selección tematica*, Tomo i, Volumenes l, 2. Enero 1959–abril 1961. Havana: Editora Política, 1983.

Declaraciones de Cuba sobre los sucesos de Granada, Octubre de 1983. Havana: Editora Política, 1983.

Foreign Broadcast Information Service, Volume VI (Latin America), 1982–1988.

The Presidential Commission on Broadcasting to Cuba. *Final Report.* Submitted to the President of the United States and to the Secretary of State on September 30, 1982.

Programa del Partido Comunista de Cuba. Havana: Editora Politica, 1987.

Skoug, Kenneth N., Jr. *Cuba as a Model and a Challenge.* U.S. Department of State, Bureau of Public Affairs. Current Policy No. 600. Washington, DC, August 1984.

————. *The United States and Cuba.* U.S. Department of State, Bureau of Public Affairs, Current Policy No. 646. Washington, DC, January 1985.

————. *A Spotlight on Cuba.* U.S. Department of State, Bureau of Public Affairs, Current Policy No.881. Washington, DC, October 1986.

————. *Cuba's Growing Crisis.* U.S. Department of State, Bureau of Public Affairs, Current Policy No. 976. Washington, DC, July 1987.

————. *The U.S. Cuba Migration Agreement: Resolving Mariel.* U.S. Department of State, Bureau of Public Affairs, Current Policy No. 1050. Washington, DC, March 1988.

————. *Cuba: "Our Last Adversary."* U.S. Department of State, Bureau of Public Affairs, Current Policy No. 1085. Washington, DC, July 1988.

United States Code, Congressional and Administrative News. 99th Congress, 1st Sess., 1985, Volume 3. St. Paul: West Publishing Co., 1986.

United States Code, Congressional and Administrative News. 99th Congress, 2nd Sess., 1986. Volume 6. St. Paul: West Publishing Co., 1987.

United States Code, Congressional and Administrative News. 100th Congress, 1st Sess., 1987, Volume 1, St. Paul: West Publishing Co., 1988.

United States Department of State, Bureau of Public Affairs. *Human Rights in Castro's Cuba.* Washington, DC, December 1986.

BOOKS

Betto, Frei. *Fidel and Religion: Castro Talks on Revolution and Religion with Frei Betto.* Translated by the Cuban Center for Translation and Interpretation. New York: Simon & Schuster, 1987.

Crocker, Chester A. *High Noon in Southern Africa: Making Peace in a Rough Neighborhood.* New York: W. W. Norton & Co., 1993.

Cuban–American National Foundation. *Cuba's Financial Crisis: The Secret Report from the National Bank of Cuba.* Washington, DC, 1985.

————. *General del Pino Speaks: An Insight into Elite Corruption and Military Dissension in Castro's Cuba.* Washington, DC, 1987.

Dixon, Edward H., and Mark A. Galan. *The Immigration and Naturalization Service.* New York: Chelsea House, 1990.

Franqui, Carlos. *Family Portrait with Fidel: A Memoir.* Translated from the Spanish by Alfred MacAdam. New York: Random House, 1984.

Gernand, Renee. *The Cuban-Americans.* New York: Chelsea House, 1988.

Gonzalez, Edward, and David Ronfeldt. *Castro, Cuba and the World.* Santa Monica, CA: Rand Corporation, June 1986.

Haig, Alexander M., Jr. *Caveat: Realism, Reagan, and Foreign Policy.* New York: MacMillan Publishing Co., 1984.

Hudson, Rex A. *Castro's America Department: Coordinating Cuba's Support for Marxist-Leninist Violence in the Americas.* Washington, DC: The Cuban–American National Foundation, 1988.

McNeil, Frank. *War and Peace in Central America.* New York: Charles Scribner's Sons, 1988.

Menges, Constantine C. *Inside the National Security Council: The True Story of the Making and Unmaking of Reagan's Foreign Policy.* New York: Simon & Schuster, 1988.

Montaner, Carlos Alberto. *Castro en la Era de Gorbachov*. Madrid: Instituto de Cuestiones Internacionales, 1990.

―――. *Fidel Castro y la Revolución Cubana*. Barcelona: Plaza y Janes, S.A., 1984.

Oppenheimer, Andres. *Castro's Final Hour: The Secret Story Behind the Coming Downfall of Communist Cuba*. New York: Simon & Schuster, 1992.

Pavlov, Yuri. *Soviet–Cuban Alliance: 1959–1991*. New Brunswick, NJ: Transaction Publishers, 1994.

School of Advanced International Studies, Johns Hopkins University. *Report on Cuba: Findings of the Study Group on United States–Cuban Relations*. Boulder, CO.: Westview Press, Inc., 1984.

Schwarzkopf, Gen. H. Norman. *It Doesn't Take a Hero*. New York: Linda Grey Bantam Books, 1992.

Shultz, George P. *Turmoil and Triumph: My Years as Secretary of State*. New York: Charles Scribner's Sons, 1993.

Smith, Wayne S. *The Closest of Enemies: A Personal and Diplomatic Account of U.S.–Cuban Relations Since 1957*. New York: W. W. Norton and Co., 1987.

Suchlicki, Jaime. *Cuba from Columbus to Castro*, second edition, revised. Washington: Pergamon-Brassey's, 1987.

Szulc, Tad. *Fidel: A Critical Portrait*. New York: William Morrow, 1986.

Thomas, Hugh. *The Cuban Revolution*. New York: Harper and Row, 1971.

Timerman, Jacobo. *Cuba: A Journey*. Translated from Spanish by Tony Talbot. New York: Alfred A. Knopf, 1990.

Valladares, Armando. *Against All Hope: The Prison Memoirs of Armando Valladares*. Translated by Andrew Hurley. New York: Alfred A. Knopf, 1986.

ARTICLES

Dominguez, Jorge I. "Cooperating with the Enemy? U.S. Immigration Policies toward Cuba." in *Western Hemisphere Immigration and United States Foreign Policy*, Christopher Mitchell, ed. University Park: Pennsylvania University Press, 1991.

Falk, Pamela S. "Cuba, 1974–1978." in *Constitutions of the Countries of the World*, Albert P. Blaustein & Gisbert H. Flanz, eds. Dobbs Ferry, NY: Oceana Publications, March 1979.

Index

ABC (American Broadcasting Company) "Nightline," 30
ABC Charter Company, 131
Abierno, Bienvenido, 159
Abrams, Elliott, Assistant Secretary of State for Inter-American Affairs, x, 14, 187; on Angola, 170; CANF and, 130; on embargo, 148; greets ex-prisoners, 131; attacked by *Granma*, 112; on Migration Agreement, 123,175, 196; and Pan American Games, 1987, 142–43; on political prisoners, 61, 110, 114, 120, 129–32, 160–62; receives Cuban bishops, 110; urges release of Orlando Bosch, 194–95; on TV-Marti, 202; leads U.S.-Soviet talks, 112–13, 122–23, 169–70, 173, 192
Abrantes Fernández, José, 28
Adega, Juan, 30
Africa, 4, 44, 84; Horn of, x; southern, x, 3, 199. *See also* Angola

Against All Hope. See Valladares, Armando
Agence France Presse (AFP), 132
Alarcón de Quesada, Ricardo: on Angola, 173, 200; on Grenada, 50; disputes INS, 83; in Koenigswinter, 155–56, 171; Mexico City, 1987, 174–75; negotiations on, Mexico City, 1986, 125–26; Migration Agreement, confidential session on, 156, 166–69, 171–73, 181 n.4; New York, 1984, 65–67, 69, 72, 75–77; on political prisoners, 35, 77, 91; on Radio Marti, 87–88, 92, 113; radio talks, 1988, and, 190–91; review sessions on, 87, 184; suspension of, 106, 113; regarding USINT, Havana, 37, 135–36, 140, 144–46, 156
Aldana Escalante, Carlos, 200
Alexander, William, 84, 99 n.11
Alvarez, Felipe, 140

About the Author

KENNETH N. SKOUG, JR., a U.S. Foreign Service Officer from 1957 until 1990, served in Latin America, the Soviet Union, Germany, Czechoslovakia, and Washington, D.C. He received Presidential Meritorious Service Awards in 1988 and 1991.

ISBN 0-275-95467-6

HARDCOVER BAR CODE